Walking Between Winds

A Passage Through Trauma
into Healing

Darling G. Villena-Mata, Ph.D.

Walking Between Winds:
A Passage Through Trauma into Healing

For more information regarding permission, contact the author at
walkingbetweenwinds@use.startmail.com
First published as a dissertation:
Reclaiming Ourselves: Societal Trauma and Its Healing

Library of Congress
Control Number TXu1-097-003
published as
Walking Between Winds
A Passage Through Societal Trauma
Discrimination's Impact on Love, Safety, Health, and Conflict
First Edition, 2003
Second Edition, 2005
Third Edition, 2009

Fourth Edition, revised and expanded: 2020.
Renamed as
Walking Between Winds - A Passage Through Trauma into Healing

ISBN 978-1-7350367-0-0 (book)
ISBN 978-1-7350367-1-7 (mobipocket)
ISBN 978-1-7350367-2-4 (ePub)

Cover design: Augusto Silva
Formatting: Polgarus Studio

Dedication

To my parents
Graciela Elisa Granizo Villena de Mata
and
José Alberto Mata Espinosa

Through your love and example,
thank you for helping me
Be
my own storyteller of my life.

Contents

List of Diagrams

Prologue

The Covid-19 pandemic had not yet occurred when this book was updated. Is the book relevant here as well?

The answer is yes.

For all too many, the pandemic is making long-forgotten fears, griefs, and traumas re-emerge, as if suddenly unearthed. Will they drag us back to an unwelcome past, or free us to deal with them once and for all?

Our sense of self and security is changing seemingly without our permission, along with our sense of what is normal. Some of those who have gone through war say that this pandemic is scarier. They could handle bombs and firefights but not this.

The pandemic is challenging us on multiple levels. It is making us ask who we are as an individual, family member, friend, as well as a nation. We may fear that the ways we have seen ourselves and acted may not work now. May this book help you find strength in a time of hardship.

Acknowledgments

Remember Who You Are

I believe that no one can go through life successfully without support from others. Offering opportunities, taking a chance on someone, providing a supportive, loving environment, and role modeling—all of these helped in the encouragement I was given to follow my heart, especially during times of changes and transformations. I also want to thank those folks who inadvertently role modeled to me what paths not to take and for the mirroring they provided me to work more on myself. They too were my teachers.

To my beloved parents, José Alberto Mata Espinosa Bolaños de los Monteros (in the last years of his life he was so happy and proud to say his full last names) and Graciela Elisa Villena Granizo de Mata, thank you for giving me the foundations of love, *cariño*, curiosity, humor, and storytelling through role modeling. You continue to be givers of unconditional love, for which I am and will be forever grateful. Even though both of you are no longer on this plane, I still feel your presence and your guidance. *Gracias, mis bonitos Mamita y Papito.* You gave me the strength to follow my dreams, no matter how off the "main road" it has been. Through your love and example, thank you for helping me be my own storyteller.

There are many more people who made this work possible

through their support of my own human evolution, for which I am deeply grateful: my family members, Fernando, Guillermo, Dianne, Chloe, Monica as well as my comadres: Nicole Valentino and Maria Greene.

To my sister-friends, colleagues, clients, former students, and participants in my workshops, presentations, seminars, and classes, thank you for your insights.

My prayers go out to all of us who have experienced difficulties in our lives, whether they are society-based, family-based, or individual.

Gratitude to the forerunners and leaders of Adult Children of Alcoholics (ACA), Co-dependents Anonymous (CoDA), and Alanon (families affected by alcohol) recovery movements. My inspiration came from these movements. I started to understand the great similarity between the coping skills and paths that participants took to heal, and the coping skills and paths of people who experience societal-scale traumas.

I came to realize that regardless of whether trauma was at the micro level of individuals and families, or at the macro level of society, all these groups and individuals have common ground from which they can learn from each other.

SPECIAL ACKNOWLEDGMENTS

Special thanks to Dana Cloud, Brooke Medicine Eagle, Peter Levine and his foundation, and to the Upledger Foundation.

Special mention to Dr. Elizabeth Kübler-Ross and her publishers.

Special thanks to Harlon Dalton for allowing me to modify his definition of racism to include other "isms" in our lives.

Special recognition to the Southeast Asian newcomer families with whom I had the honor to work and to provide service many years ago. I am beholden to them and to Dr. Reverend Paul Janke of Lutheran Social Services of Northern California, who gave me the opportunity to work with refugees and to be of service.

Ultimately, I became served through their stories, spirit, and humanity. Those experiences eventually became a major turning point in my life. *Gracias*.

A very special thanks to Susan Luton whose patience and encouragement and gentle guidance as an editor and friend helped to make this edition far better than what it was before, despite the software glitches we encountered along the way! And to my brother Guillito (affectionate term) for quick on-spot editing and brainstorming.

I thank Augusto "Ace" Silva who did a beautiful job of designing the book cover, after many changes and errors on my end. Thank you for your patience and imagination!

Not being one to ever forget, I give thanks always to Spirit or God for all the adventures in my life and for helping me through a variety of ways. Most of all, thank you for the love I never cease to experience, although there were times that I wished I had had more direct guidance!

Author's Note

This book is a layperson's version of my Ph.D dissertation, Reclaiming Ourselves: Societal Trauma and Its Healing, which I wrote in an academic style requiring citations and references. Modifying the dissertation to make it more user-friendly to nonacademics produced what you are about to read. Also, this book is written using a specific writing methodology called heuristic, which was developed by Clark Moustakas. As part of that methodology, I included myself in that study. I presented my own process and discoveries, as well as those of others, in experiencing trauma and healing. To pretend that there are no feelings or emotions about this would not be accurate and so choosing the heuristic way was the logical choice.

With this fourth edition, I expanded my focus to also address persons who are not members of non-dominant groups and whose traumas and healing are not affected by factors affecting those of non-dominant groups. Hopefully, this will show that regardless of societal group memberships, we all share many things in common when experiencing adversity and healing.

Coming from a storytelling culture and considering that many nondominant groups are from storytelling backgrounds, I found it only fitting that I would approach topics from that communication style, in addition to the linear, direct approach.

The pronouns *I*, *you*, and *us* are used, since that is also part of a reflection of the way in which many of us discuss issues that affect ourselves as individuals and as members of groups.

For many groups, explanations of the process and how we arrive at our observations and conclusions are expected in a discussion. We also tend to repeat ourselves in different ways. Usually in three's.

Food provides a good example that crosses many cultures. Would you like a second helping? No, thank you. A few minutes later: There's plenty of food. A second helping? Thank you, but maybe not. Another few minutes later: Another helping? Yes, thank you!

The first helping is of courtesy. You are eating the food that the cook (usually the mother) spent hours preparing. The second helping shows that you liked her cooking! And the third is saying, "Wow. Delicious!" The cook beams and feels proud.

I remember that when I was all of six years old our next-door neighbors invited me to join them for dinner. I was a playmate of their daughter. When the mother asked me if I wanted a second helping, I of course said, "No, thank you." She said okay and never asked me again.

When I got home, I told my mother that I was still hungry. "Could I have something to eat?" I asked. As was the custom, one did not load up on the (first) helping so as to make room for the second, and possibly the third. "What?" my mother said. "They didn't have enough food to give?" I shrugged, thinking they might have needed the food for leftovers.

All this to say, there are concepts that I will state in different ways in various parts of the book. For those who are storytellers and from cultures where repetition is part of the dynamics, it will seem fine.

It is not enough to give the bottom line. How we arrive at that bottom line is important for a fuller understanding of the mind and heart. Therefore, individual ownership of experience is shared so that the listeners will understand "where I am coming from" and know what tone and caring went with the words when discussing matters that affect all of us.

Since I have acculturated to other manners of communication, interwoven into this work are the linear or business-oriented communication style, theoretical paradigms, tables, and key points. Consequently, it is a reflection of communication styles used by different cultures and genders, for that too is part of the story.

This book is primarily meant for individual use as part of educating yourself about what it is that influences the worldviews you hold and the choices you think you are making. Since we all are members of multiple groups—some dominant in society and others not—we all have an investment in understanding how those parts intersect in our lives.

People who have experienced trauma and abuse—from the societal level, to the family level, to the individual level—will be able to relate. Additionally, health and social service practitioners, mediators, and those who work in areas of peace and trauma will find the writing beneficial in helping them develop approaches and modalities in areas of tailoring treatment paths, delivery systems, protocols, and policies.

Those who are in a relationship with loved ones affected by traumas will find the book beneficial as well. Those who are adult children of childhood abuse and other adverse experiences will notice the similarities and commonalities you have with recipients of societal traumas.

What I hope you will discover is that we all wear "hats" of different groups. It is unavoidable. At least one "hat" of yours will belong to a nondominant group in your society. We are all related in some manner, in our hopes and dreams, but also in how we cope when faced with shame, fear, abuse, discrimination, traumas, and a sense of loss of self.

May you find this book useful to yourself or to others who walk with you in your life.

Walk in Beauty.
We Are All Related.

Preface

Allowing the Heart to Guide

Never again will a single story be told
as though it's the only one.
John Berger

John Berger's quote comes from Arundhati Roy's book, *The God of Small Things*. It summarizes what my parents taught me. We are made of many stories. Our lives read like novels, with certain themes and characters highlighted and others given smaller credence and secondary roles. Life can be a series of stories, or it can be one major novel. As we look back on our lives and as we near our departure time, we will see what stories we gave our power to and what stories empowered us.

Life stories are adventures, or *aventuras*. People are never boring. "We all have our life stories," my mother would say in Spanish. "What stories are worth relishing? What stories do you, *palomita* (little beloved dove), want to pass down to others as showing off the *linda alma* (beautiful soul) that you are?"

What we choose to highlight and what stories we allow to govern our lives depend on our willingness to be creators of our lives. This is what my mother left me: While God is the almighty creator of all of us, God left us the seeds in our hearts and minds to choose storylines that could honor our souls, storylines that could honor the God that resides in us, waiting to come out. It is up to us to nourish those seeds.

I wrote the following poem after a meditation. As we heal, we search for meaning in our lives. How do we want to live our lives? We turn to finding God or Great Spirit to give us guidance. Yet many of us search outside ourselves because looking within may be too painful. Life and its wonders and sadness can be passed from generation to generation.

While we may search for God outside of us, eventually we discover that God or Great Spirit has been waiting for us to come home.

God of the Universe,
You are around me and in me.
Yet I have sought you in rituals,
in other people's cultures, in other people's words.
God of the Universe,
You are around me and in me.
Yet I have sought you frantically, fervently,
running to see you, to feel your presence.

God of the Universe,
I traveled far and wide
from my home to distant lands
seeking wisdom of you from others.

God,
I got tired and dejected.
I felt good when I was doing the rituals,
and when I was
meeting and listening to others who have seen you.
Yet.
I felt not nourished nor fully grounded,
It felt temporary.
Not long-lasting at all.
God of Love…The Divine,
I got tired and finally went home.
And there you were, waiting for me.
As I embraced myself
I found you there,
residing in me, through me, and around me,
Waiting to be noticed.

In my life adventures, I have come across the sacred and the miraculous. I have also come across life tragedies, traumas, and the unknown. How do I approach those stories that seek to engulf my very nature, my identity of being a wonderful human being and a child of God?

We met wonderful people when we came to the United States. We immigrated with stars in our eyes and songs in our hearts. We believed what people from the United States were saying of their country, and soon to be our homeland. "Land of milk and honey. Fairness. Equality for all. Equal education for all. A land where hard work will lead you to prosperity."

When we arrived we were met by wonderful people. Missionary friends, new American friends, and people from the churches we attended greeted us with civility, courtesy, and encouragement. My parents were optimistic, and they role modeled that perspective to us, the children. What we had learned about the United States appeared to be true after all—land of the free and open arms to all.

But then a larger reality set in: racism and other "isms" that would induce societal traumas. Discrimination would make its way into our lives, both as recipients and as witnesses to others being on the receiving end of discrimination's effects.

This book is about reality as I perceive it. It is the reality that holds what I call "isms"—racism, sexism, classism, heterosexism, ageism, among others. It is a book about how these "isms" can affect our souls, our beliefs about ourselves, the strategies we unknowingly develop to keep us safe; how traumas from "isms" affect us as human beings; and how healing can take place. We will explore how traumas from family and individual adverse experiences (childhood and adulthood) are similar in terms of symptoms and healing with societal traumas that have arisen from "isms" experiences.

It is also about how individuals experiencing abuse and neglect within families—whether in the dominant culture or not—have similarities of coping in order to stay safe and, sometimes, sane. It is about a struggle fought by many people to go from existing to living—whether because of societal or familial trauma, no matter in what country.

It is a book about hope and faith. It is about how we can obtain passage when we walk between the winds of traumas and changes, and transform them into life's adventures.

SECTION ONE

Discovering Trauma

... we talked with many Native American and Alaskan people and several first- and second-generation immigrants to this country.
Their family dynamics and survival characteristics resemble those of persons raised in alcoholic homes to a striking degree, whether alcohol was a factor in their childhood or not.

Jane Middleton-Moz and Eleanor Fedrid,
"The Many Faces of Grief," *Changes* (magazine)

Chapter 1

DISCRIMINATION, ABUSE, AND TRAUMA

People who have been the recipients of discrimination and abuse are often left to fend for themselves. They are marginalized and told that it is their personal responsibility to "get over" what society has inflicted upon them—or what their families have done to them.

As victims, they are seen as whiners and told, "Can't you put that behind you already?" As survivors, they become invisible again as they struggle with their own internal demons to be sane and "normal." As "success stories," they are held up as examples of what can be done "if all your people would follow your lead." Or, "Why can't you be more like them? They don't complain and they had it tougher in their families."

For many people, discrimination can lead to societal traumas. Discrimination is not an intellectual observation. It touches the hearts and bodies, the very souls of people faced with it day after day.

Societal trauma is the harm done to people not because they are individuals, but because of their membership in a particular group, whether the group is based on, for instance, class, race, ethnicity, age, gender, sexual orientation, age, religion, or body shaming. While this harm may be imposed by members of other marginalized or nondominant groups, discrimination and societal traumas serve to reaffirm various structures of dominance in society.

Trauma is a life-changing, devastating, often overwhelmingly (physically, mentally, and/or emotionally) painful, stressful experience with far-reaching repercussions. If unattended, trauma can create disruptive obstacles in the growing and healing process of an individual or of a group. Trauma involves an unresolved fight, flight, or freeze response. Stress is a low-level reaction to such a response.

The fight, flight, or freeze response is the body's way (via the sympathetic nervous system) of giving you extra strength and of making all your senses super-aware of what is going on around you. This happens when there is a perception of harm coming your way—a life-threatening harm. That threat can be physical, sexual, emotional, spiritual, etc. While you are in this state of preparing to protect and defend yourself or of getting away, the cognitive mind goes into an "either-or" view of the world. Time becomes the enemy. You have no time to think about it. You have to put things and people into categories. If your memory, experiences, or exposure to the media and others have created stereotypes of people and situations, you fall back on these to give you quick guidance for an immediate response. First responders and military personnel are trained to analyze situations very quickly so as to avoid knee-jerk reactions.

The "freeze" part of the response was added a little over twenty years ago. "Freeze" will be further discussed later in the book. Essentially, if you believe that you cannot fight your way out of the threatening situation for whatever reason, or if there seems to be no way to escape—no exit—then the body will try to make itself very still in an attempt to be "invisible" to the potential threat.

My contention is that trauma is the result of a perception that the life-threatening experience in one's life was not successfully dealt with. So the body does not stand down. It stays on alert; it does not deactivate the immune system's fight, flight, or freeze response. Peter Levine introduced this concept. It is not the life threat that creates the trauma; it is the perception of not being successful in addressing it. Think about it. First responders would be severely traumatized for any life threats they encountered.

The concept that trauma stems from a perception, rather than the actual life-threatening situation, is not new. What has been added to this conversation is the concept that Levine introduced in his earlier workshops and in his writings. He connected the psychological perception with the physiological response to that perception. (This also will be further discussed later.)

Trauma can also occur as the result of discrimination. If there is a perception of a failure of fighting or fleeing or freezing—whether it is in a physical, emotional, spiritual, or psychological sense—the group and its members will experience trauma.

Perpetrators of discrimination can knowingly or unknowingly sow the seeds of trauma. However, trauma is different from discrimination, in that the receiver of discrimination need not be traumatized.

What does any kind of trauma do to us?

It forces us to look at life through the lens of loss, grief, and concern for safety. It can challenge us to hold on to our humanity when others have forgotten theirs. Trauma pushes us to change our way of being and behaving in the world when we least expect it, or when we do not want it.

Grief can change personal ways of being in the world: routines, habits, perceptions. If the loss is of one's job or housing, and the reason for the loss involves discrimination, that loss is not simply about a job or a home (which can probably be replaced), but how one is perceived as a human being. We may question ourselves: Who are we? Who am I to be targeted this way? Shame or embarrassment may enter the picture, especially if the same type of loss repeats itself.

Any form of bigotry can also affect the soul, regardless if one is from the dominant group or a nondominant group. Words, tone, and/or energy that promise possible physical threat or some form of harm, if experienced enough, can burrow into a person's mind.

Additionally, trauma affects the body. Specific physiological changes take place when there is any perceived threat to the individual or to his or her livelihood. Like a pebble thrown into society's lake, the pebble's waves continue until they reach the edges of that lake—affecting everything in their path. Those people who are affected the most are those closest to that center of the trauma. While I see trauma affecting the waters, the emotions and the life force of people, others may view it as an isolated occurrence on land.

Societal trauma can be experienced by a whole society or by a group (for example, genocide or victims of ethnic cleansing in Bosnia, with a primary focus on killing or maiming interethnic Bosnian families).

It may also be inflicted by an entire society on a particular group of people within that society. An example is the Holocaust in World War II. Within Germany's borders, the mentally and physically disabled, Gypsies (Roma), communists, trade unionists, Slavic peoples (such as Poles), anarchists, gay men and lesbians, Jehovah's Witnesses, Jews, and other groups not deemed worthy to live were forced into concentration camps or killed in pograms. Over eleven million people died; six million were of Jewish background.

In the United States, an example of societal trauma is the legacy of Anglo European American society's maintenance of slavery, and later of legal segregation concerning Africans and African Americans. Similar latter actions were directed toward Mexican Americans, notably in the southwestern states and in California.

Other examples include the genocidal actions toward Native Americans and First Nations in North America: the reservations created for them, and the boarding schools established to wipe out their cultures. Forced internment camps legitimized for Japanese Americans during World War II. Throughout history regardless of countries one finds groups targeted within the boundaries of those countries. In the United States' history for example, "coolie" (derogatory term used often at that time) (anti-Asian), anti-Irish, and anti-Semitic laws and their enforcement, affected many generations to come. Societal trauma can be enforced at the federal, state, county, and municipal levels. While such overt "isms" may now be part of history for many countries, covert ones may continue.

There are many countries whose histories are filled with horrors done to other human beings because they belonged to groups not popular with the dominant group. Fear, hatred, shame, nightmares, and how one perceives themselves and others are passed down to the next generation—consciously and unconsciously. Even when the major horrors have stopped, if there are reminders in one's society that safety is once again threatened, those ancestral memories and one's own memories are awakened again.

By allowing "isms" to continue and by not acknowledging their continued effects of creating further societal trauma, society, through its governmental institutions, impedes the attempts of societal healing of those members affected by such trauma.

In a society that places a premium on individuality, there is no place for collective accountability for actions that might help heal group members of the trauma inflicted on them by those in power. Political leaders have sometimes given token apologies and compensation after much public outcry and political struggle. Yet racism, sexism, ageism, and classism continue, albeit more covertly.

Classism further divides "haves" from "have-nots." Stereotypes and bigotry along the lines of how much money one makes become embedded in the language we use. Think of the slurs and their accompanying emotions. The first time I heard the phrase "trailer trash," it was said by a person of that very culture but of a different socioeconomic level. The emotions and attitude that went with that phrase surprised and dismayed me. Classism has been fed.

In the area of sexism, the progress made by women to be seen and treated under the law as human beings equal to men is seen as creating a lack of morality and as diminishing "family values" by those who prefer a traditional patriarchy of hierarchical power. Is it any wonder that globally, as women seek to have basic human rights, they are being tortured more frequently, receiving more death threats, and are actually being killed in greater numbers?

Yet if women are allowed by both the macro (government) and the micro (family, neighborhoods, communities) to seek and have equal treatment, such as having an education and employment, their nation prospers more. Their communities become better for it. Those groups get nourished in many ways when half the population's productivity, talents, and abilities are utilized.

However, in some countries, by making social concerns a private affair, society sidesteps its responsibility to its members and caters primarily to those who do not raise the issues of injustice and trauma. Society avoids participating and then thrusts the responsibility of healing onto its recipients to do their own healing.

Normally, psychotherapy is used to help the client better adjust to society. This attitude presumes that society is healthy and is not the perpetrator of the ills of the client. What good does it do to help clients get better if they have to return to an abusive society, to an abusive family or neighborhood? As clients and patients, we then need to question our would-be helpers. How do our mental health practitioners view racism, sexism, and other "isms" that may play roles in our lives? How do they view the transgenerational transmission of behaviors and attitudes that might have been good for one's ancestors but are not for oneself?

Are health providers trained in trauma and/or in grief? Some say they are trained, but in reality their training may consist of one workshop, which might not have lasted even half a day, or one course back when they were getting their degree, or, even worse, OJT—on-the-job training with their clients or patients. It is important to know if you are being a "guinea pig" for such a therapist.

If you are, then ethically that therapist should not be charging you because she or he is learning from you: OJT. Or, at the very least, you should be charged much less.

I have known therapists who, after taking a course (whether for one day or three days) to get continuing education units, "tried out" what they learned on their clients or patients to get some practice. Again, ethically, they should not charge for the time since they are utilizing you to practice their newly acquired methods.

I interviewed one such therapist by phone. She mentioned that she does EMDR (more on this modality later in the book). I asked about the type and length of her training. I shared with her that EMDR has a high abreaction (that is, a high risk for retraumatizing or putting the client into a flashback).

As such, it is important that the therapist has years of experience dealing with such abreaction possibilities and knows how to get the client out of that state. She paused and then slowly said that maybe she was not the one to be listed. She had just learned a few months ago how to do EMDR. So she withdrew her desire to be on the therapist list that I was developing (for referring people who needed psychotherapy, since that is not the kind of work I do).

I sometimes wonder if she would have been candid with potential clients about her level of training. Her website made it sound as if she was experienced in the EMDR modality and others. While she may have had over thirty years of experience in psychotherapy, her training in EMDR was very recent. Nor was her experience in trauma extensive, although she was well versed in grief, as well as in death and dying. While they may overlap, they are not the same in terms of approaches and client education.

As a social service provider in the mid-1980s, I observed the fear and reluctance of newcomers from what was then the Soviet Union and from parts of Southeast Asia to utilize American mental health services. It was very understandable.

In their countries, the government used the term "mental health services" as a euphemism for torture and the imprisonment of perceived political adversaries. People would "disappear" into the large maze of psychiatric institutions.

In countries where there have been "disappeared ones," where people have been rounded up and not allowed to contact their families or attorneys, where there is no legal process, trauma will follow, possibly planting seeds of pain and generational revenge for those who experience such traumas.

People who are innocent but imprisoned—especially without due process—may develop revenge and hatred in their hearts and in their actions. These feelings may especially occur if no recompense or no formal acknowledgment by their captors occurs when they are set free.

How much of our own trauma has its origins in societal trauma?

Oftentimes we are taught that it is solely our concern and our problem to resolve those traumas that were culturally induced.

For example, does sexism play a part in the low regard women may have for themselves, as well as in the media portrayal of women? Does sexism contribute to violence against women? Many would say yes, as evidenced in the courts or in laws and the degree of their enforcement to protect women.

How many of the problems that we embrace individually are actually societally induced or societally exacerbated?

Two areas became increasingly important in my thinking of the many kinds of trauma and how to heal them:

1. Revisiting the past through the person of today
2. Adult children of alcoholics and their similarities with recipients of societal trauma

Chapter 2

REVISITING THE PAST WHILE REMEMBERING THE PRESENT

Neither racism nor classism (as examples) has to hit you or me over the head. Either one can be quite subtle. Either can even happen in the guise of helping. Since racism and classism are so prevalent in our society and often are invisibly interwoven into the fabric of how we believe and interact with people, we do not or cannot see certain words or even positive stereotypes as bigoted.

Most people of the dominant group do not see that their beliefs, patterns, and customs are being held up as the norm, while other groups' beliefs and values are, at the very least, not mentioned or, at most, pathologized or ridiculed. Racism, classism, and sexism can be silent or covert, such that those people who are not the objects of the prejudice or bigoted actions do not know what has transpired. Bigotry and prejudice do not have to appear as "larger than life"; they can come quietly and with authority in the guise of "knowing best."

In the early part of my elementary school years, I was put in a special class because of my accent. I felt branded by the way teachers and school administrators were handling my situation. My father protested to the principal when I told him of my experiences. He took time off from work to speak to her. We were a working-class family, and it was a big thing for him to miss a day of work without pay. My papa asked the principal if she could roll her *r*'s or say the "yuh" sound of the Spanish letter *ll*, as in *gallo*. She admitted that she could not pronounce either one. She finally understood, she said, and then she laughed. She would personally take me out of the special class. He beamed, knowing he had helped his beloved daughter.

After my father said goodbye to me, the principal took me by the hand and promptly led me back to that special class. I did not tell my father that she had lied and disrespected him. He would have "lost face" had I told him. She had lied. He had no power. Thankfully, I was in the special class only briefly due to budget cuts. That class did nothing to change my accent, but it did deepen the notion that having an accent was wrong, especially if the accent was not popular.

Decades later, as an adult, I told my father what had occurred. It took me that long to let him know. He told me he was sorry he had not been able to protect me any more than he did. I told him that he and my mother protected me by giving me tools, such as being *bien educada*, or well-educated of the heart, to believe in my goodness and to never give up.

My parents tried to intervene when racist behaviors were expressed by teachers or even by a principal, but their logic fell on illogical and biased ears. I eventually learned not to tell my parents what was happening to me at school because it did no good, and because I felt embarrassed that my parents were "losing face." I tried the best I could to become "small" and not be seen during my school years. I played hooky to avoid those feelings of disrespect. Eventually it was discovered that I had deliberately avoided going to school. I did not know the words to describe my feelings of anger and shame.

How my parents handled my skipping school was to listen to why and to where I went instead. I had no words, but my emotions and body language said a lot. So in exchange for not skipping school, my out-of-home working mother would take one day off per month from work to have a special day with me, her *hijita* (beloved daughter). We went to movies and ate at Clifton Cafeteria in downtown Los Angeles. We rode the bus each way. I have not forgotten her love, understanding, and awareness that her daughter needed to know that she (that is, me) was special in a good way. The one day per month, that mental and loving focus day, got me through middle school, or, as it was called then, junior high.

Racism and *classism*—what would a child know of such grown-up words, especially those many decades ago when such things were not really discussed in the media or in school? Naming a feeling is extremely empowering. It is a great relief to the person.

While my parents were unable to protect me from bigotry, racism, and classism as I grew up, they gave me tools of love. As for the rest, I was left to my own devices to save my ego, my integrity, and my heart when I was young and in school. I developed compassion and understanding from knowing that my family did the best they could, given their circumstances.

Because of my work and reflection, I discovered that the symptoms of adults who had experienced childhood abuse were very similar to those being experienced by many families in which there was no history of child abuse.

I realized that I, too, was exhibiting some of those child abuse symptoms. Why was that? My parents had never beaten or mistreated me. They never neglected me. My memories of my parents are fond ones. We were a close-knit family. Upon discussing this with other "people of color," as we called ourselves then, I discovered that all of us had these symptoms to varying degrees. Traditionally, the term *psychological trauma* describes individuals who have experienced events such as in family-based situations, natural disasters, human-made disasters, and war-scarred countries. Yet *psychological trauma* can easily apply to societal traumas, which can arise from "isms."

Chapter 3

COMMON PAIN, COMMON BRIDGE: ADULT CHILDREN OF ALCOHOLICS AND RECIPIENTS OF SOCIETAL TRAUMA

The parallel became clear to me that recipients of societal traumas, which originated from racism, sexism, and other "isms," demonstrated many of the same symptoms as did adult children of alcoholics and adults who had experienced childhood abuse and neglect, as well as children who had experienced other kinds of adverse experiences.

A friend brought me an article titled "The Many Faces of Grief," which she thought described what I had been informally talking about with other members of nondominant groups. The article validated what I was suspecting: The symptoms and grief developed from societal traumas were similar to the symptoms developed from familial or individual abuse. This realization increased my curiosity and my research into how racism affected me and other people of nondominant groups. Some of the similarities the authors highlighted in their article were as follows:

1. Multigenerational grief
2. Poor self-esteem
3. Family heroes

4. Embarrassment about parents and background, and feelings of shame toward them
5. Suppression of feelings
6. Survivor's guilt

Of all the symptoms mentioned, I recognized the strongest connection between myself and item five—the suppression of feelings. It was driven home to me when I read in the article what a client said to the authors, Middleton-Moz and Fedrid:

Other kids would tease me about being a 'dumb Indian.' I couldn't talk to my parents about it when I got home because I knew they had the same pain, which I didn't want to add to.

Eventually I, too, learned during my childhood not to share with my parents what was going on at school. It would hurt them, and I did not want them to feel helpless. I parentified myself—caretaking for my parents. I discovered that other children in similar situations did the same. After that incident with the elementary school principal, I began to learn that there are some things that are best not shared when there can be no satisfactory justice.

Unknowingly, I was following the "Don't Rules" of childhood trauma: *don't feel, don't trust, and don't talk* (not even to yourself if the trauma is that bad).

Later, when I participated in Adult Children of Alcoholics conferences, I learned that participants had had the same rules growing up as children. Throughout this book, I will bring up more similarities between the groups.

I realize that some members of dominant groups state that they know how it is to be teased and discriminated against because they experienced those things as children. That may be so. Yet while many children or adults may have teased them about being different, when they became older usually some of these differences disappeared, or else adults normally no longer shamed them for the differences.

Yet for many, the effects of any kind of trauma—in the form of bigotry, abuse, or neglect, for instance—may linger well into adulthood, impacting how we view ourselves and our world.

Experiencing bigoted comments and actions and/or being discriminated against may produce pain, hurt, traumatic memories, and contribute to the development of a child's or adult's self-esteem. Being discriminated against adds another layer onto an already hurt child or adult.

Discrimination is a double-edged sword. You are shamed, derided, ridiculed, and perhaps targeted by actions of hate and anger—not just for who you are but because you belong to a certain group of people. Your identity as an individual and your identity as a member of a group are assailed.

Discriminate means to make a distinction or to discern based on judgment. The ability to discriminate or make critical distinctions can be a valuable survival tool for survivors of trauma.

However, as this term is commonly used, it means to make a distinction not based on all the facts about a situation or person, but rather to discern based on biased perceptions and other than genuine merit. What differentiates discrimination from prejudice is that discrimination has the power or backing of some authority or agency of enforcement.

Institutional discrimination is another term used for the kind of discrimination wielded by the group(s) perceived to be the dominant power in a society. Institutional discrimination occurs by means of laws and law enforcement, media, education, and government institutions.

The media may and often do engage in discriminatory practices. Watchdog groups such as GLADD (an LGBT nonprofit organization), and ethnic and racial as well as religious groups, are on the lookout for stereotyping, the exclusion of actors, screenplays, and how the news is presented.

I remember watching a newscast describing the perpetrators of a robbery. The perpetrators were defined by ethnicity and race only if they were members of nondominant groups; but if they were of the dominant group, their race was not included in the description. While this practice has largely ceased, it took watchdog groups and other organizations to call these discriminatory practices to the media's attention.

Why was this important? It gave the false impression that there was more violence perpetrated by nondominant group members.

Prejudice or *bigotry* can come from anyone. The people expressing it do not necessarily have support from some authority, nor do they have enforcement capacity. They may not have the ability to disseminate and make widespread their particular prejudices, and their actions and words are not sanctioned by the government and its institutions. However, these prejudices can still create great pain and have long-lasting impact on the person on the receiving end.

Overt prejudice or *overt discrimination* consists of obvious words, actions, or behaviors that readily can be seen by any onlooker and recipient as being prejudiced or discriminatory (e.g., derogatory words, physically hitting someone, obvious laws that deny the civil rights of a group of people).

Covert prejudice or *covert discrimination* consists of subtle words, actions, or behaviors that are felt or seen by the recipient of prejudice but are not detected by onlookers (e.g., double meanings, a look, an energy). It was not unusual to hear others and myself use terms such as *obvious, overt, explicit, subtle, covert,* and *implicit.* When the bigotry or discrimination is done in a covert or subtle or implicit manner, the targeted person can become frustrated from not getting validation and support from onlookers, especially if the onlookers belong to members of a dominant group. "Did you not see that?" a nondominant group member would ask, and the response from the onlooker might be "See what? You're being too sensitive."

In child abuse situations it is not unusual for a child to "pick up" on the subtle energy or the gaze or the double-meaning words of an apparently congenial cousin or other relative (but in actuality a perpetrator of sexual abuse) in a roomful of oblivious adults. One can also say that the selective lack of enforcement of civil rights laws and of laws that protect all citizens in terms of justice and safety, as that lack pertains to a particular group or members of a particular group, may be covert to the outsider but very much overt to the intended person or group.

Throughout my travels, I have observed that the poor and working class are at times looked down upon by those groups whose economic levels are higher. "Trailer trash," "hillbillies," and other awful terms are used to put down people and to sustain stereotypes. Each country has its own expressions of derision. If you are in a caste society, you may be viewed as and believed to be "unclean" if you are from the lowest caste.

During the Gilded Age in the United States, the poor who were fighting for better wages and working conditions were seen as inferior—"those people from the other side of the tracks." They were labeled as lazy and stupid because they were demanding not to work seven days a week, twelve hours a day. Those labels stuck and were passed on to succeeding generations who used them (and expressed certain attitudes with their use) without realizing why those perceptions had been created.

Were it not for the unions' leaders and followers, we would not have five-day work weeks, sick leave, and other benefits. Of course, currently such situations are changing in many parts of the world—

in some cases for the better, in other cases for the worse—for working-class and middle-class people.

For those of us who have experienced societal abuse and neglect, these differences do go with us as we become adults. These differences are part of who we are—differences that contribute to the makeup of who we are. Darker skin, or some other feature that one cannot change, is a difference that can draw negative attention, not necessarily from individuals but from societal institutions. Coming from an unpopular economic class or religion can also follow us into adulthood, depending on where we live as adults or what is occurring at the national level.

I am reminded of attitudes toward "illegals," "wetbacks," and "trailer trash" or "white trash," as well as epithets toward people who wear turbans or dress in their religious attire as part of their daily wear. In each country there are slurs for those not in power and/or those who look different or act differently. Those words become part of the everyday language. "He gypped me." (*Gypped* refers to Gypsies, or Roma people.) "That is so white of you." (Or, "How very Christian of you."—meaning that you did something wonderful, and of course it is a compliment since the assumption is that only White or Christian people could be so gracious or generous.) When I was in my twenties, I recall a man giving me a backhanded compliment: "You're very bright. You think like a man!" Some of these slurs and backhanded "compliments" are now history, but not all of them. And new ones are probably being made, regardless of where you live on Earth.

Children and adolescents may emulate the attitudes and behaviors of adults in power or of people they admire. The same holds true for adults who take their cues from people in trusted leadership positions.

My recognition of the similarities between adults from

childhood family abuse and people who have experienced societal trauma eventually led me to develop methods of understanding the choices we make in "coming out" and in "closeting" aspects of who we are to ourselves and to our world.

Chapter 4

CULTURATION SPECTRUM: CHOICES ON THE ROAD TO LIVING

Sometimes the inadvertent aim of diversity training and intercultural conflict resolution is to understand how to be and what to do about *them*, whoever and whatever group that might be. I observed intercultural trainers providing how-to sessions in which ethnic and gender groups were being stereotyped. No thought was given to the issue of why some people in a group assimilated (embracing another group's values, beliefs, etc.), why others stayed traditional (adhering to one's own heritage or own group's values and beliefs), or why still others chose to be bicultural or polycultural (keeping some values, beliefs, customs, etc. of one's group and choosing some values, beliefs, customs, etc. of another group or groups). The trainers seemed to believe that everyone in a particular group was completely traditional.

How did these choices influence communication styles, values, and expectations? This culturation spectrum, as I call it, serves as a basis to help us understand why some people seem to gravitate to one area of the spectrum for certain aspects of their lives and yet other people are more set in another area. That is why no two individuals, even from the same household, are assimilated in the same ways or are traditional in the same ways as are other siblings in the family.

I found that many diversity trainers I had met ignore this topic of culturation. Without addressing this spectrum, we and others can easily fall into creating stereotypes of our own groups and of others. We also fail to address how traumas can influence our decisions along this spectrum if we do not consider the components of a culturation spectrum.

Assimilation

Assimilation is embracing the core values and beliefs of another group, while rejecting, letting go, or "closeting" the heritage, values, or beliefs from our own group. We see no value in our own group's heritage, dynamics, customs, or other expressions, and so we totally embrace the elements of the other group, normally the dominant group. Societal institutions generally encourage assimilation.

Women entering male-dominated careers or workplace settings sometimes have to "closet" certain aspects of their femaleness to be more like one of the "boys." In some cases, women have to put up with sexist jokes in order keep the job and (hopefully) advance. To fit in and not be harassed may be reasons for assimilation.

When people who come from lower socioeconomic levels work or interact socially with people in higher economic brackets, they may experience comments, looks, or tones that are not respectful of them, especially if their roots are showing, so to speak. Not mentioning one's "humble roots" in such company may be part of assimilation.

Bicultural or Polycultural

Bicultural or *polycultural,* as I define it, is the process of embracing the best aspects of all groups to which we have been exposed in our lives. We acknowledge and appreciate our own groups (ethnic, race, gender, religion, sexual orientation, class, etc.) without putting ourselves in a hierarchy of, or having competitive feelings toward, other groups.

Rather, we learn and value what other groups have to offer. Ideally, we choose the best from each of the groups as we honor those groups and their contributions to our lives. We also acknowledge that in all groups there may be customs, expressions, and dynamics that may not serve us in the best way. We do not see the groups in terms of "either-or" concepts.

Societies are organic, not static. Angles became Anglos, and then Anglo-Saxons. Families became clans. And clans became large villages, which led to cities. City-states sometimes became countries. Countries banded together and became regions, or political entities such as the European Union. Our languages also transform through time. Old English is not the English we speak now. Old Spanish is not the Spanish we speak today nor the Spanish people will speak in the future.

Furthermore, other languages have become extinct. Currently, one language dies every fourteen days, without there having been enough time for the knowledge of the speakers' environment and culture to get passed on. According to UNESCO and other organizations that track the loss of languages, some of them include concepts and words about important, promising medicinal plants— and these languages are becoming extinct!

Perhaps the fear of losing one's language and its culture may fuel some people to be solely traditional. Is there perhaps a fear of other people's languages and cultures taking over?

Keep in mind that the majority of languages continue to exist as they organically transform with the times and needs of their existing users (i.e., people). There are many words in English that have roots in non-English languages. The following are from

French, Arabic, and Spanish: Faux pas. A la carte. Voyage. Ad nauseum. Candy. Carat. Checkmate. Check. Modus operandi (what's your M.O.?). En masse. Albatross. Armada. Avocado. Arroyo. Bonanza. Canyon. Canoe. The list goes on.

The same can be said of any modern language, not just English. The language includes words that came from other countries or regions but are now completely accepted.

Life is about change and transformation. We learn from each other and we borrow, with respect, while acknowledging the source. Everyone wins if we honor and learn from each other's cultures and languages, without the fear that one group will supplant the other. If that fear exists, then it stops being a win-win. Instead, a zero-sum situation occurs, and then eventually, over time, no one wins.

Traditional

Traditional is keeping our heritage, our values and beliefs and not wanting to learn about other groups and their ways, except in those areas that affect us peripherally. Those who stay traditional have only a superficial understanding and knowledge of other groups' cultural beliefs and values, if at all. Examples are listening to other groups' music and eating ethnic foods. Traditional-oriented people often do not have the desire to know the possible plights or joys of other groups, even though they are benefiting in some form from the labors of those other groups.

One of my colleagues serves as an example of someone having a traditional area in his life. He is third-generation Chinese American. His clothing, speech pattern, accent, and work values are very much like those of the dominant group. His friends are of different ethnic groups, and he enjoys a variety of music and books. He seems to be assimilated. Yet when it came to getting married, he asked his mother to help him find a "nice Chinese girl." In that area of his life, he was traditional.

Whether differences are viewed with joy or with pain can affect what we keep or what we jettison from our lives. For example, within a family, one person may strive greatly to make his or her accent disappear because of the derisive comments of authority figures or peers. That person may choose to consciously assimilate the accent that is acceptable. Yet another person in the same family may choose to keep his or her accent because the opposite sex finds it charming and attractive. How we view our own differences influences what we keep and enjoy, and which differences we let go,

It is not unusual for a person forced into being humiliated or demeaned in some way regarding a particular trait to vilify people who demonstrate that trait. For instance, if people in power or in authority view hugging between males as a "weakness," then they may shame the individuals involved in order to force them to "closet" or "throw away" that trait. They may even pass laws. They may also encourage negative attitudes toward such behaviors. It would not be unusual for the children of these individuals, and for them also in their adult years, to have negative feelings or anger when witnessing people from cultures that allow such expression between males.

This is important. Understanding how we treat differences within ourselves—whether as gifts or as burdens—will help give us a clearer idea as to why certain aspects or traits are kept traditional, others are assimilated, and still others are bicultural or polycultural.

While there can be generalizations made about our collective groups, there are also differences within such groups. For example, some ethnic groups within the collective group come from matriarchal cultures, while the cultures of others are patriarchal. In terms of African Americans, there are regional differences as well. Also, some African Americans have assimilated to the culture of the dominant group. Similarly, there are people from the dominant group who differ based on region, rural or urban origins, ocean or mountain settings. These differences and their subcultures can be seen throughout the world. As an example, among people speaking the same language, those who come from hot climates tend to speak differently than those from very cold environments.

Education and Ageism

When we look at the culturation spectrum, we also should look at education and ageism. What feelings and thoughts are going through your mind right now? Snobbery and prejudice can arise in any area, including those of age and education. In my upbringing, education was and is very important. And, yes, the vocabulary that one uses may not overlap with that of people who have a different education. Examples are terms from the areas of law, medicine, engineering—and the list goes on and on when other academic and advanced degrees are considered. Often these kinds of professions are connected with higher economic brackets.

In a hierarchical society, individuals in professional fields such as law, medicine, and engineering are given more respect than individuals who could not or did not need to go to academic schools. The assumptions and attitudes of people who went to trade or other nonacademic kinds of schools may contain a false belief about their level of intelligence. Keep in mind that education includes the attainment of knowledge by workers such as automobile mechanics, sailors, train workers, oil rig personnel, plumbers, massage therapists, air conditioning and heating professionals—to name only a few. People who learn through on-the-job training often are at lower levels in a society that values hierarchical respect and power. Think of sanitation workers, people working in retail, and so forth.

So when we look at the culturation spectrum, where do you and I principally fit in, in terms of being honored and respected? Are we considered expendable? Are we told that anyone can do our jobs and therefore we may be seen as less valuable, which may extend to the erroneous thinking of being a less valuable human being? In jobs that are dangerous or that expose you to health hazards, how well protected are you? Is financial security less assured for you if you are perceived as less valuable than someone in, perhaps, upper management or another kind of field?

With regard to finances, how much do we embrace fear of the short-term (which is very real) versus the long-term impact on health and the untold costs of medical bills or other kinds of bills down the line? Safety now or safety later? Having a roof over your head now (or not) versus later? Where is our focus? If we are stressed, our focus will be mainly, if not fully, in the present. If we have time to breathe and exhale with calm and peace, then options may arise for our future. Stress impacts our worldview and our ability to influence it, especially when it comes to safety.

If we perceive "the other," rightly or wrongly, as threatening our ability to stay safe in some manner, then differences become threats rather than curiosity.

In terms of age, each age has its own wisdom and knowledge, its own way of marveling at the world or not. We can learn from the young to be curious and excited over what adults take for granted. The young, in turn, can learn from elders through their many stories of being on this Earth. We learn from each other, *if* we see the other person as an equal who is worthy of respect and a teacher to us, each learning more about life from the other.

Let me share a story with you. Decades ago I met a woman who became significant in my life. She was a *curandera* (healer) — but was much more than that, since she was in connection with the spirit world. She had braided grey hair and wore work jeans and a western shirt. She knew all about medicinal herbs and other manners of healing, including special prayers to God for guidance and working with the spirits.

As was the custom of my culture and family, I nodded my head and gave a slight bow — a way of showing my respect, since she was an elder. It did not matter that she was also a *curandera*.

She looked at me and got slightly annoyed. "Don't give me automatic respect just because I'm old. I may be an old fool, while nearby there may be a wise child." I was taken aback. "There is basic respect for all living creatures, which include humans," she continued. "And then there is respect of and for the individual. Know the difference!" She did not mince words. For a Latinx, she was not diplomatic with her words, to say the least, considering that we were meeting for the first time. Yet her demeanor was that of a loving, scolding aunt.

There may be a wise child or children in our midst. They are and have been in every generation. They come to perhaps keep or help the older people be on top of their game as human beings. As it is with every generation, our young people bring new perspectives on how life is seen. They bring in inclusivity. How should people be addressed and treated in society? Are we doing enough for humanity and nature? All countries have had young people lead in many ways in areas where some older adults in power may have lost their wonderment.

What's in a Word?

Recently a dear friend updated me on terms being used out in the communities. She is active in several of them, in particular those made up of younger generations. I myself have been isolated in that respect. For over fourteen years my focus had been caring for my father, until he passed on, and then I moved to a geographical area that is basically monocultural. Talk about culture shock after leaving a place that was demographically diverse! But I digress— sort of. One of the terms my friend shared with me is the word *Latinx*. *Latinx* is popular at colleges and universities, and it is also now being used in the larger society by millennials and others in the United States. It replaces *Latino* or *Latina*. Older generations may not be aware of this term. Those who do know it may or may not approve of the change. Why *Latinx*? It is gender-neutral. Finding gender-neutral words is a way to acknowledge that we are human beings and not simply people of the gender to which we belong.

While *Latinx* is used in the United States, it is not used in Latin America or Spain, at least not yet. The term *Hispanic* is rarely used now since it does not recognize the indigenous aspects of the person. And yet I still see the term *Hispanic* in many official demographic questionnaires.

"So what?" you might say. How we identify ourselves versus having someone identifying us through labels is important. "You're stupid!" is a form of someone identifying you in your attempt to understand something. What feelings come up for you when that phrase is thrown at you in a demeaning tone? I learned to say, "Well, that's interesting and I appreciate your perspective on how I'm gathering my understanding. I beg to differ, however."

Such a response includes a lot of words, certainly, but there is a reason. It helps you stay anchored in your love for yourself, while acknowledging the other person's perspective with which you disagree.

It always throws the other person off track in a gentle way because they are wanting an argument or wanting you to feel bad or both.

So care must be given not to stereotype, and at the same time to understand that there are generalizations made of all groups and subgroups. It is very important to get to know the individuals. And just as importantly, if not more so, get to know your own self and where you fit in the culturation spectrum.

Questions to Ask Yourself

What prompted you to stay totally traditional in one area in your life, while in another area you may be bicultural? What differences have you "closeted" and for what reasons? What differences have you safely expressed—and even with smiles?

Here are some scenarios. What feelings and words come up for you?

You have a Southern accent and you now live elsewhere. Do you lose your accent to fit in, or do you keep it? The same if you have a highlander or coastal or island accent.

You are from a family of engineers, yet your heart tells you to be an artist or writer. Your family members are expecting you to follow in their footsteps. Do you, or do you not? Why?

In a culture that does not encourage hugs or embraces between people of the same gender, you tend to be a "huggy" person. People make fun of you; they call you needy. Yet you are simply that way—not needy at all. However, the comments said in laughter are starting to bother you. What do you do?

You were born into an urban way of living, with so many options of things to do—not to mention all the nightlife. Yet you long for the rural life and want to grow crops. Do you give up your job and uproot yourself to follow your heart? And if you have a partner, what do you do?

You are of a minority faith in your country. Do you express your differences, such as dress in traditional attire and/or attend faith gatherings? Do you feel safe doing so? Or are you scared and try to "pass" as being part of the dominant faith in order to be safe?

Your sexual orientation is gay, lesbian, or bisexual. Perhaps you are fluid or maybe pansexual. Do you feel safe enough to tell your parents and friends? Or do you stay "closeted" except to those you definitely know you can be yourself around and will be safe?

Do you sense that how you feel about and perceive of yourself is not matching with your physical body? You come from a family that does not understand *those* people or that has myths about and stereotypes of *those* people. What do you do? Do you try to "pass" as being a member of the body you were born into? Or do you seek ways to synchronize who you are with the gender you need? What would you do?

The list of examples can go on from overt/obvious differences to invisible differences. Invisible differences are easier in some ways but harder in others. You can hear and witness what people really think of *those* people.

Coming out is a relief and you can be yourself. Yet it may carry risks in terms of your safety, housing, employment, medical care, and much more, should you live in a town, city, or country that does not protect you, or at the very least perpetuates caricatures that dishonor you and your group.

The next page presents what I have just discussed, yet in a different format. In communication, some people prefer the narrative; others prefer tables, charts, and other types of visuals. I do both, as they appeal to both sides of my brain, which is important for me as I get older. May you find it of use.

CULTURATION SPECTRUM

TRADITIONAL	BICULTURAL/POLYCULTURAL	ASSIMILATION
Keeps one's own *original* core cultural beliefs and values (i.e., those elements exposed in childhood via the family, sexual orientation, religion, gender, ethnicity/race, etc.) Has superficial understanding and knowledge of other group's cultural beliefs and values, if at all. More than likely acquainted with only the other group's music, food, attire, etc. Minimally learns of other group's culture for purposes of interactions (e.g., workplace, common public settings).	Keeps some of one's own cultural beliefs and values, but also embraces some values and beliefs of the other group, or groups. Ideally chooses the best from all cultures to which person was exposed in their lives. May hold a side-by-side coexistence of values. Choices may be based on likes and dislikes, as well as what may benefit person in terms of economic and social success.	Rejects or "closets" one's own core values and beliefs for another group's values and beliefs. Choices may be based on likes and dislikes, as well as being shamed, ridiculed, and embarrassed of group of origin (e.g., ethnic or racial expressions, class, sexual orientation, religion, etc.).

Do the majority of people vacillate between these areas? If you experienced traumas, abuse, and/or neglect, how would it affect your choice? If one of your traits was acceptable by the dominant group, would you keep it or "closet" it? If that aspect was shamed, what action would you take?

This spectrum is to assist us in questioning what areas in our lives we choose to stay traditional, what other areas we decide to be bicultural/polycultural, and what areas we choose to assimilate.

Where are you in this spectrum?

Good Cop/Bad Cop Roles

Many multicultural trainers focused on what some of my White colleagues expressed as "making the White people cry or feel ashamed for things over which they have no personal control." The effects of racism were discussed in the workshops led by the trainers; history was provided as a context for the present state of affairs; emotions were elicited during small groups; and when the workshops were over, people's feelings were still raw. No debriefing was held. Only a summary of the workshops was presented, with no long-term follow-up.

I recall my Southeast Asian staff leaving in bewilderment halfway through one such training. The workshop had broken into small groups to do experiential exercises. Group members were asked to share experiences of vulnerability: when they first felt their differences, and when they first felt negativity toward another person because of their differences. My staff members were extremely embarrassed.

To share such things with strangers! They felt that their sense of privacy had been violated. These are intimate matters. And because some of them had such horrific memories from their past, staying in the workshop any longer was too much to bear. So they left. Later my staff members told me they thought that the facilitators did not know how to conduct the workshop. They made comments such as the following:

> "Why open up one's pain and heart only to be judged as to whether you've been a good person?"
>
> "Who are they to do so? And then leave the wounds open after the workshop is over!"
>
> "These diversity trainers didn't consider cultural considerations even among their participants!"

For readers not familiar with the phrase "good cop/bad cop," it comes from television police shows. It refers to a situation in which one police officer acts as the uncompromising, relentless cop who intensely interrogates a suspect, while the other police officer in the interrogation room acts politely, sympathetic, even appearing to take sides with the suspect in a gentle, "buddy"-like manner.

In diversity trainings where the approach is good cop/bad cop, the participants may appear to "change" in terms of behaviors and attitudes. They change either due to a bonding feeling or due to feelings of guilt (depending on which "cop" approach is used with them in the training). However, the effects are not long-lasting, according to some of the participants I later met. I participated in some of those trainings and I too left frustrated.

Diversity trainings that were "bad cop"-oriented elicited feelings and emotions that were not addressed either in debriefings or longitudinal follow-up. Those experiences felt more like a demand for members of the dominant group to accept how their group acted toward the "minority groups." The concern I have with this style of diversity trainings is that some people feel embarrassed or even shamed; they "lose face." Others get angry and defensive and may shut down.

Still others may smile or break down with emotions and acknowledge their behaviors and attitudes as being racist (if they have power/authority at the job) or bigoted (if they have no power/authority). Weeks later those same people may resist deepening their intercultural knowledge.

Why undergo another public embarrassment? Providing a safe place to explore attitudes and behaviors is not a priority for some of these "bad cop" trainings. Furthermore, most of these trainings were one- or two-day workshops. Many agencies requesting these kinds of very brief workshops use them as their sum total of diversity training, thereby giving themselves and others the illusion that they have completely addressed intercultural matters and conflict.

The "good cop" approach of lightly touching on the issue of racism or sexism (or classism, if at all) involves a discussion of early experiences of notable differences and an exploration of the values of the different cultures. These workshops are basic and a good introduction, but they are not sufficient. The emphasis usually is on total safety. People's feelings and fears are not challenged from an emotional perspective.

These trainings were very cognitive and oftentimes linear in teaching style, albeit lightly peppered with stories. While these approaches provide a certain amount of useful information to some participants who are not diversity-conscious, they do not address why there might be tension from "minority groups" (aka nondominant groups) toward the dominant group—tension which to the dominant group may appear to be out of proportion or illogical. The unstated idea is "Why can't they get past it already?!"

Furthermore, these kinds of trainings do not help members of "minority groups" understand why some members of the dominant group express wariness and defensiveness toward them. The fear of creating unresolvable conflict supersedes deeper queries as to how racism and sexism (the two more popular "isms" for diversity training) affect recipients and how we as a society perpetuate practices unknowingly.

In the beginning, I provided one- and two-day workshops. I tended to use the "good cop," or soft-style, approach in my delivery. I knew what it was like to be shamed or embarrassed, especially in public. It had happened enough when I was younger, provoked by teachers and authority figures.

Eventually I decided to provide training for trainers only. In this way, agencies would not be dependent on outside trainers but, instead, would have their own internal trainers.

While these workshops and trainings are for learning about "the other group and people" through reevaluating how we perceive and experience those groups, it is step two.

Step one is being kind—being kind to ourselves as we explore how our world has treated us as individuals, no matter what groups we belong to.

As I started to include the similarities of adult children of alcoholics with those recipients of societal traumas, I saw a change in the multicultural/diversity trainings. Participants who initially had given me negative comments did seem to later change their minds to something more positive. As weeks went by, what had been discussed in the classes made more sense to these participants, especially if they shared what they were exposed to in class with members of nondominant groups. I came to realize that longitudinal evaluations were more indicative of whether a training had been successful.

One workshop participant, in fact, contacted me many months later to thank me for having presented the analogy between the symptoms experienced by adult children of alcoholics and those experienced by members of nondominant groups.

She told me she had been angry at the end of the workshop and had given me a poor evaluation, stating that she did not understand how adults with childhood experiences of abuse had anything to do with how "minority people" felt. She had considered the workshop a waste of her time.

Then, a few weeks later, she realized that she had not wanted to accept how much of a workaholic she was and how her behaviors were impacting her managerial skills in conflict resolution, especially with "minority members on the staff." Her own dysfunctional behaviors were affecting her sensitivity to anything outside her focus: her work addiction. Anything outside her addiction was not that important unless it became a crisis and interfered with her work.

I suggested to her a twelve-step program for workaholics, as well as two books: Anne Wilson Schaef and Diane Fassel's *The Addictive Organization*, and *How Can I Help?* by Ram Dass and Paul Gorman.

Having this kind of feedback inspired me to further explore the relationship between macro and micro abuse, neglect, and traumas. "Isms" can produce symptoms of a bigger picture: our uncomfortable feelings and thoughts about differences that do not conform to the dominant group's norms.

I began to understand that if "isms" were not being dealt with, then one might develop traumatic attitudes and behaviors. Furthermore, our bodies would be affected by the underlying stress, whether low-level or high-level, of experiencing these "isms" on a daily basis. Much like with people who have experienced childhood abuse and/or domestic violence, and with war civilians and war veterans, similar and even identical coping skills can be found.

We have more in common than we think and feel we do.

The approaches that I share with you in this book are based on personal and professional experiences, on stories shared by colleagues, on research, and on participation derived from the Adult Children of Alcoholics (ACA) movement. Names have been changed of course, and in some instances the individuals discussed are composites of several people who had similar experiences and with whom I had repeated interactions.

My journey into understanding the effects of racism unfolded as I further delved into my own societal healing. My understanding of how people have suffered from family or childhood adverse experiences expanded as I worked in social services. Having friends who had undergone such experiences also increased my understanding. The approaches that I gathered or developed eventually became the foundation I would use to explore an even more wholistic approach toward the effects of trauma—from familial to societal—and subsequent healing, which I will discuss in later chapters.

Chapter 5

THE DON'T RULES AND BASIC HUMAN RIGHTS

People who have been abused in their childhood by family members, regardless of their culture or socioeconomic status, will relate to this. In addition, adults who have had adverse childhood experiences that have affected their sense of self and their ability to be safe will have, at some level, learned to do this. *This* is the Don't Rules. I learned about these Don't Rules from ACA (Adult Children of Alcoholics) conferences, as well as in child abuse workshops. The Don't Rules are *don't feel, don't trust, and don't talk.*

In other words, do not feel your feelings, do not trust yourself (or others), and do not talk about it—the problem—to others (especially to *them*—whoever that may mean to you personally: to the abusers, or to anyone else who you are assuming would not understand you).

I would like to define the term *abuser*. It is a person who mistreats another sentient being, whether human or nonhuman. As a consequence, that being on the receiving end is hurt physically, sexually, or emotionally. An abuser can hurt another soul through violence, through words, through tone, or through actions. Those who have been abused as children know all too well the pain of the tone and look, as well as the words. There is no ending, no

47

beginning when that kind of abuse is thrown at another person like a weapon.

Abusers have no intention of self-correcting. So their actions continue. This differentiates them from individuals who are clueless about how their words or actions affect others, or from those who use poor parenting skills. The clueless and the poorly skilled parent, when confronted, will change their ways and are truly sorry for the harm they have done to the other person. For people in this latter group, parenting classes become helpful, as well as counseling to break the intergenerational role modeling of their parents, which has not been life-nourishing. The clueless will apologize, and some may even do research or ask others to help them understand.

The Don't Rules do not apply only to people who have experienced abuse, neglect, or other forms of adversity. They are used at the societal level as well. During our lives, some of us may also experience many incidents of prejudice, assumptions based on faulty logic, overt and covert bigotry, and discrimination. We learn to choose our battles. We learn to prioritize which incidents really matter enough to feel an emotion about them—let alone *say* anything about them.

What I noticed, and what caused a leap in my understanding, was that many people who were the recipients of racism, or any other kind of "ism," developed this same set of Don't Rules toward the perceived abusing group—in this case, the dominant group. For example, in the United States the abuser group could be perceived as the Anglo European Americans (or Whites) by Native Americans and by African Americans. This same abuser group is called Anglos by many Hispanics (also known as Latinos or Latinx).

Each country has its dominant group and nondominant groups. Whether or not equal treatment is given to each group and its members, and to what degree, will impact the perception of safety. If discrimination is still occurring and if traumas are being created as consequences, then the Don't Rules will come into play in that country.

In the case of LGBTQ (Lesbian, Gay, Bisexual, Transgender, and Questioning/Queer) individuals, the abuser group could be perceived by them as heterosexuals who have discriminated against them or have expressed bigoted words and behaviors. This is especially the case when many of the societal institutions and laws in a country still do not protect them, just as members of other groups targeted by hate crimes are not protected.

People who come from socioeconomic groups that are derided might see the upper class as elites in the discussion of economic disparity, beliefs, and values. The term *elite* may also be used to denote people with college degrees by those who have not attended a college or university, if education has been used as a weapon to belittle anyone with a "lesser" education. People are seen as members of groups, not as individuals, when there is a question of safety and vulnerability. Individuals would have to prove to the ones in doubt that they are safe.

I remember a friend from my past who came from the working poor. He was able to attend college and then go on to graduate school. When he went back to his old neighborhood, he was treated differently—as if he was the enemy. His friends had immediately assumed that he would now look down on them, so they put him down first: "Who do you think you are? Do you think you're better than us, now that you have that fancy degree?!" My friend was so surprised and hurt.

We talked about how classism reared its head among his friends. They knew what it was like to be looked down upon and shamed or derided or made the butt of jokes by people who had more economically. My friend had to prove to them that he was not that way, that he had not changed. He had not forgotten his roots or his neighborhood. Eventually, they saw *him*, and not a member of the elite.

Passing

The Don't Rules may especially be used by members of the invisible nondominant groups. Members who could "pass," that is, be mistaken for being a member of the dominant group, might be particularly careful in imparting who they are to the perceived abuser/dominant group if they feel that possible trauma or abuse could ensue.

Members of "unpopular" religions or sexual orientations might stay silent if they feel that their lives are at risk, or if their employment might be taken away, or if they might be asked to vacate their homes, or refused admittance in a hospital to see their loved ones, or denied rights and privileges the dominant group takes for granted.

Is it any wonder that if people can hide their differences, they will, when their lives and livelihoods are threatened, especially in states, counties, and towns that condone hateful actions through inaction?

Women

The Don't Rules can also be applied to women who have been discriminated against or have had negative interactions with men to the point that the rules are seen as a coping skill to be used. In these cases, men would be perceived as the abuser group, until the men in question could prove to the woman that they could be trusted and were "safe."

A man might innocently be entering into a minefield of psychological wounds and explosions, which a woman who has been hurt might be carrying with her. He may gradually realize that he is "triggering" her safety and trust issues. Inadvertently, he has become the symbol or representative for all the men in her life who have hurt her.

Whether it is societal- or individual-induced trauma, the recipient may respond in a similar fashion if there has been no healing or intervention to resolve the trauma(s). The response that I heard from my colleagues and friends who were members of nondominant groups was that, yes, the Don't Rules were and are used. The degree to which they are used and with whom would depend on the severity and duration of safety violations.

Again, if there is a perceived threat coming from any individual or someone from a group that has been perceived as abuser, the Don't Rules would be used for safety's sake.

Men of any race or ethnicity may be seen as the dominant group, due to hierarchical structures that favor males over females. Individual men may not see it that way, but the perception and practice remain because societal institutions and laws have yet to address inequalities that create circumstances and environments that may breed abuse, neglect, and trauma—from micro to macro levels. Therefore, in any country, "abuser group" may be synonymous with "dominant group" for those affected.

Much like some of the refugees I met from authoritarian or totalitarian countries—as well as adult children of alcoholics or other childhood adverse experiences, and members of the nondominant groups of a country—they were reluctant to share their feelings, their trust, and their talk with outsiders or those representing the dominant group/abuser group. Specifically, "the" authorities (e.g., social services agencies, law enforcement, and governmental institutions).

We learn that we cannot automatically trust a person of a perceived abuser group. Instead, he or she has to earn our trust. This is important enough that it bears repeating.

We need to feel sure that a person of a perceived abuser group will understand, or at least respect, our point of view. At some level, we do want to see that person as an individual and not as a representative of a group that has harmed us or our group— whatever group that may be. As long as we are part of the group that has felt trauma, safety is a major concern for us. Who is to say that I am not next? Or that you, my dear reader (or a friend, or a colleague), are not next? There, but for the grace of God go I. Or go you. So we keep those Don't Rules and any other coping skills that can help us with possible safety issues.

Based on the amount and intensity of our exposure to the members of the perceived abuser group, we may act and communicate in a way that revolves around safety considerations, which, of course, affects the level of intimacy we want to have with them. People who have been hurt or continue to be affected do want to stop being hyper-aware of tones, words, looks.

At the same time, this question comes up: "Will I be protected by societal institutions?" It takes a lot of energy to be at an ongoing low level of fear, which can spike should triggers appear in one's environment.

We learn to prioritize our hurt feelings—from "It's no big thing" and "It didn't hurt me" to "Here one of them goes again!" (said with a sigh), to "Hmm, should I tell him what I think of his attitude?" to "Those are fighting words!" to "I'm out of here!"

Many times my friends and colleagues have made comments such as "They would have you spending your whole time educating them, when they should be educating themselves to be respectful." and "Don't waste your time on people who are ignorant and want to stay that way." The same can be said of family members who wish to be kept in the dark about the fact that one of their uncles, cousins, or other relatives is a pedophile, or a rage-aholic, or an alcoholic. So we choose what to share and with whom, and we give up on those who we wished had been more open to understanding our feelings and experiences.

The concept of *bien educado*, of providing space to others so they can change their behaviors into loving, respectful ways, is sorely tried when there are triggers of impending discrimination or bigotry that drain or fatigue a person's soul. When the triggers are activated by loved ones, by people we trust, time becomes the enemy. Time is no longer a friend who had created space for you and me to use. Quick decisions must be made—again, for safety concerns. Time transforms itself into our master and we must not dally, but, instead, act fast for safety's sake.

The Don't Rules serve to keep people safe. They serve to help us compartmentalize and prioritize our lives. But at what cost? Creativity and imagination become geared toward keeping us safe. Depending on how severe the threat is, we learn to use our imagination and creativity to develop ways to avoid the abuser, as well as ways to maneuver and manipulate so that our basic needs get met.

Many people in such situations learn to "work the system." We learn what the abuser likes and dislikes. We learn to anticipate what the abuser might want. If we do any daydreaming, it may be about living in a world free from such abuse—or about how to keep the abuser either appeased or as unaware of us as possible.

We do not use our creativity and imagination in terms of risk-taking or of developing skills and behaviors to expand ourselves. We use them to be safe and to stay safe in the present and, maybe if we have time, in the future, while trying to get ahead, survive, and, with luck, maybe even succeed.

If we have "safety islands"—places or people that help us feel who we are—where we matter and where we can have aspirations beyond our circumstances, then escaping and even thriving become real possibilities.

Family abuse is a micro image of this process, and societal abuse is the macro version. Each reflects the other. If individuals in power come from family abuse and if they have not healed and grown from those painful times, then they can, and often do, perpetuate their dysfunction in the workplace and in the kinds of policies and laws they develop, implement, and enforce.

Again, if we are lucky or if we have the wherewithal to seek, we may have at least one safe haven where we can let our imaginations soar. But what if abuse is both inside the home and outside it, out in the world? What then?

For people who live in neighborhoods full of violence and/or poverty, imagination and creativity may center around the present and on short-term aspirations of "making it" without too much melodrama. If death and illness are part of our norm, joined by a belief that we have no control over our lives, we may develop attitudes and behaviors to maximize what little control we actually have. Conversely, we may not care at all, and then we become negative and dangerous high risk-takers, grabbing at what we can through any means.

The longer the abuse, neglect, and other kinds of trauma last within our spheres, the greater is the likelihood that what we have used to keep us safe changes into a monster that stops us from being us. Applying the Don't Rules stops being a protecting coping skill and instead becomes the opposite: a way of keeping us from touching ourselves and others. Thus, we become strangers even to ourselves.

The Don't Rules are meant to be temporary ways to keep you and me safe in an unsafe environment. They are meant to be retired once you leave the environment of abuse and neglect. They are not meant to add to the development of traumas.

But what do you do if society triggers possible threats? How does your body tell whether a societal trigger is going to affect you personally or whether it is just in the airwaves or on the internet with no bite? You do not know. So the Don't Rules stay active, ever hypervigilant.

The Don't Rules affect our basic human rights to perceive reality, to interpret, to imagine, and to create. When people have been traumatized, those rights are affected because of the Don't Rules. When imagination and creativity get twisted or destroyed, then the person's ability to develop new coping mechanisms is impaired. Trauma takes center stage. Reality gives way to a traumatic way of looking at one's existence. Trauma coping mechanisms and coping skills (TMCS) develop.

We stop going beyond our own personal experiences. We stop taking risks that can expand our world. Everything shrinks down to this:

Personal experiences = Personal perceptions = One's reality
= The "truth" for oneself

Gone is the creation of bridges to other people's understanding of the world, unless those people's experiences mirror our own. For example, if we are alcoholics, then we keep alcoholic friends and stay in the environment that tempts us to stay that way. If we come from fearful and limited environments, we tend to interact with others who also come from such environments. If we were born wealthy and very privileged, chances are that, unless we move in other socioeconomic circles in a meaningful manner, we will only know the world from our perch.

Being socially involved with people who you or I would normally not meet gives us the opportunity and the good grace to know other human beings—human beings who may surprise us in a good way. I think of religious and spiritual institutions whose objective is to help people, as well as individuals engaged in, for example, associations, clubs, and nongovernmental organizations. Interacting with others who we might have never met otherwise adds to our experiences, which then influences our perception of ourselves and the world, which in turn changes or adds truths for us.

We may decide to stay within the limits of our comfort zone, where we have some safety and control. We may not dare to expand our horizons if we feel that we do not have the skills to cope with anything new. We may rationalize this by not being interested or not being curious to expand our comfort zone.

By not feeling, trusting, or talking, our ability to be intimate is affected. Our own sense of risk-taking is curtailed. Our self-worth takes a hit. We learn to keep silent. Or we turn our power over to those we believe we can trust—who appear to have our best interests in advocating for us. But what if they know our "language" but are not our advocates? They say what we wish to hear and believe; but when the time comes, their actions do not reflect their words. What then? Do we allow ourselves, without shaming ourselves or others, to reevaluate and not judge ourselves? Being misled is not a failure. Yet in the world of a dysfunctional use of the Don't Rules, being a failure invites a loss of safety and a vulnerability that we can ill afford. Even though it is not life-affirming to stay with the person (or group), we stay. Why? Because we equate mistakes and misjudgments with being a failure—and with that comes shame. What sane person would want to deliberately choose to feel like a failure, to feel shame? So we stay even though it is contrary to our own well-being.

Eventually individuals in this situation will come to realize that being and doing are two different things. Being well-educated of the heart, in this particular case, means letting go of behaviors and beliefs that do not honor one's Self, one's heart, one's love and connection to God.

People who were misled, or victims of a scam, must acknowledge that they made an error—that the person they thought was like them was, in the end, only using them. The error has not changed their goodness, or their love and belief of goodness in the world. They must learn to have compassion toward themselves and, if need be, forgive themselves.

We are human beings. We are not perfect. We learn with love and compassion, and we eventually let go of what does not reflect who we are. We explore our core values and beliefs of love, peace, kindness, generosity of the heart, and respect for Self and others. Do any beliefs, attitudes, or actions not mirror and carry out those core values?

If we value courtesy and kindness, yet we are with someone whose actions and attitudes are contrary, either we have to change our core values or let go of the person who is dishonoring us.

People who have been abused or neglected are coming from a possible ongoing place of fear (stress is a form of fear) and are being overwhelmed, especially if they have not gone through counseling or some other means to help them heal, or have not created ways to stay grounded and to experience the peace that has been hiding inside themselves.

Critical thinking requires time and space, as well as curiosity, for us to question those who *appear* to have the answers, yet in our gut we sense that something is not quite right. Alternatively, we deny or ignore the red flags because we are needy and needing for someone else to do our own advocacy.

During times of stress, transitions, and not knowing what is around the corner (apart from fear of more abuse and/or more neglect), our abilities to be anchored and to carry out effective critical thinking are at an all-time low.

At such times people are ripe for "cults and charismatic con men" — as a police officer friend once described them long ago. We are too weary or exhausted and/or in the midst of major changes, and so our minds become pliable with the fear of "what next"? Of "who will take care of me"? Of "who can I trust if I can't trust myself"? So we may turn our power over to cults and the fellowship being offered. (Of course we don't see them as such; otherwise, we would not venture to join!)

Cults seek to separate people from their loved ones and allies — to make them listen only to the drums of the cult leadership. Love is given, but it is conditional. Former gang members have said to me that when their own families were not there for them (emotionally and/or physically) for whatever reason, the gangs offered them roles in their gang family. The results? They feel needed and like they belong, but with conditions. They are forced to forgo others and to see solely the gang or the cult as their everything. Everyone else becomes the enemy to them, no longer seen as people who hold different opinions or have ways of doing things differently. This is done as a way to maintain power over the members.

Their role can give them a sense of belonging, a level of self-worth, and the sense that there is a bigger cause to be a part of. In order to belong to the gang, members may willingly kill or maim themselves or others. Once they are in the gang, they may be willing to kill others in the name of their organization, group, cult, or something else. The set of Don't Rules, when used *beyond* its time, can breed an environment of distrust even within ourselves.

We are cautious even to our own selves as we hesitate to delve deeper into who we are. Many of us may learn to fake what is "normal" to others, or maybe to ourselves.

Intimacy becomes a façade, especially when we are interacting with individuals from perceived abuser groups. During a conversation I had with my friend Kate C., she said the following:

In an abusive situation, true intimacy is lost, because the abuser is fearful and the abused shuts down. A physical intimacy may still exist, but it too will have limitations. The emotional exploration between the two parties is nonexistent because the trust was broken by the abusive situation.

We learn to shut down our intimacy and our emotional connection with the members of the perceived abuser group. We may talk to them at work, or even have them as neighbors. But when it comes to being intimate friends or trusting them with our emotional life, the line of perceived abuse stops us.

In a world in which the Don't Rules apply, our emotional health takes a toll. We may explode into what the outside world looking in considers sudden acts of violence, unprovoked tears, depression, and/or drug and alcohol abuse. For those of us who have survived child abuse and wars, these expressions are considered post-traumatic stress reactions.

Yet for victims of discrimination, there is nothing "post" about any of the "isms." It is ongoing. Fresh. For people whose abuse and trauma are in the past, they too will have similar, and possibly the same, kinds of coping mechanisms and skills if they have not healed from the abuse and trauma.

Individuals who have also been affected by family abuse know that these Don't Rules are rules to live by, especially if they are living with the abuser in the household. Being vulnerable is not an option. They can share feelings and trust only if safety is assured and if what they have shared will not be held against them, either at the time of sharing or later.

As in family abuse situations, recipients of societal trauma may learn ways to appease the abuser, such as being a "hero child," a "mascot," the "invisible one" or "wallflower," or by being a scapegoat. Usually, the scapegoat tries to get help by "blowing the lid" off the secret of abuse when everything is blamed on him or her by the abuser. Or the role of wallflower may be adopted when the recipient attempts to blend into the landscape, hoping at least not to draw attention while quietly trying to heal or numb out. In addition, sometimes the abuser assigns which role or roles we are to play.

In a perceived relationship of abused-abuser, people who feel abused or oppressed often adopt at least one of the abovementioned roles: the hero, the mascot, the scapegoat, and the wallflower. There is another role to add here: the appeaser. An appeaser role can be a mixture of a hero and a mascot. The appeaser tries to adhere to the behaviors and attitudes that the abuser wants, while trying to make light of any abusive situation. Is it any different for members of abused or oppressed groups to adopt similar stances? Societal abuse and traumas are no different.

Let me continue with the family abuse-abuser dynamics. Often the siblings of a family find themselves being pitted against each other. Does this occur at the macro level? Do we find ourselves wanting the approval and the attention of the abuser group?

Do nondominant groups treat each other as enemies or competitors for housing, employment, or education, for example? How do classism and racism and sexism intersect? How do they play out against each other—or in collaboration with each other to maintain a certain type of paradigm? The answer is, much like families that are very dysfunctional, in which one child may get pitted against the other by the alcoholic parent or by the codependent spouse. Why? I leave that to you to ponder.

Furthermore, do we start to define our sense of self and worth based on what we do in relation to the perceived abuser group? An example is staying in the "closet." This means hiding our personal life and masquerading, for example, as heterosexual for fear of being harmed or discriminated against. Invisible differences are easier to "closet."

When we have been abused or perceive that we will be abused, safety becomes paramount, even if it means not being totally ourselves. Being who we are takes a back seat to learning what to do in order to be safe.

If, in our lives, all we do is learn how to behave, how to act, and what actions to take in order to feel safer in relation to those who discriminate against us and to those we perceive as being members of the abuser group, then that "doing" way of life becomes how we define ourselves. I repeat: That "doing" way of life becomes how we define ourselves.

Our identity collapses into what we do and the roles we play. We forget who we are, except within the confines of roles that we choose or maybe not choose to play. Of more concern is that we forget to explore the beauty we are inside of us, as well as the beauty we are with one another.

We lose the ability to see what is truly a threat to our safety versus something that needs exploring and understanding. We may even superimpose our past safety fears onto the present and globalize it—or perhaps project our own unresolved traumas onto others.

A safer place, whether physical or emotional, is needed if we are to be who we are. Otherwise, "being" becomes conditional, based on safety. That is, being ourselves is allowed only when safety and trust are assured.

Trauma's Impact on "Being" and "Doing"

To paraphrase Lao-Tzu, a Chinese philosopher, "By Being, all things get done." If we listen to ourselves, listen to our bodies, listen to our hearts and be gentle with what we hear, then our paths become clearer. Our actions become more focused and purposeful. When safety is present and trust exists, then imagination and creativity can take flight. We as a group, and you and I as individuals, feel free to breathe, to wonder, to hold our own perceptions, and to question the world around us. Then "doing" can come from the heart, from our being.

When some type of trauma is introduced, "doing" becomes paramount. If we become traumatized, we may feel unsafe. Our need, your need becomes what to "do" in order to be safe. "Being" is not a safe primary option.

Therefore, "being" comes out of the "doing," rather than the other way around. "Being" becomes conditional since it is no longer safe simply to "be." Reactions to trauma may take over—from partially to totally.

How life is approached and embraced becomes dictated by trauma. How do we imagine? Is it by revolving around staying safe and staying "small," so as not to get noticed by those who would hurt us? Can you exhale and breathe in deeply the imagination of wonderment and "what-ifs"? Can you soar to the skies with dreams and possibilities of a more expansive life? Or is it possible that you can do both?

When trauma becomes a daily, expected experience, then who you and I are become defined by the"doing" of what we do or do not do.

Sometimes a soul is no longer trusted by the body to keep it safe.

When trauma has been so great that the heart cannot bear the pain, the body may in turn be forced to concentrate on surviving and "doing.""Being" then becomes an untouched concept. Safety is everything, even at the expense of the "being" and of the"who."

Terrorists and Urban Guerrillas: Continuing the Cycle of Pain

Safety and appeasing the abuser become the only goals. There is a caveat, however. If the person or group members feel that they have nothing to lose, then safety is not a consideration. Why? Because they live in a traumatized existence, or live in a bullet-ridden neighborhood, or in a way of life in which death and the threat of death pervades the air and steals their souls, where hope and justice are no more than concepts blowing in the wind.

Consequently, the extreme persona of the victim can emerge: terrorists and urban guerrillas. Violence will be used — violence against symbols and people in the society that they believe abuse them. Identity may develop around the actions of being this kind of attention-getter, to put it mildly. Such people may see themselves and rationalize their actions as crusaders for a just cause of bringing down the abuser, or of trying to "wake up" the other abused people to the traumas inflicted by the abuser.

As I said, this is the *extreme* version of the victim turned "rescuer." What is ironic is that in their passion and reaction to the abuser, they themselves become the new abusers, the new perpetrators.

They create victims from neutral parties and may give justifications as to why the perpetrators persecuted them in the first place. Those who do not bother to know the history of the parties involved will not know the intensity and traumas being passed down from generation to generation.

If family abuse is occurring, we may not be able to discern who is the perpetrator and who is the victim if both are using the same "weapons"—one for offense and the other for defense—and if we do not bother to get to know the history of that family and its dynamics.

This can be seen in schools when both bullies and victims are punished, if the adults in charge do not bother to delve deeper to discover that the victims were defending themselves.

At the societal level, the urban guerrillas and terrorists seeking revenge and justice now emerge as a new form of victimizer. The cycle of violence, the cycle of trauma and pain, is unbroken. The abused becomes the abuser, thereby supporting the very societal structures of discrimination and "isms" they have sought to dismantle.

In the wake of becoming the new abusers, they give further fuel to the prior abusers to exact revenge and seek redress as the new victims. The cycle never stops; instead, it grows, leaving those who were not traumatized before now traumatized and making the healing ever more important for all concerned.

Breaking the Cycle: Advocates and Whistleblowers

If being a victim is a role *used by the person* (or by a group), rather than the person being *used by the role*, then healthy social movements can arise.

The Don't Rules can be broken. As mentioned before, one kind of victim is called the scapegoat. As this person becomes healthier and less traumatized, the tools of the scapegoat can be used to break the cycle of pain and discrimination. In social movements, the scapegoat does more than point out the abuse and the "secrets" of the family for all to see.

Scapegoats provide emotional and psychological support to other members and to the groups themselves: They are human beings, worthy of love and respect. The civil rights movement, the women's movement, the respective ethnic/race movements of nondominant groups (e.g., Red Power, Black Power, Yellow Power, Brown Power), and the gay movements of the 1960s and 1970s provided opportunities for people to realize that they were not alone, that they mattered.

More recently the Me Too movement has given voice to people who were not heard before. Men and women in the shadows of workplace sexual abuse, of harassment, of being demeaned, used, and much more are now stepping forward to tell their stories.

The social movements and our yearning to be accepted with respect, consideration, and justice are based on having our differences be legally and, hopefully, socially accepted by those of the dominant group.

Yet it is how we experience our differences and similarities, as well as the meanings we give to them, that impact how we will view our sense of self, our values, beliefs, assumptions, fears, and hopes.

If we allow trauma to define who we are and what we are, then we curtail our abilities to be truly free and responsive to our own needs.

If there is a historical account of genocide, internment camps, apartheid, and/or second-class laws, then a generation will transmit to the next generation the tools, skills, attitudes, and behaviors needed when being around a perceived abuser group and its members. A generation will teach what it means to be safe and stay safe to its children and its children's children. In addition to the ideas about safety, other beliefs may be passed down consciously or unconsciously, such as unresolved grief; fight, flight, or freeze reactions; and a desire for retribution. These concepts will be discussed later.

The Don't Rules continue on in the micro world of familial and individual abuse. These same rules live on in the macro world of "isms" and the ensuing societal traumas. What can we do to change the Don't Rules? How can we allow ourselves to develop healthier, more flexible rules, especially for nontraumatic periods or non-crisis times?

When the Don't Rules are in effect, there is an assumption that the world is in constant threat of safety violations. That may be the case if there is no "safety island" where you can be you and can exhale safely, or no space or time for peace to show its face and its gentle embrace.

If peace of the heart and health for the body are strangers or infrequent guests, it is very difficult to stop using the Don't Rules as the guiding light or mantra, which our internal voices chant to us whenever we are approached by individuals, groups, or situations.

If we focus only on a threatening world, then we lose the ability to create foundations that would include a broader base for trauma-free living. We miss out on what are non-threats, on joy, beauty, and a sense of wonderment about ourselves and others.

What foundations do we need to build in order to understand our world perceptions? What must we do to appreciate who we are, and to comprehend how we connect with others and how they connect with us?

Who we are or think we are influences our ability to imagine and wonder beyond the world in which we were born and raised. We understand that we are not our circumstances, once we realize that our identities and self-worth lie within us and not in what surrounds us.

How we treat our differences will impact how we view other people's differences. If the Don't Rules include not showing our unique loving self for fear of reprisal or shaming, then might our anger be projected onto those who do?

Family and Differences

Our family of origin influences how we carry our differences—with honor and pride, or with embarrassment and shame. Do we show all of who we are—all that is underneath the veils we wear? Or do we "closet" our differences, our uniqueness, our beauty, our connection to God, especially those gifts which are not considered within the norms of the society in which we live? Do we come from a family of engineers and attorneys, yet our souls yearn to be artists or researchers? Or, conversely, do we come from a family of artists, but our souls desire to be engineers or scientists?

Do our families support our particular paths, which may differ from their traditions and those of our ancestors? This includes choice of religion, choice of work, where one wants to live, who to marry, and more.

Do our families understand our uniqueness and the gifts embedded in us? Do they seek to understand and support that which is born in us that cannot be changed? If they do not and shame is dealt, how do we receive it? Depending on one's age, it can be devastating or it can be the opposite. If families are supportive but friends and others are not, what can buffer the slings and arrows of words and physicality?

Keeping the above questions and comments in mind, I

developed six areas to guide me through my journey at that time. I grouped these areas under a title I now call "Intra-Cultural and Cross-Cultural Approach to Understanding Ourselves and Others," which I will discuss in the next chapter.

Chapter 6

INTRA-CULTURAL AND CROSS-CULTURAL UNDERSTANDING:

DISCOVERING WHAT MAKES US
WHO WE ARE

INTRA AND CROSS-CULTURAL UNDERSTANDING AREAS

Area One: Who Am I?
Why is it important to become aware of the influences and dynamics of my own ethnicity/race, economic level, family dynamics, etc.?

Area Two: Who Are You?
Why is it important to become aware of how I and my group perceive the other groups and the reason for this perception?

Area Three: Whom Do You Think We Are?
Why should I become aware of how I think others perceive me, my culture, my gender, my class, my religion, and so forth?

Area Four: Loving Differences/Hating Them
How are differences and choices honored, shamed, or closeted by me and members of my group and by members of other groups?

Area Five: How Do I Talk To You?
What are the inter-group and intra-group communication styles and assumptions adopted by me and *them*?

Area Six: On the Bridge of Understanding
Why is it important for my health and peace to develop, understand and comprehend One through Five?

Area One: Who Am I?

It is important to first become aware of the influences and dynamics in our own lives: race, ethnicity, economic level, family dynamics, child-rearing practices and parenting styles, sexuality, sexual orientation, gender, religion/spirituality, geographic region (e.g., relative to the United States: Northerner or Southerner; East Coast or West Coast living, Bible Belt; relative to other countries: highlander, lowlander, valley dwellers, coastal folks, islanders, or mainlanders; rural, urban, hamlet, village, town, city, or metropolis).

Our relationship with touch is important to explore. What does touch mean to us? How do we express our touch—as platonic, sexual, sensuous? In some cultures and groups, touch is a communication style. Touching can be misinterpreted in an animated discussion between people from different cultures.

In some families, sensuality and sexuality are blended, the former leading to the latter. In other groups, sensuality stands alone, not necessarily connected to sex. Misinterpretation and safety concerns may arise if people are not familiar with the other person's culture. Yet even within one's own culture, there may be issues because of unresolved traumas and griefs. What do we suppress? Why?

Those same questions apply to our emotions, feelings, religion, and spirituality. How and what do we express and suppress? Why?

Of course, becoming aware of personal influences in our lives is not a weekend-long homework assignment. It is a lifelong endeavor, as we unravel the veils and effects of these elements on our lives. This model is dynamic; it goes back and forth from Area One to the other areas, and from the others back to Area One.

We hold in us many myths, many stories. If we are lucky and if we have intent, we learn what they are and we make them conscious in our lives. Otherwise, we pass these myths and stories on to ourselves and to others, as though these stories and myths are who we are—as though these stories and myths define our being and theirs.

We may have been born into stories of despair. We may hunger for food and for something or someone to nourish our souls. The stories may set the stage of our lives. But if we do not learn and understand what comprises our stories, then we are lost.

We become susceptible to others telling us how to exist, how to act, how to be, and what roles they think we should play. Within our stories are permanent fixtures, no matter what we do, such as our skin color and our heritage. Yet there are other aspects of our stories that can be transformed, added, or deleted, such as our attitudes, behaviors, generational passages of values, and perceptions of differences.

If you and I do not explore our lives in an active manner, then societal and familial traumas may be our legacy to pass down to others, and they may be the centerpiece of our lives.

We will inadvertently teach those we love to do so as well. And they will follow us, with misguided loyalty, because they have trusted us. We can make our lives stories of traumas, which impede our growth, or we can perceive them as adventures for our souls.

Who am I? This question is very important. By responding to it we have the opportunity to discover whether we wish to live out our existence of other people's stories, or whether we wish to become our own autobiographers, recreating and developing stories that honor us and others.

I will use my family and myself as examples for Area One. In my family, God was and is seen as being everywhere—not only "out there" but also inside of us. We were and are God's gifts. Spirituality plays a major role in our lives. It is the context in which we live our lives. We are all connected, regardless of bloodlines, friendships, or being strangers.

Members of First Nations and many people of other indigenous cultures would say that we are all related— "in all our relations"— in how we treat others with love and respect and how we treat ourselves in kind. It is a circle of life. We all come from the Creator, and therefore we are all related.

In my family, discipline was carried out through storytelling (*cuentos*), sayings (*dichos*), and talks. My parents listened to their children. They were not afraid to acknowledge errors in their judgment. After all, *¡somos humanos!* (we're human!). Apologizing was a human thing, and it was role modeled by the adults in our extended family. Words of apology and questions such as "How can this be done better?" and "How do you feel?" were part of our language. Being *bien educado* extended to the children. We were not shamed, although a bit of guilt went a long way in developing our sense of conscience! The measure of our success was how well we did with others in loving them as well as ourselves.

While materialism was pursued, it was not at the expense of our souls. Differences were celebrated, and similarities helped us bond.

Yet through no fault of my parents nor a lack of their trying, it was not an ideal family life. Societal influences and their standards and norms differed in ways that pushed me to assimilate in some areas and in other areas to acculturate. Sometimes my "embracing" of other cultural ways clashed with what my parents were accustomed to. Yet they were the first ones to say that there is good in all cultures and groups—as well as bad, which does not serve the individual or the group. So it was a matter of whether my choices were from the best the groups had to offer, or whether I was taking on the less desirable values, attitudes, behaviors, and traits, according to the perception of my parents.

Area Two: Who Are You?

In this area, you become aware of how you and your group perceive the "other" groups, as well as the reasons for these perceptions. In other words, how do you perceive the other groups' cultures, religions, spirituality, economic levels, their traumas and problems, and what they hold dear? Why? Where did your beliefs come from? Are they from actual experience, hearsay, history, personal interactions, and/or group interactions? Social media? Opinions of others? How do you perceive their version of what success and respect mean?

At one of my workshops, a participant who was Chinese American talked to me during the break. Although he was a second-generation American, he retained many of the traditional values passed on to him by his family. Outwardly, he seemed assimilated in terms of attire, mannerisms, and some business values. He thanked me for the workshop thus far. It had given him a better understanding of what had happened to him the week before at a manager's training class. In that class, one of the exercises had been to write down and then share where one would be in five years in terms of success.

He said that all of his colleagues (women and men of the dominant culture) had reported that they would know they had succeeded if they had a newer car, bigger house, additional academic degrees, advancement in their career, and more money. When it came to his turn, he said he would know he was successful if he was a better father, better son, better husband, and a good contributor to his community. His response was met with complete silence. A few of his colleagues smirked, and the facilitator said nothing and quickly went on to the next exercise. He told me he was embarrassed and angry at that point.

"What kind of people have such values—materialism over relationships?" he told me he had thought at the time.

After my workshop, he realized that he had judged his colleagues on the basis of his own cultural values, as well as the shame he felt at the way the facilitator had handled his response to the question and the disrespect shown him by the colleagues who had smirked. He did not like what he felt—anger and prejudice toward the others. He had carried it over to the workshop I was facilitating, ready to judge others who were different from him and ready to defend himself.

I told him that not everyone in a culture places more value on materialism over relationships, and that I was certain he could recall Chinese Americans who felt similar to his smirking colleagues. He agreed, although he replied that such Chinese Americans were exceptions. He appreciated my coverage of the biculturation spectrum (as it was known then). His parting comment to me was that he had much to learn, including to be more curious before judging anyone, including himself.

Keep in mind that Area Two is based on Area One.

Area Three: Who Do You Think We Are?

How do you think others perceive you? How do you think they perceive your culture, your gender, your sexual orientation, your religion, your socioeconomic level (aka class), and so on?

Their stories need not be our stories, nor do we need to make their perceptions and language our guiding light for how we conduct our goodness and expressions of our self-worth. Stereotypes may be plentiful, especially during times of national stress and in times of war. We may even turn against each other, especially if we perceive that a member of our own group is displaying a stereotype, which may invite retaliation or reinforce discriminatory practices and attitudes.

One example is diction. Growing up bilingual, at times when I was tired I would mispronounce *that* and *this* or confuse the pronunciation of the *b* and *v* sounds. It took effort, especially when I was young. As an adult, I began to pay particular attention to such matters, especially around members of the dominant group or in professional situations. Why? It went beyond speaking correctly and being seen as an articulate person.

It went directly to my feeling that I was representing my group. How I conducted myself would reflect on how others would perceive my gender and my ethnicity and maybe my class, depending on the situation at hand. This fear was not just my imagination. It was true—true enough to keep me alert in my younger years.

I remember thinking as a teen how ironic it was that oftentimes some people who prided themselves for being from individual-oriented cultures would be "group-oriented" when it came to stereotyping and generalizing.

Times have changed, and now not all people hold a person accountable for his or her group. As more people continue to integrate the various employment fields, and as more diversity can be seen in the workplace, in housing, and in other areas, people in general do not hold what someone has done in a negative way as representing his or her whole group. However, during times of stress and fears, stereotyping increases, as does the fear of not being safe, both for the perceiver and the perceived.

When a Timothy McVeigh or some other person of a dominant group transgresses the law and morality, the blame is usually squarely put on that person and maybe on his family, but not on his ethnic group or race or gender. During the search for McVeigh, law enforcement in Oklahoma did not round up nor incarcerate all Caucasian, blond-haired males in their twenties who were ex-military. Nor did the media make us all scared of McVeigh's groups and affiliations. Yes, society did not stereotype all men who had physical features, a background, or a religion similar to McVeigh's.

But wait a moment. When an African American, Arab American, gay or lesbian, or Latino, Jew, Muslim, undocumented worker, or some other member of a perceived unpopular nondominant group (or whoever is the "soup of the day," so to speak) transgresses, it is not unusual to hear the whole group being blamed directly or indirectly.

It is not unusual for members of that nondominant group to feel they must speak up and reassure the dominant group that not everyone of their group is like the perpetrator (e.g., Arab Americans or Muslims after the September 11, 2001, attacks).

It is also not unusual for those groups that might be mistaken for the "transgressor" group to make it known to the world that they are different. (For example, during World War II, Chinese Americans put up signs stating that they were of Chinese and not Japanese ancestry so as not to get harassed or, even worse, killed.) Decades later, it was not unusual to hear jokes from comedians about t-shirts being made that said, "Hey, I'm Mexican" — implying that "Since I'm not Arab American, don't hurt me or trash my business or house."

The LGBTQ community provides another example of nondominant groups needing to speak up. It is not unusual after a serial pedophile is arrested for gay organizations to provide facts, figures, and other educational information to the public via the media to remind people that pedophilia is about power, domination, and control.

If sexual orientation were the reason for pedophilia, we would all be reluctant to allow our children around any heterosexual males, as the great majority of pedophiles are of a heterosexual orientation, rather than from the gay community. The main emphasis is that, in reality, pedophilia has little to do with sexual orientation and, I repeat, almost everything to do with power, domination, and control over a lower-power person (namely, a child).

Another example of people who do not wish to be identified with the targeted group are those who are permanent residents. Such people are quick to state that they are not "illegals" or undocumented workers, so as not to be the recipients of negativity.

The list goes on.

After September 11, 2001, fear of "the other" and disinformation increased. *Who are these people who wish to harm us? Or do they wish to impose their way of living onto our own? Do they have the same core values, same hopes and dreams?* How many of us take the time to know what is true? How many of us default to believing the opinions of others as though they are factual?

What we have been seeing are more people in the dominant group voicing their concern and showing unity with the affected group. For example, after September 11, 2001, some Christian women started wearing burkas and other types of attire to demonstrate unity with Muslim women who were being attacked. Also, there were demonstrations of interfaith support and more interfaith discussions to improve communication among and between faiths.

Times have changed, but not enough to quell the fears or to let go of coping skills for those of us who are in nondominant groups that have been abused or neglected (for example, indigenous groups). Nor is it enough to give up our perception that the world is not quite that safe yet, even in our own society.

If we can acknowledge that fear, that perception, then it will be easier to see how our perceptions and those of other groups have affected our sense of who we are. And maybe the stories will not own us, but instead will appropriately guide us.

Members of the dominant group may also find themselves having a reaction or in a responsive mode similar as those of members of nondominant groups do, if by chance they have differences that are not welcomed in their group. Furthermore, should members of a dominant group have close relationships (platonic and non-platonic) with members of nondominant groups, they may see up-close and upfront what happens to their friends.

Area Four: Loving Differences, Hating Them

How are differences and choices honored, shamed, or "closeted" by you and your group and by other groups? Yes, this bears examining again.

The obvious issues that come to mind are invisible differences. One example of such a difference is being Muslim, Buddhist, or Jewish in a predominantly Christian society. Another example is being a sexual orientation minority, as are gay men, lesbians, and bisexuals. A third example is being a gender minority, as are transsexuals and intersex individuals. Members of any of these nondominant groups may not feel comfortable enough to freely make themselves known publicly via attire, practices, and expressions, if there is a sense that it is not safe to do so.

Therefore, some may "pass" for being a member of the dominant group.

My cousin has blondish hair, fair skin, and looks like a model. She once overheard two men making derogatory comments about Latinas. As she did not look the "type," they felt they were safe to make bigoted remarks in public. Much to their surprise and chagrin, my cousin, who was walking ahead of them, turned around and shared her feelings.

There are times when those of us who are able to, do pass

physically for being a member of the perceived abuser group (in this situation, the dominant ethnic group). Those who pass often get an earful about what people truly feel. We witness more than we would like to from bigoted people. The question then becomes, Do I say something, stay silent, or leave? Again, saying something depends on how safe the situation is and how safe one feels inside.

If you and members of your group are targets of hate crimes, bashing, or shame, or if you are seen as morally "less than," it is difficult to announce to such a world, "Here I am!" It is no coincidence that the largest suicide rate for teenagers is among gay and trans youth. It is no coincidence that many "throwaway" kids (tossed out by family members) are nonheterosexuals or do not measure up to their family's standards in some way.

To "come out" — in the sense of one's sexual orientation, religion, gender, or any other difference that is shamed, ridiculed, bashed, or looked down upon — takes an act of courage and a certain level of self-worth.

A person from a lower socioeconomic class may find it hard to interact in a social setting with members of the upper class, whether socially, in higher education environments, or, in some cases, in the workplace. A hierarchy of privilege and worth may play out. ("Janitor versus CEO" comes to mind.) Stereotypes may occur on both sides as a quick way to assess a person's morals, intelligence, and worth.

The choices we make in our lives are sometimes affected by how our differences and similarities are regarded. If there is a fear of reprisal — such as a loss of employment, housing, medical benefits, access to a loved one, custodial loss of beloved children, harassment, or, worse still, rape, torture, beatings, or death — is it any wonder that for the sake of survival many individuals who have invisible differences will opt to pass for being a member of the dominant group?

How do we view other people's differences? If in our upbringing we have been protected from other parts of society, then going outside our comfort zone may bring surprises.

I was about twelve years old when I went to visit a friend and her family. Prior to this, most of our family friends had been from Latin America and from some parts of Europe. The friend I went to visit was a girl around my age, whose heritage was Anglo European and Anglo American for many generations. I recall my shock when I saw her quickly kiss her parents on the lips as we were leaving her home.

"Incest!" I thought. In my family, children kiss their parents on the cheek, never on the mouth. "Too sexual" is the implied meaning of the latter.

Furthermore, when my friend's oldest brother was leaving to go back to college, he gave his mom a peck on the lips and his father a handshake! No hug or kiss on the cheek for his beloved father?

"Have they been fighting?" I wondered. No words or gestures of love or affection that I could hear or see had been demonstrated. It felt sterile. "No cariño," I thought. No tender energetic caring or love expressed. That visit opened my eyes to the fact that other families might possibly show love and affection differently.

I told my parents about my experience and they laughed. They said that not every family from that group expressed their affection for each other in the way I had observed. Up to this day, many decades later, even though I have assimilated in some ways to the dominant culture, it would seem strange and uncomfortable to kiss my parents on the lips. Not my cup of tea. Since that first exposure, I have had no problem witnessing such affection between children and their parents. I know that among some families it is a cultural expression of love and bonding.

There was one emotion that was not shown in my family, even

though it is part of being a human being: personal anger. The expression of anger had to be directed at some type of injustice in order to be honored and accepted. It was not an anger expressed with rage or screaming, although it could be loud or passionate.

Anger was not directed at people but at situations that dishonored everyone involved. Yet if the anger was about ourselves or what had been done to us personally, it was not condoned. We would assess, evaluate, understand, and find compassion. We would look at what was underneath the anger, if that could readily be done.

In my lifetime, I have noticed that some people are not able to differentiate between anger and passion.

I remember when a colleague of mine was giving a presentation at a conference. She was quite passionate on certain topics. Audience members who were Latinx or African American understood. Yet I noticed that there were some members of the dominant group who appeared uneasy and showed signs of not liking the presentation. I knew almost at once what was going on. During the question/answer portion, I opened it up. (I was co-presenter.) Sure enough, they thought she was angry, and specifically angry at them. My friend was totally taken by surprise. She is African American and immediately thought that some people in the past would view her as an "angry Black woman," when in reality she was being passionate.

At the presentation, we discussed what was passion and what was anger. It seemed that for some people the only time they saw passion was either in sexual activities or when someone had blended passion with anger. They did not know to separate the two, or how to do it. In families and cultures in which passion is restricted to certain activities, people belonging to those families and cultures will project their interpretation or definition of passion onto the person of the other group as having expressed it in a similar manner.

Being Ill-Mannered, or *Maleducado*

Pobrecitos. No son educados. Son ignorantes. No tienen sentido. "Poor things. They aren't educated (about how to be with people). They're ignorant (meaning, clueless with regard to behaving with love toward others). They have no sense or feelings (that is, an understanding that what they say and do affect another person and his or her self-esteem)." These statements were made by both my parents to help me understand why people behaved in such a *maleducado* way—or, poorly educated of the heart. *Mi mamá y papá* taught me not to hold anger or revenge in my heart. Rather, we were to have sympathy and ask God to help those people to be better human beings.

Anger is a messenger during times when other emotions are, for whatever reason, reluctant to express themselves outright. Anger is the attention-getter when I have not paid attention to the other parts of me. Fear and/or being hurt are two emotions that can be masked by anger, if they do not feel safe enough to give voice.

As I dealt more with the effects of racism and classism on myself and on people I knew, anger might have been the attention-getter. While anger might have been the first to be expressed and felt, it was being *bien educada* (if one is female) or *bien educado* (if one is male) that could help me progress and, importantly, without harming my health. For anger constricts the vessels and indeed does harm to the body, in particular to the heart.

Anger is meant to be short-term and only when the true emotions do not come forth. As the go-to emotion or as a way of living, anger provides a disservice for the person feeling it. And for those listening, they may get lost in the tone and intensity of the anger to the point that the message becomes lost or garbled.

As I have gotten older, I have noticed instances of ageism, especially among health providers. I have found myself not being heard or taken seriously by younger people as well. Feeling anger or frustration does not enter the picture for me most of the time, because I know that it muddies the water of understanding. I have learned to be assertive and take steps to advocate for myself. Yet there are times I have failed at that moment to stand my ground, then later quarterbacking what I could have said. I am gentle with myself. I learn, and then I move on.

Area Four is important because it is here that we have the opportunity to reclaim or discover, for the first time, our differences. Our differences and those of others are simply part of the tapestry of life that God gave us.

Our lives change when we deny these different gifts, when we are forced to disown them based on other people's biases. Our lives become more a biography or a canvas of someone else's image, and less the autobiography or painting of our own making.

A little bit of us dies if we are forced to let go of something that gave us joy or was a part of our identities—such as our names, our accents, our language, our religion, our attire, the way we spoke, how we dreamed, and who we loved with our hearts.

Differences can add to the richness of the human experience, or they can be used to create hierarchies, pitting people against people. As we grow into adulthood, choice becomes important as we select how we want our lives to be, what we keep, what we decide to embrace, and what we choose to bring to our lives. It is at this area of self-reflection that we explore what was discussed earlier as the culturation spectrum.

Appropriation

The term *appropriation* is often used by nondominant groups in reference to the dominant group. Historically, and even today, we can see the dominant group take and modify the other groups' customs and expressions into the dominant group's image. Shamanic workshops in three easy weekends or getting a degree in shamanism are examples that often make wise women and elders of indigenous cultures shake their heads in sadness. Taking something from another culture or group without acknowledging that culture or group is part of appropriation. Taking and yet being dismissive of, or clueless about, or outright discriminatory toward that culture or group whose products or ideas are taken is part of appropriation.

It is in the taking of what we want and not giving much thought or feeling to how we can inadvertently be perpetuating a form of "ism" and inequality that leads some members of nondominant groups to say, "That's typical of them" — and then both actions close the doors to each other's hearth.

It can be argued that appropriation is often done by people who have stayed traditional in their own group while taking something from another group. Had they been truly acculturated, they would have asked permission from the group to use their concepts, ideas, or products. They would have given acknowledgment to the creators of those concepts, ideas, and products.

It would be a form of consensus, or horizontal discussion, a form of giving credit, rather than a hierarchical taking of someone else's work or ideas.

Conversely, there are nondominant groups that are traditional as a way of life and not as a stage or process. Members of such groups usually keep to their own groups and venture into the dominant world only if they have to when doing business or carrying out other affairs.

The fear of bashing and/or classism can contribute to creating enclaves or segregated housing. Little Tokyo. Chinatown. Little Italy. People stay with their own groups. Sometimes it is out of fear of integration and not feeling safe. Other times it can be the result of a transitional decision for newcomers until they get more accustomed to a new environment. It can also be the result of redlining by real estate agents, which was still happening until relatively recently.

Locations of businesses may also be within the same group's neighborhoods, although not always. Often, though, this kind of traditional way of living has its historical roots in safety concerns that originated when lynching and bigotry were the norm.

Meanwhile, the members of dominant groups that are traditional may be that way not because of safety but perhaps because they do not desire, or do not find value in, exploring beyond their own groups in terms of housing, or because of the low value of housing in areas where members of nondominant groups live. Conversely, there is gentrification: the pushing out of low-income people in order for people of higher incomes to move into the area and live in more expensive homes. For example, tech companies in some regions have been seen as fueling gentrification, driving housing costs higher than what the "original" residents could afford.

The outcome remains similar. If we do not find a way to meaningfully interact with others who look different from us, an increase in stereotyping may occur. If we create enclaves, we stay in our bubbles, not knowing what is beyond our comfort zone.

In reality, we do not live as archetypes, of being in one area of the spectrum or in another area. It is not an "either-or" situation unless we have been severely affected by trauma and safety concerns so much so that we corner ourselves into protective shells.

There are many areas in our lives in which we keep the beliefs and values of our own group (that is, stay traditional), while in other areas we may have assimilated.

These are not separate categories but rather points on a continuum. Our decision as to where we are in this spectrum can be influenced by prejudice, discrimination, and trauma arising from some form of "ism." I have seen this in myself and in others as we go back and forth in this culturation spectrum. Too often, discussions of assimilation or bicultural processes in academic circles are unidirectional, with the outcome sometimes being "assimilated." Often the words *assimilation* and *acculturation* are used synonymously.

I invite you to use the culturation spectrum as a tool.

Does it hold true for you in some of the choices you have made? Were any of your choices of staying traditional, being assimilated, or becoming acculturated (bicultural or polycultural) based on any of the "isms"? On the other hand, were your choices made out of joy and a desire to select, rather than a need to move from one to another? Did you gravitate toward certain behaviors and attitudes because they furthered your unfolding of the beauty that you are?

For those of you who felt that your group was forced to assimilate, are you now resentful of having had to do this, especially with regard to the values and beliefs of a perceived abuser group? How does that feeling affect your soul, and your eventual attitudes and trust toward that group and its members? Was too much "given away" by your group?

What is interesting is that there may be a fear held by the dominant group of being "overwhelmed" by the influx of nondominant groups in their communities. Could part of their concern be of becoming assimilated themselves? Are they scared of losing their culture, as many of the nondominant groups have (most notably, many First Nations people—"non-rez" in particular—and African Americans who descended from enslaved people)?

Finally, I sometimes wonder if our young ones, our youth who rebel in accepting White or Anglo ways of talking and succeeding, are in their own way trying to keep something that is theirs. Alas, what they may inadvertently keep are the trappings of classism and poverty, oftentimes mistaking those behaviors as being their cultural expressions. Learning about what is cultural and about what is heritage will go a long way for those young people who unknowingly are throwing away the very avenues that can lead them to themselves.

For me, understanding why I gravitated toward certain areas within the culturation spectrum helped me to better grasp how those selections impacted my communication styles, as well as to listen to others without judgment.

Area Five: How Do I Talk to You?

What kind of intra- and inter-communication styles do you use within your own groups and with members of other groups?

Do you talk with men differently than you do with women? Do you speak with the same ease with members of the dominant group as you do with members of your own group or of other nondominant groups? If so, why? Do concerns of trust, familiarity, vulnerability, and a sense of safety play a role in why you choose the kinds of styles you use?

I find myself "talking story" (as a Hawaiian friend would say) with my Latino and Latina friends, as well as with my African American friends. I find pleasure doing this with my Persian and Irish friends as well.

When I lived in the South (in the United States), storytelling was part of having an afternoon visit. In fact, I am this way with other group-oriented people who are still in touch with their storytelling style. It gives me a sense of "home" not to have to speak so directly. Music, food, and exploring tangents are all a part of it.

In these groups, at some point we get back to the main story. We always manage to keep an eye on the main road while we take side roads. Everything is related. With most women I can also "talk story" regardless of whether they are from the dominant or a nondominant group. Storytelling is a bridge I love to cross and linger on, as are fine food and good company. Time is an ally and a friend that allows us to share our tales.

I talk straight to the point with linear-oriented people. They are all business with no time to dally, not even to spend time with themselves. Appointments are required with linear-oriented people, who seem—at least to me at times—to have gone to the extreme as far as boxing in and confining spontaneity. This linear way is my way of talking with many men, as well as with some women, of the dominant group. I speak and write in a linear way with those who have assimilated to the linear style of communicating. It is also a style of writing for certain fields.

What other intra- and inter-communication styles do you and I use? If I feel that there is no safety foundation, no trust lines connecting me with you, might I be hesitant in sharing all of my feelings and stories with you? Yes, of course.

Until I can feel that you respect my way of talking and of sharing my heart, you might get a linear-style, abbreviated version of my truth. And if I perceive you as an active member of a perceived abuser group, I may tell you where I have been and not where I am going. Information is power, and it will be guarded and used according to rules of safety. Friends, colleagues, and former clients of mine who have been traumatized by discrimination and/or are adult children of childhood abuse can readily relate to this kind of thinking and action.

If you and I experience a sense of safety, trust, and mutual respect with certain persons, we express ourselves through our "home" language, including our body language. We use certain terms, certain tones and looks and body movements as we talk and share our feelings. For storytelling cultures, exaggeration is used to magnify the thrust or important part of the story.

On the other hand, understating the issue and employing diplomacy are used to deal with conflict or sensitive matters. I have received positive feedback throughout my life for my diplomacy and politeness, which I perceive as part of my cultural heritage. I enjoy and find value in those traits and I have kept them. I have shared that part of me with all groups—dominant and nondominant.

Yet I also had to learn other tools for conflict situations: to be more direct, linear, and assertive at times. While diplomacy and storytelling worked most of the time with most people, there were others who did not understand this approach. (They possibly misperceived my diplomatic approach as manipulation.) It literally was emotionally painful for me to be "rude" and be blunt in order for them to hear and understand my concerns or issues. I felt that I was "hitting them over the head with the obvious."

My judgment came in: "Why could they not pick up what I was trying to say in a gentle, indirect way?" I felt that I was being *maleducada* (ill-mannered). Furthermore, I needed to feel internally safe and grounded, in the event they would be offended by my "rudeness." In the majority of such situations, it was fine when I was very direct.

Although I perceived myself as being rude and brash, they saw it as normal and direct, as "not beating around the bush." To them, being direct was seen as being "honest." Had they been traditional Latinx, my blunt manner would have been perceived as disrespectful. In polite society and in many parts of the Southern states of the United States, the bluntness or directness might have been seen as disrespectful, or as acting like "one of those Northerners."

There they go again!

When I was working with Southeast Asian colleagues, I noticed that "yes" had more than one meaning. If being asked for a response, they might say, "Yes, I hear what you're saying." Or "Yes, I understand what you want me to do." Or "Yes, I agree." The tone of voice, the nonverbal look, and the body language helped me to understand which "yes" was being used, or if all of them were. Courtesy and not having anyone "lose face" is very important in many cultures. It is also very important when using diplomacy. Why? It gives space for the person or all the persons involved to change behaviors and attitudes without feeling that who they are and their identity are being attacked or derided. For those not accustomed to this way of presenting the honesty, it may seem like "beating around the bush," or trying to deceive, when in fact those people are trying to be gentle in their answers, which may include the rationale that leads to the bottom line.

On the other hand, I have noticed that my friends and colleagues at times change their communication style with members of perceived abuser groups (typically the dominant group, whether in terms of race, gender, ethnicity, or class) when there is some sort of conflict or disagreement. There are times that we do not want to be viewed as "there she (or he) goes again!" Sometimes we are ignored, or else too much import is given to our words. Either extreme distorts our message.

Whether the input is ignored or dismissed, or whether it is

pushed into the spotlight and distorted, it is not uncommon to hear from other "minority" colleagues that they hesitate in expressing their comments if no trust and safety have been established first with those in power.

In my late twenties, one of my female friends, after observing my interaction with a White male authority figure, commented on my communication style: It changed around Anglo men. It was not until then that I became fully conscious that I had changed my tone of voice and mode of eye contact.

Why had I done that? What was going on inside me to elicit a change from how I was communicating with my friend to how I was communicating with the Anglo man? I realized that at some level I did not trust myself to be myself with him. I was genuine but had engaged in a role that treated him as a "big brother."

In my family, the unspoken rule that my father gave my brothers was to care for their sister (i.e., be protective). He gave a different rule to me: to care for my brothers emotionally. Somehow, I was subconsciously behaving in a way to elicit brotherly feelings from the White male colleague in an effort to get his collaboration in the project we were discussing. I had pulled a coping skill to get help.

My school experiences of racism and classism had left their marks with regard to my interaction with Anglo European American men. I realized that with African American and Native American men I did not do this—only with Anglo European American men and some Latino men. With Latino men, it was because I enjoyed feeling like *una hermana* (a sister) or *prima* (cousin); it was cultural. Now, of course, since I am much older and more aware of how I communicate, I do not fall back into certain coping ways.

Exploring why we do what we do without judgment, but instead with curiosity, opens opportunities for growth and deeper understanding.

Area Six: On the Bridge of Understanding

Understanding and comprehension are developed based on Areas One through Five. This is a dynamic model, going back and forth as new information comes in and as insights occur. This process is lifelong.

Also, it forever goes upward in a spiral form. As we become older and hopefully wiser, we will come to comprehend that there is no "we" and "them," but only all of us.

Chapter 7

WHAT IS IN A NAME?: BRINGING THE WORD HOME

Even though these areas or stages that I described to you in the previous chapter are helpful, for me this process did not bring into focus the picture I was sensing. There were other pieces missing that would help complete that picture and bring it into clarity. One of the pieces was that *societal trauma* was used as a term more to discuss world wars, or ethnic wars in various regions of the globe.

Societal trauma can bring fresh new traumas or second-generation traumas, such as those experienced by war veterans and Holocaust survivors. Yet as I stated earlier, *societal trauma* was not a term used to address any of the domestic traumas created by the society at home. The common words were and are *discrimination, hate crimes, racism, institutionalized racism, classism, ageism, sexism,* and other kinds of "isms." For me, these latter words lost much of their emotional meanings of what human beings experience because of discrimination and its legacy.

As long as we utilize the term *societal trauma* to address traumas outside the boundaries of our own society, we participate in the ongoing denial that societal traumas do not occur in our own back yard. Our back yards are replete with historical and ongoing societal traumas—no matter what country on this planet we are exploring.

People here in the United States are also being traumatized, maybe not as overtly as those from war-torn countries or by genocidal practices that in some parts of the world still go on, but in covert ways via economic practices, governmental and educational institutions, civil rights limitations, assimilation, and mental and medical health practices that undermine the confidence and overall health of the recipients of traumas.

When I was working in a child abuse prevention and intervention program, I encountered family members who did not want to seek counseling. Some considered the concept of mental health counseling as appropriate only for people who were truly "crazy in the head." Others (such as Ukrainians and Russians) had experienced psychotherapy as a tool used by the KGB or other authorities as a means to send them to prison. *Psychotherapy* was a euphemism, and it actually meant subjecting the person to torture and "re-educating" them into what the government believed.

The infamous re-education camps of Vietnam are one example. After the fall of Saigon and after the North Vietnamese took over the southern part of Vietnam, people who had allied themselves with the Americans and the fallen regime, as well as educated middle-class professionals, were prime candidates to be sent to the re-education camps. They were "debriefed" and "deprogrammed" of their beliefs and values. Then they were "re-educated" with the beliefs and values of the communist totalitarian government. Psychology and its practices through psychotherapy and psychiatry are still bitter fruits for many people, in that those tools had been used to manipulate and demean them.

Authority figures in those countries had the power to put you away, to pathologize you, and to demoralize you. In those countries, authority figures were not ones you would look forward to seeing for help if you were not part of the "norm" or were not perceived as "normal" as defined by the dominant group. If you were different or you had differing opinions from those of the regime, the government was not your friend.

In the United States and similar countries, the government does not put people away for being different. However, what does exist are institutions that lack the training and understanding in how best to serve their diverse communities. Often the lack of services can block or hamper helping those who are troubled by, or held back due to, traumatic experiences related to discrimination.

Authorities who are set in their ways, or who are too slow to comprehend the existing urgency of taking care of the multitude of issues that arise from societal traumas, can give the impression that racist or bigoted attitudes are the reasons. Often it is not that, but rather ignorance and the lack of comprehending the effects of societal traumas on the overall well-being of individuals. While the intention may not be bigoted, the results may still seem the same.

My mother said to me long ago, "*Palomita, las personas enseñan solamente lo que saben. Algunas veces, no saben mucho, pero creen que saben todo. Paran de ser estudiantes de la vida y de la gente.* (Translation: "My little beloved dove, people teach only what they know. Sometimes they do not know much, but they think they do. They stop being students of life and of people.")

This can also be said of any traumas that a person has or is suffering from. Not everyone in the mental health field is trained in trauma work and healing. Often it is limited to OJT—on-the-job training. While continuing education units are required, this does not mean that all mental health care providers will avail themselves of courses that are current or cutting-edge.

In some of the work I did as a trainer, the people who had the hardest time opening up to new ideas were those in positions of authority. They were invested in being right or appearing to know;

yet they had closed down their hearts, along with their minds.

Throughout my years of working in the fields of social services, mental health, intercultural issues, and conflict resolution, I have heard many comments made by members of nondominant groups about whether or not to trust members of the dominant group or to see them as individuals. Often these comments were prompted by the members of nondominant groups being tired of or being discouraged about "educating those people about our lives." The following comments in particular have stuck in my mind because I have heard them so often during my adult years from members of such groups regarding the dominant group:

- Racism is a disease, and healing the traumatic effects it has on us can't be left up to the very people who inflicted it.
- What do they know about being poor? About struggling and figuring out how to pay the bills? They don't bother to come and talk to us in a deep way.
- Rural communities like ours have it tough economically, and there aren't many medical services. We're the forgotten ones.
- The people themselves who have been the victims and survivors of this kind of trauma can't depend on those responsible for their situation to work in good faith to change their ways toward their victims.
- If they're conscious racists or sexists, they won't want to change their power structure.
- If they're clueless or deliberately resistant to exploring the fact that they're carriers of such a disease, then we can't expect any help from them. We can only expect their anger over our trying to hold a mirror up to them that shows

their actions and behaviors. It will be up to those in their own group to educate its members.

- All we can do is heal ourselves, coalesce into a unified group of all nondominant groups, and push for political and social change.

These comments reflected the weariness of educating the members of the dominant group. Weariness of educating people from programs and organizations that supposedly serve all groups but provide very little training or required academic courses concerning the groups they are servicing. Outright anger to quiet exasperation toward members of perceived abuser groups often would come with feelings of "burnout."

As demographics continue to change, the dominant group is slowly becoming a numerical minority. And this scares some people in the dominant group. I am reminded of conversations that I had with Afrikaners (Whites from South Africa) when Nelson Mandela and others were in power. They were scared that the Blacks would treat them the way Afrikaners had treated them. They feared a bloodbath at worst, and at best becoming the recipients of the practices they had forced upon the coloreds (of mixed descent) and the Blacks. Yet that did not happen when there was a transition of power in government.

Things are changing, but slowly. In today's world, in one form or another, we all are members of some kind of nondominant group, one whose voices and needs are not being heard nor met. Societal and individual traumas still exist, and the consequences of such traumas are expanding. As long as the effects are not addressed, the coping skills developed out of those traumas will be passed down from generation to generation, continuing to interweave themselves into the fabric of cultural customs.

SECTION TWO

The Effects of Trauma

In applying its force, the immune system is essentially blind.
It simply knows it [the invader] does not belong there,
and will relentlessly, blindly pursue it
until either it is cleaned from the system
or until, in extreme cases,
the immune response finally destroys the host [the body].
—Candace Pert,
Molecules of Emotions: Why You Feel the Way You Feel

Prelude

STRANGER-NEIGHBOR IN OUR MIDST

In 1998 in New Hampshire, along with other members of the Organization Development Institute, I met with representatives of Northern Ireland to discuss alternative means to resolving the Northern Ireland conflict at the community level. The comments from the representatives of the Unionists and Republicans at these meetings were heated.

Aside from the historical, cultural, and economic clashes, the emotions of anger and revenge seemed to fuel both sides of the conflict. These emotions were forms of witnessing and showing loyalty to those who had died and been maimed.

For the Unionists, the Republicans were terrorists, killing and maiming those who opposed their complaints. The Republicans at the meetings saw themselves in a war with Unionists who had treated them as Blacks had been treated prior to the 1960s in the United States.

Many proposals were being offered and passionately discussed. Prior to the onset of the talks, I had been planning to offer a proposal and perspective similar to that of my colleagues, but through the perspective of trauma. As I do before undertaking anything of importance, I meditated and prayed before writing my outlines. Every time I sat down to type, I drew a blank when I tried to force myself to write in a linear fashion about conflict resolution in terms of trauma's influence.

Finally, I let go and allowed myself to write what my heart really wanted to write. The outcome was a freestyle poem and an essay. I have learned enough in my life to follow my instincts. What I noticed in my writing was the term *stranger-neighbor*, which I had never used or heard until I found myself using it in the poem I eventually named "Stranger-Neighbor." (Looking back through the years, I realized that this poem could also be discussing how our bodies might distrust our minds. Conversely, will our minds and desire to live and not just exist be sabotaged by our bodies' perceptions?)

Stranger-Neighbor
You look at me
wondering
what if?
Can we find common ground?
After years of not trusting,
not feeling safe with one another.
Acrimony fills the air.
Exhaustion trying to extinguish it.

What if?
A certain move from you
and I jump.
Ready to fight or flee.
Can safety be ever established long enough
to have trust develop?

Can trust flourish when bitter memories
of loved ones having been
murdered, maimed, hunted, ridiculed

are only yesterday's memories
that the body and mind cling
to remember
as a form of witnessing and honoring their lives
of having laughed, having loved, having embraced Life?

Peace.
I don't know what I would do with it.
How to be with it.
How to act towards you
and towards me.

Peace.
Where would all this energy of 'hyperness' go?
How would I make those dreams, those nightmares stop?
How would I know to touch
a stranger-neighbor?
Help me shift gears.
I too want to live again.

So there I go to the meeting, wondering what the attendees would think of my poem and essay. My colleagues had presented their proposals which were in report format. Then it was the turn of the representatives from Northern Ireland. My ear caught not only the representatives' passions about the emotional aspects of the conflict, but also the terms they were using to describe each other — and one of them used *stranger-neighbor*! Also interesting was the fact that one representative started his talk to the group by sharing an essay and quotes; another interspersed his talk with quotes and poetry.

When I finished the first part of my talk with the poem and the essay, there was silence, followed by murmurs. How can we trust each other if we feel that the "face" the other side is presenting may not be real, but rather a "mask" used to deceive? How can we forget the deaths and the maiming? All that is needed to "trigger" anger and vengeance is to see "so-and-so" walking down the street, knowing that he or a member of his family was involved in a bombing or a shooting in which a family member had been killed.

At that point in the meeting, I realized that since their cultures and mine were storytelling ones, it would make sense to use the communication style that touches the heart best. It is often through the heart that a common language can be found, one in which stories from different lands share common themes.

Since I come from a storytelling culture and family, much like my Irish colleagues I met at these meetings, I used stories to outline the fight, flight, or freeze reaction to life-threatening situations and the impact it has on how we grieve.

I asked everyone there, "How can you resolve your conflicts if you perceive that you're still in a life-threatening situation? How can you make choices if you're still grieving and you believe that grief (specifically when tied to anger) is a way of living and a way to honor the dead?"

They had not thought of anger as part of the grief process, nor had they been introduced to the fight, flight, or freeze responses in terms of conflict resolution at the community or national level. They knew, of course, that the Good Friday Agreement included a section for a budget intended for victims of violence and for social healing. That section stated (paraphrased here) that since trauma was induced at the societal level on all citizens, then societal-level healing would be done, with no individuals feeling that they alone would bear the brunt of the action of healing. Yet they had tended — as I had for many years—to think of their healing solely in emotional terms. The body had not been mentioned in our talks until then.

Why were there not prior talks about the human body at the negotiation levels? Why were there not more discussions about grief's impact on witnessing and revenge? In our informal gatherings, we discussed these things.

Somehow, the connection of how trauma's impact on the total well-being of a person could affect conflict resolution had not been made. Resolving a conflict has to include physiological reactions, not simply the cognitive and psychological aspects of problem-solving. The body's reactions to threat and survival must be addressed if long-lasting peace is to occur at the individual and community levels.

Coming home from those meetings, I knew what the next leg of my journey would be: to learn more about the human body's reaction to societal trauma and what "triggers" or provokes the body into a traumatic stance. More pieces of my puzzle of understanding societal trauma's effects were about to be put into place, as well as how individual traumas may be fueled by macro issues.

Chapter 1

OUR BODIES' ATTEMPTS TO KEEP US SAFE: FIGHT, FLIGHT, OR FREEZE RESPONSE

Most of us may be familiar with the concepts of fight or flight. We are crossing the street, and when a car comes out of nowhere we run out of its way. We flee. Someone is going to hurt us, so we run. We see a tsunami coming toward us, and we run for our lives hoping to outrun it. A group of people is shouting bigoted comments about your group, and you get the heck out of there.

You fight when you cannot flee or when you feel that you can win. You attack a cougar that has your pet in its jaws and is dragging it from your back yard into the hills. You fight like a parent protecting his or her young.

In other cases, you may physically fight or you may verbally fight. In civilized society, verbal fighting is much more acceptable than assaulting someone. When you physically fight, law enforcement is notified.

Whether you decide on fight or flight, your heart is pumping fast. Your limbs go cold while your chest gets hot. Your senses get hypersensitive to any words, motions, looks, smells, sounds, and touch that are potential life threats. Safety alarms go off. Your otherwise peaceful body has a built-in response to protect itself.

And then there is the freeze reaction. You find yourself not able to fight or to flee. You shut down instead. Your breath changes and your body temperature changes. Trying to become invisible, so to speak, you hope that the threat will stand down or pass you by or lose interest in you. You try to hide within your own skin. Your heart tries to go into silent mode (except in your own ears of hearing it), quietly breathing or taking short breaths, if that. You are like a deer in the headlights: motionless. This may serve you well, depending on the situation at hand, or it may not.

At some point, when the perceived danger has passed, the body shakes and shudders; it also sighs to let go of that extra energy needed for fight or flight. If you have frozen, the body now revs you back up.

Trauma not only affects our hearts and souls and how we treat ourselves and others, but at a very fundamental level it also affects our temples in which we reside—that is, our bodies. To comprehend how trauma affects the human body, I needed to understand the role of the body's immune system. I wanted to explore the "microworld" of the human body in relation to trauma, specifically, the physiological mechanics that result in a fight, flight, or freeze response, which I will soon discuss.

To understand how trauma affects us, especially the body's reactions, I drew a diagram.

I envisioned life-threatening situations as gobblers, almost all mouth with jagged teeth, threatening to gobble up our uniqueness and the gifts that God has given us. When we perceive a life-threatening situation, our bodies activate our defenses (our immune system) to protect us and to give us the strength to fight, to flee, or to "play dead" (freeze). If we perceive ourselves successful in thwarting off this perceived life threat, then traumatic reactions do not occur.

However, if we perceive ourselves to be unsuccessful in fighting off or escaping the life-threatening situation, then any kind of trauma may develop, whether the source of the trauma comes from the societal, family, or individual realm. Our bodies will stay on alert for future acts, even for future generations. This ongoing alert will affect us at all levels, including psychologically and physiologically.

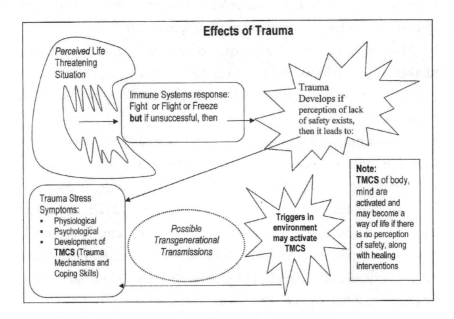

Trauma mechanisms and coping skills (TMCS) are born. I coined the term *trauma mechanisms and coping skills* because that is what we do, both at the unconscious and conscious levels. If the trauma lasts longer than a generation, we will consciously and subconsciously, as well as possibly physiologically, pass down whatever TMCS we have developed to our descendants—that is, to the next generation.

In other words, if either triggers or future indications of another threatening situation are present, they will stimulate TMCS. Can TMCS become a way of life or become the primary methods of everyday coping? Definitely. This can happen if there is no healing or intervention, or if the person and/or the group on the receiving end perceive their environment as an ongoing war-like condition.

Essentially, when you and I perceive threats, our bodies go into action. It does not matter if the threats are physical, sexual, emotional, verbal, or spiritual. If the external situation is perceived as stressful—which is a lower form of a threat—then the human body will take action in a fight, flight, or freeze manner but at a lower level.

If neither a fight nor flight option is available, the body may go into a freeze mode, pretending to be dead, or "playing possum," in the hope that the attacker or situation will lose interest and go away. The physiology and state of mind might display aspects as though of decay, much like what an opossum does when cornered by a coyote.

To paraphrase Peter Levine's concepts, the opossum's line of defense is to be "dead meat," to emit a decaying smell and to make its body rigid. The coyote, as a predator rather than a scavenger, is out for fresh kill and will not bother with something that death has started to devour. Smelling and observing that the opossum is "dead," the coyote will leave. Shortly thereafter, the opossum takes itself out of the "freeze" by shaking and shuddering and then continues on its way. No ill effects, no second thoughts.

Animals do this. For example, polar bears shake, shudder, sigh, and grunt, as do some domestic animals. Human children do it too.

As human beings (especially adults and late teens), we have forgotten how to shake, shudder, and sigh. Levine's major contribution was in connecting how animals and humans "release" their fright (so to speak).

In one way or another, our bodies will find ways to protect us from perceived harm. Reacting to harm arising from the effects of "isms" in our lives can be included in this fight, flight, or freeze mode. Our bodies are a microcosm of what occurs in the larger world. Our bodies will respond similarly.

Field Generals and Headquarters

Imagine, if you will, that you are on a battlefield, observing an incoming threat. The field generals must act quickly: attack, retreat, or lie low. These generals have no time to ask headquarters which action to take. Headquarters has given them the power to act on their own, should the threat be perceived as imminent. The soldiers and other personnel know to follow the commands of their generals without any questioning whatsoever.

At this stage, time is experienced as the enemy, with no time to analyze, to question, or to ponder. One prays that the generals and troops are well rested and well trained.

Eventually, when the threat is over, debriefing occurs, along with memos and reports to headquarters. Headquarters can formulate new policies and procedures, especially if the threat was not situational nor a one-time occurrence. That information is then transmitted to the people in the field. Communication between the field and headquarters normalizes and the soldiers can rest, taking a much needed leave of absence, in order to return for another period of possible threats.

However, if the threat is perceived as ongoing and time is still seen as an enemy, those in the field may never get a chance to adequately inform headquarters. At best, a partial communiqué is sent out. The loop of commands and responses stays at the field level.

If there are severe bombardments or attacks on the roads from the field to headquarters, communication is hampered. An incomplete assessment of the enemy's movement may occur. If earthquake-sized attacks crumble the communication highways, headquarters may never know about such attacks until the roads have been repaired.

We can apply this analogy to the human body, with the unconscious and conscious minds not communicating with each other. If the threat is persistent or visits our lives often enough, our limbic system will turn over the commands to the unconscious mind, which handles the autonomic system of the body. Reactions, not responses, occur. TMCS develop.

Safety and immediate needs take precedence, with functions being rerouted away from any long-term goals not having safety at the forefront. If trauma has affected the cerebral spinal fluid and the endocrine system, at some point it will become necessary for these communication highways to become vital once again. The cerebral spinal fluid's rhythm must normalize and the endocrine system must recalibrate.

Trauma can act like an earthquake, cracking the roads of the cerebral spinal fluid. The cerebral spinal fluid has its beat, much like the heart and the pulse do. I have experienced this beat as a swaying from side to side when the fluid is running smoothly. When it is not, I am reminded of a tornado touching land because of the disarray, misplacement, and tearing apart.

TMCS: Choosing Our Battles

Whatever the type of threat to the person, the body will respond as quickly as it can, given its experience with similar threats. If it is a new kind of threat, reaction time may be slower or it may be faster. Each individual is different.

Racist or classist or sexist comments or actions can be viewed in themselves as life-threatening. They can also be perceived as preludes to life-threatening situations or actions. TMCS take over. A certain look or tone of voice from a member of a perceived abuser group can set off alarms for the field generals to react quickly: to attack, in the form of anger, sarcasm, or intimidation; or to withdraw, either leaving the scene, possibly without explanations, or storming off in a burst of emotions.

In either case, the heart beats faster, the breath changes, the palms get cold and clammy, and the perception of the event zeroes in on the trigger—that voice or tone, movement, words, or smell. Senses become hypersensitive to the environment. Safety comes first.

Everything else in that situation that does not pose a threat is ignored or downplayed by our senses. Any pleasant and/or safe memories of that person or group are minimized since they are not considered a threat. The focus is on those memories and current actions and behaviors that do present a threat. If the racist, sexist, or other "ist" action is seen as an overwhelming or severe threat, the body may choose to freeze, becoming immobilized, incapable of fighting or fleeing in any form.

How does the body know when a situation is life-threatening? In nanoseconds, the body will refer to the memory for reference. The striatum recalls which action is required to get the body out of harm's way or to help the body remember what kind of defense to use to thwart the assailant.

Memory, emotions, and biochemicals are primarily activated to protect the body and to minimize any traumas. These reactions are designed, physiologically at least, for short-term actions, not for prolonged use. The use over a long period of time eventually affects the overall health of the person, including interfering with the ability to establish healthy intimacy and/or trust, and the ability to discern who is friend and who is foe.

The Reptilian in You

The limbic system is also known as the "reptilian brain." When there is a life-threatening situation, it is the limbic system that is first activated, not the neocortex, or higher brain.

Part of the limbic system is the amygdala. When activated, it adds emotional meaning to the situation the person is facing. Heightened reactions may occur if the bodymind gets "triggered." "Hey. Boy!" can mean one thing to an African American man but nothing to an immigrant from another country. I recall a story that my father shared with me when he worked for a major printing press in Los Angeles. This was in the early 1960s. In Spanish, "*Hola, muchacho*" translates as "Hello, boy." Grown men use the term *muchacho* as endearment, of being buddies. One day at work, he saw a co-worker whom he had gotten to know and like. He said, "Good morning, boy!" That co-worker looked at my father with shock and anger and walked away.

Confused, my father asked his supervisor what had just happened. His supervisor said that in the United States, the word *boy* is used to put down and infantilize Blacks (as they were called then). His co-worker was Black. My father was beyond upset and embarrassed, but mainly he felt deep sorrow that he had inadvertently caused pain. He went to his co-worker and explained that the word for *boy* in Spanish is an endearment of friendship among men back in his country. He profusely apologized for having hurt him.

All ended well, as they had developed trust prior to the incident. They had "seen" each other as human beings, co-workers, and friends. That is partly why it had been such a shock for my father's friend when he heard the word.

The phrase "You girls," when said by a man to a group of women, may bring annoying looks or smiles, depending on the women's age and experiences with men. Neutral comments may bring inadvertent tension and low-level stress or sad reminders, or they may hold no connotation at all. On the other hand, they can contain positive feelings for the person on the receiving end.

So if what we experience through our senses (e.g., see, hear, or sense) causes us to believe that there is a possible safety violation, then time becomes the enemy. Then we may not slow down enough to decide whether it is truly a potential threat or steps leading to an eventual threat. If time is the enemy, then the body must act accordingly.

As the body continues on its full alert for any danger to it, biochemicals such as catecholamines (epinephrine and norepinephrine) are released, creating hyperstress reactions. Hypersensitivity to sounds, movements, and smells might ensue, as the body's five senses become elite teams, radar-scanning the environment for incoming attacks.

There is no time for the immune system to ask the upper part of the brain (neocortex) for permission to take action. Fortunately, the immune system is equipped with the same "language" (neuropeptides and command structure) that the brain uses when communicating to the rest of the body.

Neuropeptides were discovered to be everywhere in the body, most notably in the lymph nodes and in areas that correlate to what Eastern practitioners of yoga call chakras, or "energy centers." Peptides, which are informational carriers, were once thought to be developed only by the brain. In the last decades, several scientists, notably J. E. Blalock and Candace Pert, have disproved this belief. They discovered that the brain sends information to the immune system (e.g., neuroendocrine, nervous system, spleen, and lymphatic system) via neuropeptides, which "hook up" (that is to say, chemotax) onto the receptors of the immune cell surface. At the same time, the immune system sends information to the brain via immunopeptides.

Pert's discoveries added to the voices and findings of other scientists that emotions play key roles in helping peptides select which information to give to the immune system. This important finding adds to the field of trauma because it addresses how the body chooses.

For example, an abusive, uncaring boss is shaming Leslie (not her real name) in front of other employees. Her desire may be to hit her boss, run away from the office to a safe location (such as the women's restroom) and regroup, or she may simply freeze, trying to shut down her systems ("I wish I were dead and not having to endure this verbal onslaught.").

The limbic system would assess priority by going through memories of related issues. In this case, fear of losing her job and health benefits when she is the sole provider for her family, with one ailing child, would take precedence over the need to quit, file a complaint, or tell her boss what she really thinks. So she freezes.

By contrast, Lan (not her real name), who is a single parent, has savings, and has skills that other employers desire, tells the boss how inappropriate he is and quits, after filing a complaint. In nanoseconds, the body had chosen which course of action would most benefit her survival, specifically in this case, her financial survival. Lan verbally fights back but in a civilized manner (so future employers need not be concerned).

Anytime there is a tearing away of safety, whether it is at the macro or micro level or both, decisions are made as quickly as necessary to help the person stay safe. There is no time to contact "headquarters," and no time to double-check whether the threat appears imminent.

Depending on the individual's personal history, as well as the group's history, TMCS are created in accordance with that person's personal and group survival. The body stays tuned for certain looks, words, types of movement and touch, on the lookout for safety violations. To add to that, smells and tastes may have become associated, reminding the person of the original trauma.

For the body and the mind, *safety comes first.* Health is on a rung farther down. Peace may become an unknown concept, especially if the person or group has never visited that state of being. It need not be our own personal group that sets off the alarms and bells for incoming threats. It can be another group that reminds you that "there, but for the grace of God, go I." If there are enough triggers in the environment, even though they are aimed at another group, our bodies will sense them and wonder, "Will my group be targeted next?"

In totalitarian and authoritarian societies, people who dissent or are part of the scapegoated group have disappeared without a trace. If you are a family member, it is awful: the grief, the not knowing, fearing the worst, hoping for the best. Do you file a missing person's report? Probably not, if you do not trust the laws and law enforcement in your society.

People in such societies have to learn to adapt if they are going to exist in that kind of system. Part of the heart goes numb. Grief is never too far away. Or it has become a guest in your home, so to speak. Fear also resides. One experiences very little freedom, perhaps none, to exhale and love life. Yet moments and places that bring joy and peace are deeply appreciated. Distractions that bring laughter are sought. What cannot be controlled is met with sighs of resignation: "It is what it is, so move on."

In these totalitarian or authoritarian societies, subsequent generations also have such feelings and attitudes. There is nothing with which to compare their way of existing. These totalitarian societies strive to control what is introduced into them, such as internet sites and social media that would cause comparisons to be made with other kinds of societies or government. Since communication is controlled, the paradigms stay intact and are never challenged.

Consider the above, which is at the macro or societal level, and now apply it to the micro level—specifically, your body. What happens to us if we stay only in our comfort zone or we just blindly accept what we believe about ourselves—beliefs that do not nurture us, elevate us, help us grow as human beings? What if we simply act without thinking, and feel without understanding what we tell ourselves about ourselves? What if we pass down from one generation to another what has never been questioned since it now serves us?

My parents would say to us children, *"Somos tu papá y tu mamá y somos seres humanos. No sabemos todo."* ("We are your father and mother and we're human beings. We don't know everything.") Then they would shift to English and say, "Question authority figures for the actions they take, always with respect and kindness. But do question, for no one has all the answers. Including your own selves." My beloved parents gave me and my brothers permission to ask them when we did not understand their rationale. And sometimes they would say, *"Tienes razón."* ("You have reason." In other words, "you're right.") They would then change what they were asking of us if it made sense. Or they would say, in Spanish, "That's a good idea. Let's do that." Often, though, we did it their way with the loving understanding of the why behind it.

I learned a long time ago that when my body does something, it has a reason—even though I might not understand it at the time. Therefore, I learned to ask it, "Why does the pain still persist after all this time? Why is a certain part of my body acting up in fear or not feeling well?" And I listen to my body's response. Through the decades, I have gotten better in understanding its language and forms of communicating. My beloved body has been with me since inception, and it has morphed and transformed along with me. So it stands to reason that I should learn how to listen and communicate with this beloved companion.

So now let's get back to the societal level, because we are all affected. One way or another we all matter, whether we would prefer to believe that another person's sorrow is not our responsibility. Eventually, hopefully, we see that it *is* our responsibility. We no longer live in isolation, due to travel, international commerce, and advances in communication, to name the major factors.

If we are plugged in, we see human beings in other countries far from ours. We see their plight. Maybe because we are too stressed in our own lives, it is nothing more than information. Or, when news of their plight reaches our little corner of the world, maybe many of us start to take notice. How will this affect us? If we come from individual-oriented families, we may believe that each person is responsible for himself or herself, not others. If we come from group-oriented families, we may see them as people to help—provided we believe that our own group is healthy enough to embrace more members.

From refugees fleeing for their lives, to immigrants wanting better lives, to people of our own nation being displaced to other provinces or states due to natural disasters (which are increasing in number and intensity), all of these are occurring with more frequency. Will we ourselves be next? If so, how will others then treat us?

Refugees and asylees fleeing from a life-threatening situation and who are able to find safety in another society can finally exhale, smile, and live a life they wished they could have had in their society of birth. But if there are triggers in their new homeland, what then? Is there enough safety to calm their hearts and their bodies? Will they have to flee again? Or will they be able to forge a sense of belonging, in peace, in the new land they wish to call home?

For the younger ones, it is easier to exhale. Yet for the elders, they long at times to return home—once safety is secure back there for living, eating, breathing in peace. They want to be at home. Over time, they realize that going back may not be possible if safety has not been secured and if the means to survive are not there. So the grief of not being able to ever return may take place *in addition* to leaving loved ones behind. There are many griefs they have possibly faced or will face, including being separated, tortured, raped, physically assaulted, demeaned, and losing their sense of culture and life. Yet flee they did. They fled for their own lives and the lives of their children. They had no other option if they were to survive.

Unlike refugees and asylees, immigrants leave their country but not under life-threatening circumstances. They select which country they wish to immigrate to, with proper papers given by their government and reviewed and considered by the consulate of their selected country. They go to their selected country to make it their home. In some countries, the government arranges for host families to assist them in acclimatizing to the homeland. In other countries, instead of host programs, churches, mosques, synagogues, and other religious entities help the newcomers. In still other countries, it may be secular organizations that help them. Depending on which country they are emigrating from, it may take a few years or many years of waiting to be accepted.

Migrant workers leave their own country and go to another one to find work. They travel back and forth between the two countries.

In some countries, the government has established guest worker programs. These programs help to ensure that the migrant workers are not being taken advantage of in terms of wages, basic human rights, housing, and medical care (when they get injured or sick, as some do because of the nature of the work). They take jobs normally not filled by the country's own residents for whatever reason.

Displaced People

Now let's look at the internal movements of people inside their own country. People flee from one part of their country to another part. We call them displaced people. These displaced people flee if they have the money and the means. If they have access to transportation. If they have a place to go for the long run. If they can find jobs (now that theirs have been destroyed). Those at risk for not being able to leave are the ones without transportation, the elderly, and the poor. There are, of course, people with other reasons who do not flee, despite the droughts, floods, domestic violence, shootings, starvation, and/or violence in their part of the country. Trauma may follow or be waiting for them—if they are unable to secure safety and support.

It is common among women who escape domestic violence to have tried many times before they succeed. Sometimes they are killed if found out by their abuser; other times they are sweet-talked into coming back because the abuser promises that it will never happen again. But it does happen again. For those who do succeed in fleeing, they may have to move out of their town or city, maybe even their state or province, in order to be safe. Often they change their names. Depending on their government, their name may be changed, with legal documents reflecting the new name. Still, the fear of being tracked down by their abuser is there, especially in the beginning years of their new life. In some cases, the abuser loses interest in her because he finds another victim, another woman to abuse.

The aftermath of abuse—neglect and the threat of being killed or murdered—can stay with a soul. It takes time for the body to stand down, to breathe in and slowly exhale. The body and mind may still be in the headlights, like a deer in the dead of night. Not moving, transfixed. Trust and judgment are questioned. The ability to successfully take care of oneself is questioned as well. Going from victim to survivor is a road that winds and winds, until finally the woman can see a highway to go on, toward living once again, or maybe for the first time in her life.

Another possible source of traumatic development is natural disasters. Such disasters are on the rise: tornadoes, floods, hurricanes, droughts, earthquakes, fires, increased insufferable heat, or a one-two punch of tsunamis with earthquakes. People become displaced. An exodus away from the disaster is experienced. The hope of returning, once infrastructures are rebuilt and it is safe to do so, exists. After some disasters the resulting mass devastation, which looks like a war zone or the site of an atomic blast, makes it almost impossible, or maybe never possible, to return. How to start over with work, school, a home, local support?

Who suffers the most? Who is least likely to be able to escape to safer areas within their own country? The poor, the elderly, and those who cannot flee due to health constraints. A lack of finances, of transportation, and other limitations hamper their ability to leave a situation. What is left in the aftermath of a disaster? Possibly infrastructure damaged, businesses destroyed, power lines down, water contaminated, hospitals affected, little to no food available, and schools closed. If loved ones have died, or sustained injuries— with limited support to help them—those who are left behind are in shock and grief, and their health is slowly affected.

They wait for help to arrive, which may take days or months—and in some cases even years. In the meantime, deaths and injuries mount up, and opportunistic diseases appear.

Those who find themselves displaced and *are* able to move to other locations are greeted with additional unknowns. Depending on how many have been displaced to a particular place, will that community welcome them with open arms, or is there fear that the newcomers may prove to be competition for limited resources?

If the aftermath of the disaster can be remedied, then those who are displaced can return home. It may take weeks perhaps for the move back. But as weeks turn to months or years, doubt takes a toll, especially for those whose identities and connections remain in the devastated area. For others, they will settle in their new surroundings, their new homes. And exhale. Until some trigger of another similar disaster is heard or, even worse, felt.

The body remembers. Unless there has been an order to "stand down" from red alert to green alert, the body is forever vigilant—even at a low setting.

The Limbic System

According to Pert, "CRF (cortical releasing factors) is the peptide of negative expectations since it's stimulated by negative experiences." An inference can be made that societal trauma could therefore stimulate CRF activity. However, as of yet no major study has been done with societal trauma in mind as it relates to CRF (other than childhood trauma and, increasingly, the effects of terrorism). Keep in mind that if there is a perceived life threat, the focus and attention shifts to the limbic system. The perception of a life-threatening situation stimulates a fight, flight, or freeze response. There is a perceived energy about to impact and force itself into the body's systems. The immune system becomes activated, setting off a cascade of biochemical and electrical responses to activate the body into a superhuman endeavor to fight or to flee, or at least to freeze or "play dead."

On the next page, you will see a diagram of the brain. Recall that when we are activating the limbic system (the back of the brain), the focus is on the threats, and not on what does *not* threaten us. Unless you are specifically trained, such as first responders and military personnel are, to use your higher brain and your limbic system simultaneously, chances are that using time as a friend diminishes. For now, time is the enemy, since you quickly want to assess the situation and act. But what if you are exhausted and stressed as a first responder or as a soldier? Would that affect your ability to use the higher area of the brain while also being in the depths of the fight or flight response?

Limbic System — A Cursory Look

Below are some of the structures involved in creating a 'fight, flight, freeze' response. Not all of the functions for each structure are noted.

Amygdala: Attaches emotions and meaning to sensory input (e.g., is the person or situation or both life-threatening? Or, is it harmless?

Hippocampus: Releases dopamine to increase alertness and focus on relevant facts and memories; evaluates spatial and temporal connection to the situation.

Olfactory bulb: Because of its proximity to the limbic system, the sense of smell becomes one of the major senses to elicit memories and their emotions.

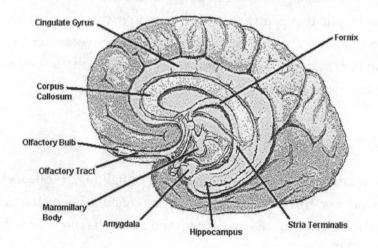

The hypothalamus selects which of the responses—fight, flight, or freeze—to activate. It will then release CRF to the pituitary, which in turn secretes ACTH to the adrenal gland. The gland in turn releases adrenaline and other steroids, such as corticosterone, for healing and damage control.

Why is all of this so important to understand? Because a trauma can be caused by overwhelming emotions that have been stored in a body part.

The whole body is one big "brain" that has memories, meaning, and emotions impacting the physiology and biochemistry of the body, notably the immune system. If traumas last long, the immune system goes into overtime, trying to keep the body safe and healthy. But if trauma is either too overwhelming for the body or too prolonged, the immune system could well turn against itself.

One thing is for certain: Traumas left unattended will tax the body. Traumas left unhealed will affect our nervous and neuroendocrine systems. Long-term trauma can eventually affect the entire person.

Trauma need not be the size of an elephant; it can be that annoying daily mosquito taking little bites of you and creating daily stress. Understanding how the body experiences a perceived life-threatening situation is important if we are to make any headway on decoupling societal trauma from "isms." Also be aware that these kinds of traumas, if experienced during childhood, can add to any adverse experiences that the child may be having.

"Freeze" and Releasing Energy

When a creature is not successful in fleeing or fighting, it collapses or disassociates. However, even though the creature has collapsed or disassociated, the process of fighting and fleeing has not stopped.

When the energy created by the body's need to flee or fight still remains, as Peter Levine has observed, a third possibility occurs: pretending to be dead through immobility, or the "possum" response.

> ...the 'freezing response' (also known as the 'immobility response' or 'playing possum') ... serves two purposes. First, it may fool the attacker into losing interest, allowing us a chance to escape. Second, we will not suffer any pain if we are injured or killed while in this state, because in immobility, consciousness seems to leave the body.
>
> Peter Levine, *Waking the Tiger*

From a freeze state, the person eventually awakens by literally shaking off the energy created by the perception of the threat. Signs of trembling, sighs, shaking, possibly groans or other audible and physical manifestations, as well as a body temperature change, are observed as the energy is released. So why are there so many traumatized individuals after the freeze reaction? The problem is that not very many people allow themselves to go through this shaking-off period.

Humans often have a difficult time letting go of their control over something that makes no rational sense to them. And in a world where emotions and bodily expressions are seen as less than logic, reason, and intellectual pursuits, then allowing oneself to sigh, moan, shake, or to express any other physical expressions without a rational reason present may feel unsafe or uncomfortable. It may look odd to anyone watching you go through these sounds and movements.

Yet no one thinks twice of witnessing or experiencing any similar sensations at funerals, sports games and rallies, during sexual intercourse, and at certain churches, where even rolling on the floor and "speaking in tongues" are acceptable. Unless these expressions are sanctioned in some manner, the person might feel embarrassed, out of control in a negative way, or too "weak" to control these expressions.

The shaking-off period of uncontrollable body reactions or biological arousal cycle, especially in today's society, is not considered the norm. Additionally, the biological discharge of the energy may feel overwhelming to the person, regardless of the fact that those discharges are meant to help recalibrate the body and assist the person to safety.

For Peter Levine, who popularized the *freeze* part of "fight, flight, or freeze," trauma is not the life-threatening situation; instead, trauma is the "stuck energy" created to deal with the life-threatening situation. If a person does not allow himself or herself to discharge that energy, the energy remains in the body, eventually wreaking havoc and affecting both physiological and mental health.

The energy inside may even start to behave like a ball in a pinball machine, bouncing around while trying to get out or to diffuse. As long as this energy resides inside the body, the immune system does not go back to a non-crisis stasis. The person's mental and psychological states become affected by the continuation of the extreme effects on the central nervous system, the neuroendocrine system, the lymphatic system, and other systems. Why? Because the perception of ongoing life-threatening acts is still very much alive in the body.

With this observation in mind, it is understandable that groups that have experienced genocide, torture, forced marches, relocation camps, reservations, internment camps, active discrimination, apartheid, hate bashing, and other societally induced traumatic events would be at high risk of retaining "undischarged" energies if they have been unsuccessful in fighting or fleeing from their abusers. They would also have unresolved "stuck energy" if their freezing ("playing possum," or "playing dead") had also failed to keep the abuser from attacking or from returning.

The fight, flight, or freeze actions described above are designed to be short-term responses to threat, since the activity taxes the body with the flooding of biochemicals and electrical activity.

Debra Niehoff, a noted scientist, contends that physiological damage is often severe when a person cannot find a way to control or modify the source of the stress. Her observations would seem to support Levine's observations that getting rid of the source of the fight, flight, or freeze response becomes paramount. And when that cannot be achieved, the immune system is left perceiving that the source still actively wants to do harm to the body.

The immune system, therefore, stays on red-alert status—or on yellow-alert at the minimum. There is never a complete absence of an alert. Relaxation becomes a dim memory, as the mind and body stay vigil, having never been told that the major battle or war is over. But what if there are still skirmishes? Still signs of possible threats? Then bodymind would be foolish to go to green alert, which would mean that all is well.

"Outside" Energy—It May Not Be Yours

While Peter Levine sees the energy in the system as a result of the immune system's fight, flight, or freeze response, John Upledger does not. Instead, he sees the energy being injected into the human body by an external force. The internal damage to the person lies in the trajectory of the force. This is in opposition to Levine's observation that the body creates the extra energy for the short-term use of dealing with a fight, flight, or freeze situation.

Upledger, founder of the Upledger Foundation, was a doctor of osteopathic medicine. In his work, he began to notice patterns in the body that led to the above conclusion. He and his institute have trained thousands of practitioners in craniosacral work (CST). This is a bodywork-oriented therapy in which acupressure points are used at the cranial and sacrum areas, as well as at other meridian points.

It is through craniosacral work that he discovered traumatic energies in the body, which were released upon the patient's spontaneous movement into body positions. Somehow, the acupressure points stimulate the memories and actions experienced at the time of the original life-threatening event. Upledger noted shaking, trembling, audible sounds, and heat being generated after the patient had placed himself or herself in the body position. He named the letting go of such energy SomatoEmotional Release (SER).

For Upledger, trauma was "an energy of injury which penetrate[s] body tissues." The force behind the entry into the body and the trajectory lines into the body can determine the degree and intensity of the trauma. For example, body organs that are in the line of the trajectory of the force would in all likelihood be detrimentally affected.

Additionally, he saw this energy as "energy cysts," which are formed by the trapped energy. These energy cysts are the culprits wreaking havoc within the body. Upledger observed that the person's emotions, general attitude, and worldview play significant roles in the level of the cysts' potency. Negative emotions, such as anger, amplify the energy cysts. These cysts are also seen as obstructing energy flows along acupuncture meridians, with referred pain to the nearby areas.

Later in his research and observations of patients, Upledger noted that there seems to be another kind of energy cyst present that is not necessarily based on external forces injecting themselves into the body. He eventually realized that there is another kind of cyst that generates itself in the body, which calls to mind Levine's observations.

Body Postures: Shake, Shudder, and Sigh

These two experts from different fields had observed the same kind of biological reactions when the recipients of trauma finally allowed their bodies to release the energy. Both observed that the body would go into a body posture that then allowed the energy and memories related to the trauma to depart. Both observed that when that body posture was allowed to occur, the person would shake, shudder, and at times sigh.

Much like what Levine had observed in the wild, humans, when allowed to finish that process, were left without their traumas. It appears that there is a basis for some kind of biological discharge that, when finished, brings a person back into equilibrium without traumatic implications.

Based on Levine's and Upledger's findings, an extrapolation can be made that societal and individual traumas can create energies that are absorbed or taken in by the recipients. I am reminded of rape victims who, immediately after the violation, have an intense desire to take a shower or somehow to be cleaned by literally washing away the feelings and sensations that are left inside. At some level, are they viscerally experiencing those fight, flight, or freeze energies? Might they be trying to get rid of the feeling of the energies?

Both Levine and Upledger described similar outcomes when the energy is discharged. They agreed that the energy is stuck, or trapped, needing to be released. Yet they differed as to what constitutes that energy, although Upledger later expanded his findings.

I believe that they are describing two kinds of energies: one internally created by the immune system and the other created from outside the body.

Societal traumas born of discrimination and intergenerational grief can possibly carry within them these cysts and unresolved stuck energy. It is not sufficient to address racism, classism, or any other "isms" without considering how they have affected our bodies' physiology, as well as what steps can be taken to get our bodies out of a crisis state and back to a more relaxed state, despite the ongoing societal triggers of ongoing discrimination. More research is needed.

Again, there can be more than one kind of energy at work here: the energy created by the immune system to give an extra boost to get the person out of harm's way, and those energies left by the abuser/perpetrator or abuser/situation. Levine observed that energy at some level occurs in response to the immune system's fight, flight, or freeze response to a perception of a threat.

However, Upledger's energy of injury may not be created each time the person physically experiences something traumatic or life-threatening. A situation that is simply based on perception, and not on any outside physical or other kind of directed energy toward the person, may not create Upledger's energy of injury.

Interestingly, for some cultures the notion of giving someone the "evil eye" or "throwing energy" at someone is considered very real. Energy as a tangible weapon is not new, nor is the concept that a perpetrator can thrust or leave a mark inside his or her intended victim. For these cultures there is a belief that the energy is, in fact, a spirit that enters that victim's body.

Chapter 2

SOUL RETRIEVAL AND EMDR

In some indigenous cultures, a ritual called "soul retrieval" exists. One of the soul retrieval beliefs is that a perpetrator's spirit has entered the victim's body, pushing out elements of the victim's soul, or that elements of the soul had to flee from the body so as to get away from the invading spirit or energy. For instance, a healer of a H'mong clan (a group from Laos) told me that the H'mong believe that the evil spirit may enter its victim's body or will deposit some mark of territory within that body. It is not unusual for the victim to be halfway out of his or her body prior to the healing.

To the outside observer, we may see that person as being somewhere between "spacy," not quite comfortable in his or her body, to the other end of the range, catatonic. The healing performed consists of getting that spirit or that energy mark out of the body and reassuring the victim that his or her spirit can fully return to a clean home—the body.

The person whose soul needs help is seated and told to not move at all, except to follow the healer, shaman, or spiritual medicine person—depending on what culture is involved—with their eyes only. The person needing to be healed hears the healer's chanting and sees the healer's ritual dancing. It is a form of exorcism: getting that energy out so that the whole soul can fully and safely come back in. As the chanting and dancing occur, the immediate and extended family, friends, and others form concentric circles around the person. They chant to the person, lovingly addressing him or her by name to come back to the body and expressing that he or she is deeply loved.

Eventually, the person's eyes start to react by following the practitioner. At some point, visible signs of the departure of the unwanted spirit or energy are seen. The person shakes, trembles, and perhaps gulps or sighs. The eyes start to show recognition of being home. The soul retrieval is finished.

The immediate and extended families approach the person. Cheers follow the hugs and words of "welcome back." The others attending then join in to congratulate the person for returning home. A big celebration is in order, for the person has indeed come home.

I asked one of the H'mong healers if the visceral signs of trembling, shaking, or sighing happen with each retrieval. His response was that it depends on the severity of disruption that the outside or intruder spirit had caused inside the victim's body. The deeper the trauma, the greater the likelihood of the visible signs of the intruder spirit's departure. Once the intruder spirit has gone, the person's own soul, or parts of the soul, that left the body can return to the body, or "temple."

The soul retrieval ritual or treatment this H'mong healer (and healers of other cultures I have spoken with) used is very similar to one of the techniques used in the EMDR (Eye Movement Desensitization and Reprocessing) method used by Dr. Francine Shapiro and her associates: the eye-hand/finger motion.

In the H'mong healing session previously described, the person who has been affected follows only with his or her eyes (without moving the head) the entire body of the healer, who is chanting and dancing around him or her.

By contrast, with the EMDR technique, the psychotherapist's client will watch only the finger or hand of the psychotherapist. Whereas the shaman invites active witnesses who love or care about the victim to an open area, the psychotherapist's client is treated in an office, with only the therapist and the client in attendance.

Unlike with the indigenous way of healing, in which there is no request or need for the victim to recall any part of the trauma, the psychotherapist's client is indeed asked to hold an image or some representative thought about the trauma. In the healer's case, there is no need to recall the trauma at the cognitive level—for it is being recalled through the body. The important goal is to get the energy out.

Using EMDR may run the risk of abreaction, that is, retraumatizing the person and sending her or him into a flashback of believing that the trauma is occurring all over again. Instances of abreactions have been reported, but only in small numbers and usually, although not always, when novices have performed the process. Practitioners of EMDR must be well versed in how to ground and stabilize their clients, should the clients become retraumatized.

There has been energy work done throughout generations within indigenous cultures. Both their healing practice and Shapiro's treatment involve stimulating the information processing system of the brain, at the very least. The basic philosophies, however, could not be further apart: energy release versus cognitive reprocessing.

Shapiro's work has an underlying belief that trauma occurs because the person's system has been overwhelmed and is unable to process those memories appropriately.

The healer's belief, on the other hand, is that the body holds the key and the avenues for releasing energies left behind by the perpetrator or perhaps by a *susto* (Spanish for "frightful situation" and addressed by *curanderas* and *curanderos*—indigenous healers). It is these energies which have traumatized the whole person. By restimulating the body's functions, such as the victim's eyes following the shaman's body moving around the person, as well as stimulating the hearing of what is currently occurring ("I love you." "Come back." "Your body is safe now."), the affected person's body reawakens to the fact that the original trauma is gone. With the bodily realizations, any energy from that trauma is released with the help of the healer, who actively is pulling out the unwanted energy.

Figuratively, the body needs eyes and ears to see and hear the present. Due to trauma, the body may stay stuck in that moment, in that period in time—not realizing that the person has grown and now has a supportive social and/or physical environment. The energy of the past, when it is released, can now walk through that door into the hall of memories and be date-stamped and shelved accordingly, yet without the intensity of emotions that were designed only for that (past) period of time.

By releasing the energy, the body and mind will recalibrate naturally. Cognitive processing is secondary in the healing from trauma. The cognitive is recalibrated when the body goes back to well-being after the energies, which have been causing havoc, have been discharged or released.

Normally, in a non-crisis situation, the person learns of the outside world first cognitively; secondly, through feelings; thirdly, by emotions; and, finally, via body sensations. However, in a crisis or life-threatening situation, it is in reverse order because of time and safety concerns. The limbic system, which has the closest association with the body, is first to react, not the neocortex. The body has to react fast. Could it be that there is a greater likelihood of abreactions when cognitive and psychological concerns are primarily addressed?

When the body and its sensations have been addressed first, there have been no reports of abreactions. Primarily addressing and releasing the energy seems to be the most beneficial for the client, as evidenced by the soul retrievals done by healers and by energy-oriented workers such as Levine and Upledger.

Whether the energy of trauma is internally or externally created, the energy remains internally active until released. The energy injected into the person by the threat has still not left the body. The body's immune system stays on alert, trying to eject the perceived foreign invader.

How can this discussion of energy be applied to groups? Can societal traumas be said to create such energies in the bodies of the individual recipients? More research is called for. Yet it is undeniable that a growing body of evidence suggests the need to pay more attention to the biological dimensions of social conflict and societal trauma upon our bodies.

This is not the complete story of what happens to recipients of trauma, whether it is societally induced (macro), family induced, or individually induced (micro). However, it is enough to invite you to explore the fields of energy work, immunology, and bodymind modalities. The effects of trauma on our bodies eventually impact the rest of our well-being.

Chapter 3

TRAUMA STRESS REACTIONS: NORMAL RESPONSES TO AN ABNORMAL WORLD

Besides the impact of energy that can lead to psychological and physical concerns, as discussed in the prior chapter, what are other effects of the physiological changes in the body due to trauma stress?

- hypervigilance of the surrounding environment
- hypersensitivity (of all five senses)
- sleep disturbances (insomnia to keep vigil, or sleeping all the time as a way of fleeing)
- distortions of hearing, smelling, touching, vision, and taste

An example of distortion is having the hearing concentrate or focus on any words or sounds that portend danger, while minimizing the hearing to any words or sounds that do not. Therefore, some words sound like they are being shouted while other words are barely heard.

A skewing for anything that may signify danger occurs, with the other non-danger words, smells, sounds, and movements being ignored. Conversely, if the person is in a freeze reaction, the distortion may be that the senses are barely experienced, or perhaps experienced in a tunnel-like sensation.

- changes in heartbeat
- dehydration
- numbness in body extremities
- breathing set for fight, flight, or freeze mode

In the 1970s, Robert Ader discovered that mental processes alone could manipulate the immune system. Ader conducted an experiment with rats. He mixed sweetened water with an immunosuppressant liquid. The rats drank the combination, became nauseous, and developed intestinal distress. Additionally, their immune systems became compromised. Later, when the rats were given only sweetened water, they reacted as if the immunosuppressant liquid was still included. What was astonishing to the researchers was that the rats' immune systems were debilitated as well!

Can reaction to traumas be extrapolated from this experiment? Anything present in or around the source of the trauma can be perceived as being the original source, with all its "power." If this is the case, then anything associated with the source of the fight, flight, or freeze response is perceived as a renewed attack, and thereby can "trigger" or evoke reactions similar to, if not the same as, those the person had expressed at the time of the original trauma.

This would explain situations in which someone is "triggered" into a series of fight, flight, or freeze reactions by people, places, dynamics, or situations that are reminiscent of the original trauma-inducing source. Suddenly their bodies are put on red-alert status. Considering that "isms" (sexism, racism, classism, etc.) are still present in our society, as are triggers, it would stand to reason that recovering or healing from "isms" and their societal traumas could be difficult. The question then is "Is it memory, or is it happening again?" when a trigger occurs. If an individual has been hurt and traumatized because he or she is a member of a group (e.g., women, or being poor, or due to one's race or religion), or the group as a whole has been traumatized (e.g., targeted for a mass shooting), anything in the environment that is associated with the trauma may serve as triggers.

Triggers: Incoming Threat, or Is It Memory?

What sets off the fight, flight, or freeze reactions of the body, along with any skills to cope with the impending threat? What "triggers" someone to switch to crisis reactions? By *trigger*, I want to reiterate that I am referring to something or someone that evokes or stimulates these reactions.

Is it a memory, a reminder of the past trauma? Or is the current situation providing cues and signs for another similar threat? Depending on the severity of the loss and the attachment to what was lost, the person will determine in nanoseconds if she or he has the luxury to see time as an ally or as an enemy. Time becomes a key player, as does the meaning attached to the perceived loss before and during the trauma.

What did the trauma signify? What did the loss mean to the person and to the group? Life? Dignity? Security? Safety? Freedom? Job opportunities? A place to live? A place to worship? To be able to love whomever? To be oneself?

The case of a woman being raped or assaulted provides a typical micro example of triggers occurring. (While this is a micro example, the analogy to macro trauma is applicable.) Anything that has been associated by the victim as belonging to the experience can be a potential trigger for her in any part of her life. If the rapist wore bright red or smelled a certain way, had a particular tone of voice or a manner of movement—any of these things can "trigger" the victim. If the victim was assaulted in an elevator, she might find herself avoiding elevators in general because they remind her of the awful event.

If the triggers evoke strong fight, flight, or freeze reactions, the fear may affect her confidence to judge appropriately.

Depending on the level of how successful the victim was in fighting, fleeing, or freezing, the potency of the trigger will then be affected.

The victim's judgment will primarily be based on safety and how successful she is in being safe. She may find herself not wanting to leave her apartment. She may develop other habits that she perceives would help her be safer. Her intimacy with people who wear bright red will be slow in coming, if it occurs again at all.

Certain people will have to prove to her that they are safe and trustworthy. She will also be hypervigilant for any comments that may indicate that a person is not respectful of her or of women in general (i.e., not respectful of her particular group).

How do triggers apply to those of us who are recipients of societal trauma? Any action, demeanor, or attitude evoking memories of discrimination that has created humiliation, shame, physical pain, or a life-threatening environment can create those triggers. As with individuals who have experienced childhood abuse or neglect, these societal-level experiences may evoke fear and safety concerns. Will it happen again?

When a woman is battered or raped and there is no real redress, a trigger is created. When Asian American individuals are denied promotion due to a "glass ceiling" for their group, a trigger is created that only a certain percentage of their group is allowed to advance in certain fields. When a gay man is assaulted, with no serious follow-up action by law enforcement, a trigger is created to not trust the police for help. When a church, mosque, or synagogue is burned down, triggers are created. When a police officer beats to death a member of your group, existing triggers are reinforced and new ones created. Stereotypes are created about "those people" — in this case, police officers — much like stereotypes of other groups. One member is seen as representing the whole group.

When White individuals are seen as perpetrators by virtue of their group membership, until they can prove they are trustworthy and safe, that too can create triggers for them — unless they can appreciate why they must prove themselves. Much like a man dating a woman who has been hurt by men, that man who loves that woman will understand and set out to prove that he is not like those men who had hurt her.

When any of these or other things are done, and there is no perceived justice and action to diminish the damage inflicted by these events, triggers will be created.

"There, but for the grace of God, go I." Simply being part of a group that has and continues to be treated as second-class in some fashion may be enough for an individual to get "triggered." If we get "triggered" often enough, either as individuals or as groups, eventually we will develop responses or reactions that can be subtle or overt as ways to keep us safe.

Our environment becomes a world of triggers, and it is our task to develop ways of coping and surviving. Still, others will seek violent means to draw attention to the plight of the groups. A range of reactions from mild to severe can ensue. All these ways are the result of societal trauma that has not been addressed, where healing has yet to occur in a sufficient manner. How sufficient depends on the individual as well as on any group that has been affected.

Trauma Mechanisms and Coping Skills (TMCS) to the Rescue

When trauma enters our lives, our world changes. It is not as safe as you or I once thought it to be. We become more wary of situations and people that may cause a future trauma. How will we act? How will we feel, should that occasion arise? What have we developed to protect ourselves while also providing ways to find our own version of happiness? Will we experience trauma again? As my niece once said to me, "There is nothing 'post' about post-traumatic reactions because there is still racism. There is still classism. There is still sexism."

The earlier part of this section discussed the physiological dynamics of going into a fight, flight, or freeze response. It explored some of the reactions that arise from those dynamics, especially if the immune system is still on red- or yellow-alert. Long-term effects of fight, flight, or freeze reactions engage the psychological aspects of who we are and the perceptions we have. The long-term effects become lenses of trauma through which we peer.

Fight, flight, or freeze (both physiological and psychological) reactions are normal ways to react to an abnormal, traumatizing event. There is nothing pathological about it.

The process becomes pathological when these reactions I call trauma mechanisms (physiological, psychoneuroimmunological) and coping skills (ensuing beliefs, attitudes, behaviors, and actions) adversely affect our continued growth and our unfolding of who we are—loving gifts from God. Initially, these trauma mechanisms and coping skills (TMCS) are healthy responses to genocide, torture, hate crimes and bashing, and other expressions of "isms."

TMCS are also created when family and individual traumas have occurred. By individual, I mean that the perceived life threat happened not because you were a member of a group. The responses become unhealthy as time goes by, as the grief process is impacted, and as the development of trust and intimacy become skewed toward safety issues.

When I was in junior high school, I learned to blend into the walls, so to speak, if I could. The term *wallflower* may be remembered by adult children of alcoholics or adult children of dysfunctional families in which abuse existed. For me, it was school. My family and friends were my haven, but the outside world? Not so much.

I did not volunteer answers. I did not raise my hand in class. I wanted to "shrink," hoping I would not get noticed by my teachers. I was not always this way. In grammar school, I was a verbal child. However, racism, classism, and stereotypes silenced my voice.

I developed coping skills as responses. So at school, I became a wallflower as much as I could. I also learned to speak in a different way to authority figures, in particular to Anglo European American authorities. I spoke with deference and with smiles or by nodding my head to appear that I was in agreement with what they were saying. I did not volunteer information. I was super-alert to certain words, tones, and movements that in turn would set off my coping skills. I found my internal mechanisms changing as well. My hearing and sight were skewed toward any words or movement portending threats to my self-esteem.

My breathing changed when I thought I was being shamed or threatened. I found myself being anxious and tense about going to school. "Being who you are is not good enough" was the message that I got from a few teachers. It was not okay to be me. Yet something inside myself loved me enough to help me develop coping skills. My beloved body, in its own way, developed physiological mechanisms to keep me alert for any more possible incoming traumas.

Safety and love were with my family and friends. I was verbal and more carefree in my mannerisms and facial expressions of delight. I saw the adults in my family as my guardians and mentors. My home was a place to be who I was. Joy, peace, love, caring embraced me there.

I learned to "wear two hats" — one for outside the home and one for my home. Other bicultural friends have told me similar stories. Yet for still other friends, it was the reverse. They found a haven in the outside world, not with their families in their homes.

Looking back at my childhood and young adult years, I realize that not only were we bicultural in our upbringing, but we also had to have *dos caras*, or "two faces." Psychologically, I and others had to divide our demeanor and communication styles into two: one for "us" and one for "them." One face is real and the other face is a mask that the wearer designs as a protection from "them." Our two faces are forced upon us by discrimination or abuse at home, or by engaging with certain parts of the outside world. We create those skills and demeanor for the sake of our bodies' and our hearts' safety.

So what do you think happens if a child has no safety — both in the outside world and at home? Where is his or her safe haven? Is the child's "beingness" put on the back burner, or "closeted," only to come to the forefront or out of the closet, when there is a perception of safety or acceptance at some level?

It is so important not to forget that those faces or masks are coping skills. If we forget that one of those faces is a mask for protection and we allow the mask to become who we are, then we run the risk of becoming a caricature of ourselves. We become that wallflower. Or we may become "mascots" trying to amuse the perceived abuser groups, or the abuser in our families. Or we may do anything to get approval, even risking our lives, to show that we are equals.

Of concern is that these masks may be put on and used for everyone and everything. For example, the mascot may become a people pleaser to everyone, not just to the perceived abuser. By becoming those masks, we lose ourselves. We risk losing seeing our beautiful faces in our mirrors to reflect back the love that we are. And the longer we see ourselves as being those masks, the more our identities are those masks, those behaviors, those attitudes. Should anyone question or challenge our masks, we then may feel that they are threatening our very identities as human beings. Separating who we are with what we use is essential, if we are to create space for us to be more of who we are: human beings.

Roles People Play: Adult Children of Abuse and Recipients of Societal Traumas

To reiterate, if this seems reminiscent to you of some of the roles that children and adult children of alcoholics adopt, you are not mistaken. I saw these roles being played out not just from survivors and victims of childhood familial abuse, but also from people who had experienced societal traumas. Even whole groups or subgroups may adopt these roles as avenues of keeping safe.

Substitute "model minority" with "hero children." Substitute "angry, violent people who riot" with "scapegoats" or "problem children." Substitute the term for those who consistently denigrate their own members through humor, or who are unable to tolerate serious discussions without inserting jokes, with "mascots." Substitute those who are rarely discussed in the media or are forgotten by the rest of us with "lost children." Often the forgotten ones, or the "lost children," are the indigenous populations, the lower castes, the rural, and the poor. The similarities continue in terms of roles and coping skills. Whether at the micro or macro level, coping skills are developed to keep ourselves safe and to help us to continue onward in life.

The trauma mechanisms and coping skills (TMCS) are often passed on to the next generation. Why? Because "isms" continue to exist and, with them, ensuing societal traumas for many. Memories are not of the distant past, but of yesterday.

Traumatic events have no time to be catalogued in our bodies' memory stacks. They are put on the reference table for easier access. When historical traumas have visited groups as a whole, it takes longer for the group as a whole and for individual members to put away these memories if there are present traumas and "isms" that keep the old ones alive.

Chapter 4

MEMORY, PERCEPTION, AND TRAUMA: IS IT REAL, OR IS IT SPECIAL EFFECTS?

Memory becomes a vital player when threat comes knocking at your door. Your body selects the appropriate memories that can help to get you out of harm's way. If you have learned to move away from an object that is flying toward you, then you should thank the striatum in your brain. The striatum had accessed a motion from a memory, which had told your body to duck in the past. If, in the past, a certain gesture precipitated your being hurt, then your body will now access that information and tell you whether that is the same kind of gesture. If it is, then the memory of action that saved you in the past might save you again.

Memory is not only important to the survival of the individual, but also to the survival of the group. A body's memory of trauma can be passed on via the immune, neuromuscular, and neuroendocrine systems. Even when the descendants have no cognitive knowledge of prior traumas experienced by their ancestors, their physiology appears to have kept the memory. Does this mean that aggression that is needed in the "fight" part of survival can be passed on, especially if an ongoing "ism" or a historical trauma is tapped into? Might aggression be one of the many tools for survival? This may be the case.

Deborah Niehoff studied the effects of violence upon our immune system, our biology, and possible transgenerational transmissions of physiological responses to violence. Her studies found that our nervous system is indeed not only affected by violence, but also learns to automatically respond in a fight or flight manner over time. Furthermore, if survival is the norm for that individual or group, this safety method may be passed down to descendants.

I think of prison systems, where the environment nurtures aggression either overtly or covertly. I think of gang life, of high-crime areas, and of hate crimes. These environments create predator and prey energies. We learn to fight for our lives, to cower, "play dead" and freeze—or to escape by any means possible, including through drugs and alcohol.

If a trauma lasts for a long time or is perceived to do so, then an overriding concern with staying safe or safer starts to affect other areas of our lives. These areas include trust development, risk-taking, intimacy development, judgment, communication styles toward the perceived abuser, the grief process, and conflict resolution. Some people might avoid perceived threatening situations. Others may take unnecessary risks. The boundaries we create to stay safe and to place appropriate limits according to intimacy levels (e.g., stranger, friend, lover, sibling, child) are utilized even with safe people who have done us no harm.

Boundaries: Fences Make Good Neighbors or Prison Walls

Normal boundaries in some cases may be distorted by trauma or be taken over by boundaries created by trauma. Those who have been abused at the micro level understand this all too well.

For example, between child and parent, there are particular expectations and norms of what constitutes healthy behaviors and attitudes within this kind of relationship. When these healthy boundaries are crossed or violated, the abused person's psyche is adversely affected, such as in incest relationships, where sexual intercourse and sexual energy are injected into what should have been a non-sexualized area. Confusion of what is appropriate love might develop. Younger victims may not have the cognitive development and the words to frame and understand what has transgressed. Emotions dominate in the early years. Individuals from each age range carry their own unique type of struggles in coping and in being believed, especially by other family members.

The meshing or destruction of those boundaries can lead to future hurt, grief, and poor judgment. When sexual harassment takes place at the workplace, the boundary that holds the norms of behaviors and attitudes between employee and supervisor cracks. Safety is compromised and trust diminished. Productivity is negatively affected. The reputation of the organization is challenged as an ethical and safe environment. The harassed person may become traumatized if appropriate action is not enforced. If the abused individual perceives that no justice has occurred or that she or he has been ignored, traumatic reactions may ensue.

At the macro level, a society and its citizens have a contract. A society also has boundaries that hold beliefs, behaviors, and attitudes. In the United States, two such beliefs are that "we are all equal under God" and "we are free to pursue life, liberty, and happiness." The Constitution, the Bill of Rights, society's laws, its institutions, and the media, which seemingly promote diversity and tolerance—all of these imply that we should trust and feel safe in our society. "Our society is the greatest on Earth. People migrate here to live. Just how many migrate out?" And so on. Each country has a vision of what it sees itself to be. Each country has a self-perception of how well its values and laws work, as well as how it views and protects its people.

When a societal trauma occurs, boundaries are affected. Boundaries cease to be flexible due to prevailing winds of change. Rather, they are torn, distorted, and ripped in various ways. Some societal traumas are like hairline fractures, felt only by the group; others are overt multiple fractures seen by all.

As a response to the trauma, new boundaries are created to help us maintain a sense of safety. We develop either too many psychological and emotional boundaries, or not enough. In the end, if we are able to heal, some boundaries created by the trauma may still remain, while other boundaries will have disappeared.

If, in society, there are reminders that other societal traumas might occur, the affected groups will keep those boundaries created by trauma. They would be foolish to discard such boundaries if they feel that they are still in harm's way and if their perception is that society is essentially doing nothing to eradicate the roots of societal trauma—namely, the "isms." It does not matter if their feelings are based on overall facts or on feelings based on slices of trauma.

For example, someone who comes from a rural area may be skittish when interacting with people from large cities. This can be due to stereotypes, or to the fact that urban people, although unaware of the damage they are doing, use bigoted words.

Much like at the individual level of abuse, neglect, and other situations that are traumatic, the person might keep her or his trauma walls for protection. If you are dating a person who reminds you of someone who was abusive to you earlier, then the new person in your life may have to prove to your satisfaction that you can open up your heart, be vulnerable, and risk not being hurt. What it boils down to is this: Are you safe enough to open up?

Whether it comes from societal trauma or from individual adverse experiences, we want to enjoy life and be safe doing that.

Boundary Creations, Self, and Trauma

Normal Sphere of the Self

Normal boundaries are usually created for distinguishing what is me and what is you, as well as for safety and intimacy development of the physical, emotional, mental, and spiritual aspects of the Self. Boundaries encircle the SELF. The person has enough flexibility to keep himself or herself safe. Boundaries are assets, not hindrances, to healthy intimacy within the Self and others.

Cultural influences (e.g., ethnicity, religion, gender, sexual orientation, socioeconomic level) influence where the boundaries are placed, the expressions of those boundaries, and their level of flexibility.

Trauma Boundaries Are Added

The person creates additional boundaries as reactions or responses to the traumatic experiences. These heavier boundaries or trauma boundaries develop when trauma has overwhelmed the normal boundaries. The normal boundaries may have portions missing before the trauma or because of the trauma. These heavier boundaries originate with the purpose of reinforcing and protecting the Self around the areas where trauma has entered the person's life.

When there are "triggers," these heavier boundaries may reappear, expand, or take on "a life of their own."

How temporary or permanent these heavier boundaries will be depends on the following:

1. the flexibility, amount, and location of the normal boundaries prior to the trauma(s)
2. how much empowerment and intervention have taken place to strengthen the Self during the trauma and immediately after the trauma
3. any additional ongoing traumas or triggers; if these occur, even more trauma boundaries may be created, thus constructing a fortress around the Self

Sometimes trauma blows a hole so close to the Self that there are no "eyes" to see it and, therefore, no boundaries are placed.

Going Back to Normal?

If there is recovery and healing, a person may retain some of the trauma boundaries and discard the rest. The remaining trauma boundaries are kept with the normal boundaries. By and large, the majority of the transitional and crisis-created boundaries are released once trauma leaves the person's life. If trauma is still around, the person will keep larger amounts of traumatic boundaries for safety. Alternatively, the person will create and modify existing trauma boundaries. Part of the healthy boundaries may thicken, so to speak, much like scar tissue.

What matters is perception. Holding on to the perception may occur if the expressions of social justice have not made their way to the practical everyday lives of the members of the affected group. The more a group is traumatized, the more its members will be reluctant to take risks in going beyond their comfort zone, going beyond what is familiar to them, if they feel that the unknown poses a potential for further trauma.

Trauma oozes into our general way of perceiving the world. We may even use trauma mechanisms and coping skills as the primary way of handling life. Trauma may seep its way into our culture, into creating customs and rituals, with the underlying purpose of helping us feel safe, of not "losing face," and of finding some semblance of comfort, even at the expense of our hearts and our freedom.

If we love our children, we may teach them tools that served us in getting through the howling winds of trauma. The question then is to find more effective tools that can help us transform societal traumas in our lives into adventures for our souls and in our hearts.

Chapter 5

INTERGENERATIONAL TEACHINGS: THE AIRPLANE SCENARIO — TRUSTING YOURSELF OR TRUSTING THEM

Societal trauma has many faces and several ways to enter our lives. One of them is through intergenerational teachings. What do we say to our children and other loved ones when trauma may be part of their legacy through "isms"? What do you say when your family has been affected and you want to provide your children, grandchildren, nieces, or nephews with tools in case they experience something similar? How do we prepare them? Or do we say nothing at all?

I wanted to understand how intergenerational passage, as well as post-trauma effects, influenced us. And God answered: I experienced a near airplane crash and the aftermath. Close, but fortunately no cigar, as the saying goes.

I use that "scenario" and the subsequent societal trauma metaphors to show how a memory of a traumatic event can affect one's perception and reactions, and also what a person might give as information to current loved ones. What emotions and perceptions and any words of safety do we pass down to the generations that follow?

Let me preface this with the fact that, in the end, everyone was fine. We landed safely. I also want to state that this experience further helped me to understand how much power we give to authority figures versus trusting our own instincts and observations.

One day, I was on an airplane that was having engine trouble. At the time, little did I know that my experience would serve as a basis for understanding how members of society might respond to societal trauma. I began to use my experience by sharing it in classes and workshops that I taught in terms of intercultural issues, racism, and abuse. I took my experience and turned it into an interactive scenario for role-playing.

After the scenario was set, I assigned students their roles, some acting as flight attendants and pilots, and the rest acting as passengers. They immediately assumed their roles. A debriefing after the role-play was included, as the scenario proved to spark strong emotions—something I had not initially anticipated. The scenario was as follows:

You are a passenger on a major airline. Everything seems fine— friendly flight attendants and self-assured pilots. There are two unaccompanied children sitting in the seats in front of you. A gentleman sitting next to you flies small planes. You chat a bit and start to relax in your seat. As the plane takes off, you notice unusual sideways shaking. You have a sense that something is not quite right. You disregard what you are sensing and try to breathe more easily. As the plane reaches an altitude of 36,000 feet, there is a tremendous shuddering and shaking. You hear one of the engines stop, then the other. Finally all engines stop working.

The plane lurches and nose-dives toward the ocean. You are thrust forward as the plane goes down. You hold on to your seat so as not to lunge forward even more as the plane continues to go straight down. Your hearing becomes acute and you feel yourself turning cold. You sense your breathing going erratic as you try to make sense of what is occurring.

Seconds seem like minutes, and you become increasingly terrified. Aside from the sound of the plane shuddering and shaking, you hear the whimpers of the children seated a few rows in front of you. Everyone is holding on to their seats as the luggage compartments open, spilling their contents into the aisles. You hear some people praying. The lights go off, except for the emergency lights.

"God, please don't let there be pain!" you say silently to yourself, pleading, bargaining for something. (In my case, I said that in the three languages I knew. I wanted to cover all bases with my prayers!) Finally, you resign yourself to the fact that you are going to die by crashing into the ocean. An inner peace starts to take over. You have accepted your fate. You are in God's hands and, yes, you are at peace. All of these feelings and reactions are occurring in prolonged seconds, maybe a few minutes at best. But it feels like an eternity.

Suddenly, the engines come on and the plane swings up, gaining altitude, until finally it seems to stabilize and the lights come back on. Relief overcomes you. You smile nervously and turn to the passenger next to you to talk about what just happened.

As you do, you notice a line of passengers heading toward the restrooms, the flight attendants taking care of the children, and one attendant helping a man needing the oxygen bag overhead.

The man next to you confirms that it was the engines. It was obvious to you and to him, and, I would dare say, to others. Yet you ask a passing flight attendant what happened, seeking reassurance and wanting more information.

"Nothing to worry about," she says, annoyed. "It was just air turbulence." And she walks away. You stare at her in disbelief. It was not air turbulence, and why are we not turning back? We hear other flight attendants respond with the same thing: "Just air turbulence."

Soon one of the pilots comes on the intercom. Okay, you think, now we're going to find out what happened to the engines. He says, "Welcome to Happy Airlines [obviously not the real name]. We hope you have a pleasant flight. The current temperature in Sacramento is seventy-five degrees." He continues as though nothing unusual took place. *Nothing is mentioned.*

That is what happened. This is the scenario I set. Then my students took over. The comments of the "passengers" to the "crew" reflected disbelief, shock, and anger. Some "passengers" pretended to cry, some were silent, some bargained. In almost every reenactment that I did, at least one or two of the "passengers" wanted to speak to the pilots to demand a truthful explanation.

At this point in the scenario, we did a debriefing: what they observed, what was said, how they felt at that moment. On the chalkboard I listed the emotions and thoughts going through their minds. We came to realize that what was being expressed seemed to be the areas of grief as described by Elisabeth Kübler-Ross in her book, *On Death and Dying.*

I then presented my students with the following: Suppose that the policy of the airline is not to tell you the complete truth. Furthermore, on occasion there will be near-misses and actual crashes, yet the airline's policy is to downplay any scary event that might happen and not to advertise its safety record.

Now let's further assume that the plane is a metaphor for our society and that the flight attendants and pilots are the authorities that enforce the (government) policies concerning its passengers during times of peace and times of crisis. Keeping in mind what you know from the previous scenario, what, if anything, would you say to those you love who are about to embark on this airplane/society as to what to expect and how to behave?

The comments proved to be very interesting because, essentially, I was talking about what one generation would say to the next. What would one part of the group say to the other part of the group about their experiences?

Some said they would not tell their children or other loved ones. They would let them find out for themselves, and then the loved ones could decide how to react. Others said they would tell their loved ones not to trust what the flight attendants/authority figures said.

One student said she would tell her loved ones how to prepare for death if that happened. Still others said,"Protest at the airline headquarters! Don't go quietly like sheep! Trust only the other passengers of the plane/society." Some said, "No. Say nothing to the airline employees; just do as they tell you." Others said, "No! Have passengers join together and demand that the planes be checked out more carefully. We can't leave it up to the authorities to inspect for safety!" And finally, a few said, "Get someone or something else with greater power outside the airline/society to advocate for the passengers."

It was fascinating to observe how everyone reacted. There was a range of emotions, feelings, coping styles, and perceptions with regard to how to handle the situation. Yet one thing was certain: The trust toward the authority figures was low to conditional. The authorities would have to prove that they were on the side of the passengers.

I ended this exercise by finishing my story: We completed the flight and landed safely. But that flight created something that no other flight had for me, as I sought to believe the "authorities" on that plane over my own perceptions and those of my fellow passengers. The following morning I heard on the local news that we were right: It had been the engines. The media validated my perception and feelings that something indeed was wrong. I stood vindicated.

Later, a similar situation occurred under a similar set of circumstances and with the engines shutting down in-flight. That plane did crash. When I saw the coverage on the news, I said to myself, "I was lucky." Little did I know then that by saying and believing that I was lucky I set in motion the beginnings of PTSD (post-traumatic stress disorder). On subsequent flights I became very jittery whenever the airplane underwent turbulence.

What is interesting is that from the time I was eighteen months old I have flown on many, many planes. I have been on a prop plane whose propeller got struck by lightning and caught on fire—and I did not have any post-traumatic stress reactions afterward. I was on a plane in which the carrier door was broken; we were delayed for six hours at an airport in Mexico but ended up flying on that plane with the broken door somehow "taped"—and I had no post-traumatic stress reactions. On one flight the tip of a wing broke when we landed in Colombia before taking off again to our final destination. We kept on flying to the next city, Quito, Ecuador, where pilots have to bring planes down almost vertically and then step on the brakes so as not to run off the landing strip. I experienced no traumatic reactions then either, even though it was a "hairy" ride!

With each of those earlier situations, what had been different? At the time, the only thing I could identify was the kind of communication on the part of the pilots and flight attendants. During each of those earlier situations, we had been told what was occurring. With confidence, and in some cases also with humor, they kept us informed. In every instance, they apologized.

Moreover, in most cases, some kind of token apology in the form of free drinks, meals, or a coupon toward a future flight was issued. In a superficial manner, there was some acknowledgment, some validation of our perceptions, and some light form of debriefing among the passengers and the flight attendants.

But there was something different about my most recent experience—something that caused me to develop post-traumatic physiological responses of fight, flight, or freeze. I was not assertive during that "Happy Airlines" plane trip. Yes, I queried, and I shared with other passengers my disbelief and incredulity toward the pilots and flight attendants. But I hadn't been assertive.

After that, I underwent Somatic Experiencing. With it, I came to realize that my body and I also wanted to be angry and be assertively insistent for the truth. I did not do that at the time of the incident because I was feeling vulnerable and unsure of myself. I trusted those in authority to be forthright with the facts and to show some sort of human connection with us, the passengers. It was a new experience to have the flight attendants and pilots not be honest with us about the situation, as the flight attendants and pilots had done during my prior experiences with airplanes in crisis.

Furthermore, I had been taught as a young child not to make waves, in terms of my own needs, to anyone outside the family who was in an authority position. In my child's mind, to be persistent and assertive on behalf of my own needs would not be *bien educada* (i.e., well-behaved) behaviors with people outside the family. In other words, I was not to draw attention to myself if it pertained to my own needs. Advocating was permissible for others, but not for myself or my own feelings. I had kept that instruction alive—well beyond my childhood years.

And yet, as the years went by, my parents would be the first to tell me to stand up verbally for myself. I had forgotten that being *bien educada* meant to be that way toward myself as well.

How might it be for those of us who experience societal trauma, such as the Armenians, who are made out to be fabricators of stories about the Turkish government regarding the Armenian holocaust? Even today, the Turkish government refuses to acknowledge the atrocities committed by Turks against Armenians.

Or how do members of First Nations and other indigenous groups feel when the full extent of their pain and fear is minimized or dismissed? How is it for a group to face discrimination and the legacies of displacement, being treated as second-class human beings by those who are bigoted and by policies that do not fully honor the current issues faced by them?

How many of us in the general public keep ourselves informed of the plight of indigenous people, let alone advocate on their behalf? Have we forgotten them?

Are they the macro version of the "lost children" role that manifests itself in alcoholic families?

Those of us who experience being forgotten by the majority of the society or by our own families might easily want to keep any trauma mechanisms and coping skills alive.

While I was not too thrilled about being in a near airplane crash over the ocean, I realized the value of that experience and the subsequent understanding I received from my students and our interactions.

I interpreted my trauma as an interrupted adventure that had to become fully adventuresome, lest I get stuck with that story as my guiding light.

By utilizing my experiences, I transformed that event as part of my soul's adventure. By eventually undergoing Somatic Experiencing, thanks to my friend Gina Ross (founder and president of International Trauma-Healing Institutes) I further translated that event into adventures for my body. At the end of the session with Gina, my body was able to let go of the fight, flight, or freeze reactions that were still actively playing in my person. By getting into the body position that my body ideally wanted to be in at the time of the life-threatening experience, I was able to complete the cycle by shaking and sighing.

By role-playing how I wished I had responded to the flight attendant, verbally and physically (looking her in the eye and using a strong, firm tone of voice), I felt the last of the captured adrenaline rush released through final sighs and body relaxation.

We tested how I would feel on future flights by visualizing my entering a plane and feeling turbulence. No reaction of sweaty hands or stomach churning. Breathing continued being normal. Relief. (Still, after the tragedy of 9/11, a bit of that old feeling was reactivated. I was able to dispel that remaining fear by doing self-hypnosis and EFT [Emotional Freedom Technique created by Gary Craig] days prior to boarding an actual flight.)

From my plane experiences I took away tools to help others and myself. Intergenerational transmissions of grief, witnessing, vengeance, and trauma mechanisms and coping skills took life into the classroom. As long as there are traumas and triggers in society, people will continue to keep TMCS in their toolboxes. As long as there is family abuse or neglect, or if adult individuals find themselves in relationships of domestic violence, traumatic coping skills will be created and maintained. Whenever safety has been violated and trust broken, the recipients of trauma will find ways, even if it means creating "safety islands" in order to maintain their sense of self.

Chapter 6

TRANSGENERATIONAL TRANSMISSIONS: THE INVISIBLE HITCHHIKERS

If we did not come from healthy families and if we are recipients of societal attitudes that treat our group(s) as second-class citizens, then the stories we develop may come to be centered on the story of trauma, not on the story of living.

The stories of the family and of the group might get passed down to their descendants so that someone can fulfill what the ancestors could not. Life then becomes the fulfillment of the dreams and sorrows of previous generations. Any trauma in the past replays itself in one form or another so that the children and their children's children can have the opportunity to vindicate their ancestors. However, there is more to this.

Even if the person knew nothing of the traumas of his or her ancestors, there seems to be a "family repetition" of similar happenings around the anniversary date or age of when it happened before.

There are two kinds of passages from generation to generation: intergenerational transmission and transgenerational transmission. Intergenerational transmissions "are spoken and overt customs, words, expected professions and marriages, rituals, habits," and, as Anne Schützenberger continues, "the transmissions [that are] thought and spoken about between grandparents, parents, and children." These kinds of transmissions are known. What occurred in the airplane scenario described in the previous chapter is an example of an intergenerational transmission.

The other kind, transgenerational transmissions, is not talked about. It is the body that keeps them as "family secrets," unspoken, kept quiet as they play out when "triggered." Like Schützenberger, I noticed these patterns with victims and descendants of survivors of abuse. These transmissions are not known, but yet somehow the traumatic effects of the past catch up to the present, haunting the descendants as ghosts and as the possibility that the trauma can happen again.

Somehow, the legacy is carried from one body to the next body, unspoken but clearly felt. The body's immune system carries the echoes of the past, with the genes viewed as the ancestors' library to draw from in times of need.

Others have also noticed these transgenerational transmissions. Maurice Apprey wrote about how "destructive aggression" can reemerge generation after generation in various forms. Members of one generation of a family may find themselves manifesting such destructive behaviors in the form of being suicidal, or of committing or being murdered, or of experiencing incest or physical abuse. It is, as he puts it, "as if the injured group has accepted the message that they do not deserve to live and therefore must die in one form or another."

Apprey calls this process "transgenerational haunting," stemming from the original trauma of slavery and the forced loss of identity for many families. I would add that this can be said of conquered groups of any country. How the "loser" is treated by the "victor" influences these thematic unconscious transmissions.

As each generation receives its legacy, the theme might be

watered down or differently expressed. In my own family, my mother had a cancer that required a hysterectomy. Many years later, she had emergency surgery due to a burst gallbladder. For me, I had fibroid tumors which required a myomectomy. Years later, a hysterectomy was required due to the severe growth of the benign tumors in my uterus, which was affecting my back. Months later, I had gallbladder surgery.

There were decades between the occurrence of my mother's two ailments. For me, it was within a short space of time that both issues arose. While the illnesses and subsequent surgeries were life-threatening for my mother, it was not the case for me. Ironically, I saw my operations as releases, whereas my mother saw them with fear. I welcomed them because they were leaving me with a clean bill of health. I was, in fact, joyful at times, which surprised some of my friends—and me too. I felt that through these health challenges, I began to appreciate other parts of me that I had taken for granted.

I took those opportunities to reevaluate parts of my life and to delve further into my faith and spirituality. My strength increased, as did my love for my body and my witnessing of what my beloved body had done throughout my life. Like a snake shedding old skin, I felt reborn. This was my physical case of transgenerational transmission. How I identified the similarities with my mother and how I responded to them liberated me. This same process can be used for societal trauma.

Another example of transgenerational transmission is a case that Anne Schützenberger mentions in her book: a thirteen-year-old girl named Myriam. As the girl fell toward a metal fence, she was impaled on an iron bar. At the hospital, she was discovered to have ruptured her hymen and perforated her duodenum. As weeks went by, the little girl grew agitated. In her attempt to explain her anxiety and what she was experiencing, Myriam drew a cartoon-like sketch of what had happened to her to show her parents and the psychologist assigned to her. The sketch was a phallic metal fence. Myriam's mother saw the drawing and withdrew, telling the psychologist she (the mother) had a secret that Myriam did not know about.

It turned out that when the mother was thirteen years old, two men had raped her. Additionally, an investigation into the family's history uncovered that Myriam's maternal grandmother was raped at age eleven and again at age thirteen.

Myriam knew nothing about her family members' trauma, since the rapes had been kept from her until after she started to investigate. It would seem that as the generations went by, the theme of rape was present but being diluted with each generation's experience. Nevertheless, the theme of the trauma and its effects remained.

In my case, I had a milder version of the health issues my mother had experienced. I did not get cancer, but I did get heavy-duty fibroids. Yet a hysterectomy was still the result. In my mother's case, her gallbladder burst and she had to be taken to the hospital for immediate surgery. In my case, my gallbladder burst during surgery. (The symptoms had already led me to make a surgical appointment.)

There have been numerous studies that explore the effects of intergenerational and transgenerational transmissions. Yet there remains a lack of such studies on generations affected by racism and other "isms."

Study after study, such as those carried out by Danieli and Yehuda, show that the physiology or, specifically, similar biochemical responses, of many Holocaust survivors appear to have been passed down to the descendants, individuals who had not experienced the original trauma themselves.

I have discussed transgenerational transmissions. Let me now shift the focus to intergenerational transmissions, specifically revenge. Can revenge be passed down from generation to generation, in an effort to seek justice and retribution? Of course it can. It can be seen around the world in countless wars. Among the many reasons that countries stay in prolonged wars or start new ones is retaliation—historical revenge or recent revenge.

Chapter 7

REVENGE: STREET JUSTICE, OR LOYALTY TO A TRAUMATIC STORY?

For many people, the notion of "forgive and forget" reminds them of other platitudes they have heard, such as "Why cry over spilled milk?"; "It's over and done with."; and "Forget about it. Forgive the person and get on with life." For other people, these platitudes are invalidations of an event of extreme significance to them.

When social justice has not been delivered, such platitudes cause nondominant groups to feel irritation, anger, even hatred, because what they are hearing is that group members who were abused, killed, tortured, shamed, and so on, were and are not worthy of being remembered and given honor; that those who have been affected by such negative actions are not worthy to have justice be sought on their behalf and on behalf of their surviving families and groups.

Revenge is born out of anger, pain, tears, and helplessness. Revenge becomes an active tool that the person can use to move forward. Revenge thaws the feeling of freezing or immobility and provides a perception of action—of fight. For many, revenge may be the only option if they perceive that the societal systems of law and enforcement have not done their job, or that the legal system is skewed against them.

Often society uses the term *revenge* in a derogatory manner. Society may consider people who desire revenge as half-crazed, brainless, bloodthirsty "animals" bent on murder and retaliation.

But what drove these individuals to seek revenge? If there are perceived viable alternatives through the legal systems, why are those alternatives not used? The key words are *if* and *perceived.* From the avengers' perspective, if they have not experienced social justice through legal alternatives, then their perception is that they have no choice but revenge.

The scholar Susan Jacoby argued in her book *Wild Justice: The Evolution of Revenge* that in reality society uses the term *revenge* in a negative way to avoid societal responsibility for the lack of social justice to those members who have been wronged.

Revenge, justice, and *retribution* are words people do not want shoved in their faces. They do not want to be reminded by those who complain. In fact, the "complainers" are seen as "disturbers of the peace." By labeling people who seek revenge as being on the fringes of society or as malcontents, society may be inadvertently increasing these "walking wounded" and, possibly, ironically increasing the number of "walking time bombs" who are seeking ways to explode and be acknowledged for their plight.

Societal trauma affects us not only psychologically and physiologically. It also affects our emotional ability to bury the dead and begin life anew. Revenge becomes a possible reality when there are ongoing triggers and actual discrimination that may develop into traumatic situations for those involved and for those witnessing.

Revenge can be the poor person's sense of seeking justice when societal institutions of laws and courts appear tainted, biased, or indifferent. When I was attending the 1998 and 1999 meetings to discuss alternative means to resolving the Northern Ireland conflict at the community level, while listening to the Irish representatives I sensed something: When revenge enters the picture, onlookers to the conflict might see the same action differently.

One will see a "freedom fighter." The other will see a "terrorist." One person will experience the conflict as "war," while someone else will view it as "terrorist attacks." Revenge muddies the water. Who is the victim? Who is the victimizer? Violence drowns out the voices of those seeking justice. The onlookers only see what is before them. One attacking the other. Innocent lives caught in the cross fire.

Is it any wonder that pacifists such as Mahatma Gandhi and Martin Luther King, Jr., chose nonviolence? It then becomes clearer who is the perpetrator, who has meted out harm. The onlookers take away a different perspective—and with that, perhaps curiosity as to why people are clamoring and protesting.

Anger fuels revenge, and both of these give witness to a social injustice, to a wound. When there appear to be a lack of acknowledgment and a denial of justice, then those who have felt wronged will pass down, along with the transgenerational transmissions, the need to be vindicated.

Death, maiming, hate, and fight, flight, freeze responses lead to the never-ending cycle of trauma not only at the group level but also at the individual level. This is because everyone is affected.

I wrote a poem after meditating on revenge and what I had heard from people who had been societally wronged. Revenge can take on a life of its own, demanding that we feed it or be branded as disloyal to those who have died or been maimed. It can manipulate us into believing that we will "save face"—ours and those of people who have been wronged—if we follow the ways of revenge.

The Whisper

It whispers to me
in sounds and in dreams.
It whispers to me
not to forget.
Not to forget
those who have died,
those who are maimed,
those whose lives
are now simply
a flurry of steps hurrying to just survive.
It whispers to me,
in smells and in taste,
the smell of blood
and the taste for revenge.
No thought of peace
could enter this mind.

For the whispers
cloud all else
including my voice, my heart
my sweet dreams … wanting to Live.
When will the whisper end?

Revenge need not be part of a legacy, for it robs us of our soul's desire to live and be happy. Yet for people who have not felt vindicated, often revenge is seen as the only tool that those in power will listen to.

If revenge is carried down from generation to generation, it may become a way of life and a way of exhorting justice, unless neutral and respected third parties present options for justice. When will the whisper end?

For many of those who have experienced hate crimes, or overt and oftentimes covert discrimination, the whisper may not ever end, as long as there is denial and a lack of honesty in acknowledging that traumas have existed and continue to exist. In litigious societies in which people fear being sued and shamed, then denying or embracing the illusions of equality can become a matter of safety and financial protection.

Chapter 8

TMCS AND TRAUMAS: FEAR AND SAFETY TOOLS

Each time we become wounded,
our feelings of being unsafe increase.

Lee L. Jampolsky,
The Art of Trust: Healing Your Heart and Opening Your Mind

As long as there are "isms," family traumas, and individual traumas, then trauma mechanisms and coping skills (TMCS) will be kept and used. For many individuals, they experience both the macro and the micro versions of trauma.

The societal traumas may in fact slow down the healing of individuals and their families, keeping them and others in a victim or survivor mode of existing.

While there may be no more U.S. internment camps for Japanese Americans, there are still triggers in societal practices, such as "glass ceilings" and beliefs in which they are perceived as the "model" minority that makes good in the "American dream." (Read: "hero" or "perfect student," which is a heavy burden to carry.) Often, all Asian American groups are lumped together. This single categorization obliterates the reality of individual Asian cultures and their subcultures. As with any other groups, there are members who are economically struggling, or whose health does not fit the picture of "making it." It blurs the uniqueness and differences of each culture when stereotypes and assumptions are made by those outside the cultures.

As long as there is a specter of "rounding up the usual suspects" of certain groups whenever there are national, state, provincial, or local crises, there will be an underlying fear: internment camps, re-education camps, being "disappeared," or something else that a totalitarian or authoritarian country would use. Some of these methods are of the past, but not all of them. Will it happen where I live and during my lifetime?

Today, there may no longer be physical genocide going on with regard to First Nations or Native Americans by governments. Alas, though, there are still killings of other indigenous populations in the world. Furthermore, forced displacements continue to occur when the indigenous group's land is desired for its oil or minerals, or to be used by other groups. Triggers that remain are stimulated by ongoing racism and classism. Fear of losing the safety of their spiritual beliefs and practices may "closet" some people from not showing their faith. Others may continue to express themselves, braving the fear of those who do not understand their faith—much like during ancient Roman times when Christians chose either to stay hidden or to express their faith. Alternatively, they may intertwine their faith with that of the dominant group.

For indigenous peoples, how to hold on to their cultures and spiritual expressions? A mixed bag exists. One of the last places where their cultures are allowed to fully express themselves, yet are economically stifling, can be found on the "rez," that is, on reservations. Echoes of the voluntary and forceful taking of children to boarding schools still remain in today's populations, along with the aftermath of cultural identity confusion, alcoholism, violence, and health problems.

Beginning in the late 1800's, the U.S. government implemented policies whose effect was the systematic destruction of the Native American family system under the guise of educating the Native Americans in order to assimilate them as painlessly as possible into Western society, while at the same time inflicting a wound to the soul of Native American people that is felt in agonizing proportions to this day.

Eduardo Duran, *Native American Postcolonial Psychology*

Those Native American people, neither fully assimilated nor fully traditional, yet not encouraged to be acculturated (that is, to embrace the best of both cultures), are said to be "in-between" people. Deborah Hunt-Esquivel describes these "in-between" people as neither fully comfortable with or accepted into the White population, nor fully comfortable with or understood by their own people. Forced to reject their own heritage, yet not fully embraced by the dominant group, they return to their lands as strangers in their own skins. Their souls finding no haven in either culture, they become strangers unto themselves.

Genocide need not be a physical *annihilation* of a group. It can also be the destruction or the killing of a culture and its many subgroups of people, a way of living that does not disappear through time on its own but rather is forced to disappear by societal abuse and its practices.

As a consequence of the persecution and repression of homosexuality and cross-dressing by missionaries and federal agents, berdachism [gay and lesbian expression] lost its role in the social and religious life of native peoples.

'Relocation' and 'allotment' policies during the '50s and '60s imposed a cultural isolation on many families, fragmenting the social framework that supported the existence of these practices...the traumatic impact on Indian culture led to changes in berdaches' cultural expressions and confined their sexuality to a totally private dimension in a closed familial environment.

Massimiliano Carocci,

in *Past Is Present: Some Uses of Tradition in Native Societies*

The persecution of unfavorable cultural expressions and beliefs as perceived by the oppressor leads to attitudinal and behavioral changes of the oppressed persons and their groups, in this case, being Native American, as well as gay men and lesbians. Assimilation then becomes an important way to erase a group and indoctrinate its members into the worldview of the dominant group.

TMCS can also become attempts to establish and maintain some semblance of identity in the face of assimilation. Historical trauma and its aftermath contribute to the identity formation to many members of discriminated groups.

A sense of group identity exists for the Lakota people. This group identity is part of the culture and is not inherently pathological; however, historical trauma may have led to some features of that group identity being formed upon the status of being persecuted and oppressed. Lakota identity may incorporate the devalued self-image projected onto them by the oppressors.

Hilary N. Weaver and Maria Yellow Horse Brave Heart, "Examining Two Facets of American Indian Identity: Exposure to Other Cultures and the Influence of Historical Trauma," from *Voices of First Nations People*

Eons ago, or so it seems at times, a woman shared a story with me. Growing up, she had been severely abused by her father. Her mother, also victimized, felt helpless to do anything about it. The woman told me of a story she had heard of a mountain lion caged in a cell, wide enough only for it to take two steps then turn around and pace again. The mountain lion repeats this same pattern of pacing even after it is set free in the wild. For her, old patterns designed for keeping her safe, which no longer worked or in fact created more anxiety and ill health, revisited her from time to time when triggers appeared.

People who have been mistreated, abused, or traumatized in some manner for a prolonged period adopt this "cage" mentality and pacing. I observed this among adults who were victims of childhood abuse, as well as among individuals that had been tortured at the hands of their government.

Those who have been incarcerated know this too. Their identity becomes caged in and set in a pattern. Once they are freed, it takes time for them to realize that the bars are no longer there, that the abuse has stopped. Yet every time there is a hint of abuse, the vision of bars becomes real and the old pattern recommences: pacing as though in a cage.

Being free can actually invite anxiety if these people have no individual or group to guide their identity formation to a healthier way of being. When the abused group is subjected to ongoing pressure by the abusive group to conform to the latter's ways, assimilation may be seen as the only way to survive, even at the expense of self-esteem and self-image. This is what happened in the case of many of the First Nations and Native American children who went through the boarding school experiences.

Earlier, I discussed the culturation spectrum. The concept of assimilation normally has been seen as the end goal for the person who is not of the dominant group. The concept of acculturating, keeping the best aspects of one's heritage and embracing the best aspects of the dominant culture, often has *not* been seen as the goal. Rather, it was perceived as part of the process toward assimilation. In many cases, these two terms were used synonymously. For me, this is troublesome, especially if these ideas are held by clinicians or those who influence policies that impact our lives.

I came across an article while doing my research for this book that I want to share with you. It demonstrates the attitude of researchers when they approach a subject from a single perspective. People do not make decisions on one basis only, nor are they influenced by only one source in their lives. As members of groups who do not normally share in developing the societal norms of the dominant group, we are often told to become part of that very group in order to be acceptable.

In "Psychodynamics of Acculturation: A Mexican-American Experience," Ricardo Ainslie provides a case study of Gabrielle, a young woman in a Mexican American family who wanted to follow the ways of the "contemporary" society in which she lived, despite the sadness and desires of her parents to have her maintain her heritage.

While I agreed with Ainslie on many points, such as generational conflicts, what I found disconcerting was his belief that assimilation was and is a desirable goal. He offered no real discussion of why the young woman felt she had to assimilate into a town whose history smacked of racism and classism.

In fact, the author states, "Though tattered by middle-class standards, the Villa living room *actually* [italics mine] felt quite warm and comfortable." Wording such as this reflects the author's bias. Why should a poor working-class family not have a "warm" living room? Furthermore, his perception that "separation-individuation needs" could only occur through assimilation denies the fact that all cultures have their own versions of individuation.

Ainslie holds the North American concept as the norm. He concludes that Gabrielle's move away from her parents' culture and the generation they represented, was "a successful accommodation to the new social world"—that her parents' ways of living "represented an obstruction to a *healthier* [italics mine] engagement with life." And while he notes "immense guilt" on the part of the daughter, his only conjecture was that it might exist because of her individuation away from her parents and their way of life.

Could it have been guilt for having adopted the values of success and ways of life of the group that had inflicted, and continues to inflict, racism and classism on her parents? Or could it be survivor guilt for having successfully gone forward in the new world while others of her group (family) remained behind? Survivor guilt can arise in children whose families have experienced societal trauma caused by cultural disrespect. In summary, the author failed to explore the impact of racism and classism on this Mexican American family.

TMCS are all designed to keep the person or group safe while also creating a space to enjoy life in some capacity. Strategies to stay safe, including wanting to be "invisible" or "to pass," may be part of the tools we use not only to survive, but also to create and maintain contentment or peace in some areas of our lives. When there has been oppression in the past, and elements of that oppression continue to the present day, maintaining TMCS are natural until there are better ways to honor the dead and until better methods are created to reestablish group and individual identities.

As I mentioned when discussing the airplane scenario in Chapter 5 of this section, if the possibility of future trauma remains, people are reluctant to forget. So TMCS have to be ready at a moment's notice, should the situation arise.

It is often a journey simply to identify and understand how societal- and individual-based traumas can affect our own lives and the lives of those we love. Once we are on that path, it becomes more apparent how our total well-being is affected. Effects of trauma impact us on many levels: our sense of identity; our allegiance; our duty, if any, to right the wrongs committed against our parents and grandparents; our sense of membership in groups that have been affected; and whether we ourselves are comfortable in being members of, or wish to distance ourselves from, our own groups.

It is important to note that if our bodies are in an active state of alert for incoming threats—real or not, impending or reminders of the past—it becomes more difficult to heal. The mind and the body become absorbed in the trauma. The trauma may become the person's life focal point. In the case of groups, many of them become preoccupied with the "isms" and the societal traumas. Why? Because we, they, you, I might never know when the next "hit" will occur, when the next incoming expressions of the "isms" are going to affect us, or affect someone we love, or affect a member of one of our groups. By understanding our bodies, our reactions, and other effects of trauma, we make progress toward taking back our lives and starting down roads of healing for ourselves and our groups.

For many of us, trauma has affected the rhythm of our hearts and the intimacy we wish to create. Can we heal from the effects of trauma? Are there ways to release trauma's energy? How does faith play into healing? Can we rewrite our life stories and give new meanings to our lives? What can we learn from members of nondominant groups that have been discriminated against but have not developed societal trauma? Do the dominant groups or the perceived abusers in one's life play into the healing of trauma? How can we heal as individuals from trauma? Do we have to wait for our groups to heal? Can we heal if we continue to live in a family that is abusive?

In the case of society, where do we go? Many countries have their legacies in which traumas created at the societal level are either ignored or minimized. Other countries have stepped up and continue to do so to address the historical wrongs that still plague the present. For many countries, the past is not history. The past affects the present. Do societies have to heal in order for *us* to fully heal, so that we can throw away the TMCS?

For individuals experiencing traumas from families and adverse situations, do societal attitudes affect their healing and growth? If so, must society also evaluate what role it plays upon its citizens, upon *you*?

SECTION THREE

Healing from Traumas

*The society in which we live needs addictions, and
its very essence fosters addictions.*

*It fosters the person who is not dead and not alive,
just numb, a zombie.*

*When you are dead
you are not able to do the work of the society.*

*When you are fully alive,
you are constantly saying 'no' to many of the
processes of the society:
the racism, the polluted environment, the nuclear
threat, and the arms race...*

*Thus, it is in the interests of the society to promote
those things that 'take the edge off,'
get us busy with our 'fixes,'
and keep us slightly numbed out.*

Anne Wilson Schaef and Diane Fassel,
The Addictive Organization

Chapter 1

SHARING YOUR HEART: BEING IN THE PRESENT

People heal in various ways. Just as there are many kinds of traumas, so are there many avenues for healing. What I will now focus on are elements needed for individuals and groups to bring along as they enter the passage that goes through trauma. It is a road between the winds of change and the winds of trauma.

My approach regarding trauma embraces the concept of the soul. I realize that this inclusion of such an ethereal part of who we are runs counter to how traditional Western science approaches healing. However, it is impossible to separate mind, body, and soul. I will not be delving into the multitude of definitions of *soul*. That in itself would be another book and would go on a tangent away from trauma.

What I will provide for context is a working definition of *soul*: Soul is the immortal segment of who we are as human beings, which is part of the greater Spirit known as God. When we are in touch with our souls, when a person is said to "have soul," for me, this signifies that the heart is singing; is giving wings to love and be loved; and is experiencing joy with delight and sorrow with respect. Soul transcends the body, the intellect, and the personality. The person's heart (figuratively speaking) is not dependent on memory or physiological functions to exist. Soul is alive and continues to live, although it leaves the body—even when the body dies. Soul defies quantification, yet it makes its presence known.

The best way I know how to describe a soul's manifestations is through an example. Many years before my mother Graciela (*Grace* in English)—or Gracielita, which is an affectionate term—died, she had a series of tiny strokes, known as TIAs, which affected her memory. Later I found out that she had been misdiagnosed with having the beginnings of possible dementia, when in fact she had had hyperparathyroidism for many, many years. The symptoms included dementia-like cognition and behavior issues. (In regard to her misdiagnoses, that is another story, one not germane to our discussion here.)

At first it was affecting her very short-term memory; eventually, it also affected aspects of her long-term memory. In a matter of months, the *mi mamita* I knew and loved was no longer there. Gracielita's personality had changed. Instead of having a mother who was bright, intelligent, witty, as well as the best storyteller of our family, I found myself facing a woman who could not add two and two without confusion, a woman who constantly repeated the same question several times within a five-minute period. Her storytelling days were disappearing. It was like a death for me to see her change so very much.

Then one afternoon, while she and I were in the kitchen watching my father cook dinner, she turned to me. She said that she did not know what was happening to her and that her memory was slowly going. She was very lucid in understanding her situation at that moment. She apologized for not being a good mother anymore. She cried.

I embraced and held her. I told her that it did not matter if her memory was failing. What mattered was our love. Being a loving mother is not based on her duties, I said, but rather on how she approached life and the love she gave us.

Despite her loss of memory, she never, ever stopped showing her love for us nor her laughter and joy for living. Even when she had to ask me in a whispered voice who the person was before her, she never stopped being gracious and loving toward anyone. She never stopped caring. Her love was always present with us.

Her intellect and all the related faculties may have started to leave her, but not her love and joy for people—not her humor or laughter or love for dancing. I looked at her and I felt blessed. She never stopped sharing her heart. Whatever it was going wrong and dying within in her did not take away what mattered the most. She was the epitome of what being in the present meant. She enjoyed those around her, familiar people and strangers alike. She showered us with love up to the moment of her death years later.

Her love was not connected to her memories. It was connected to her heart, to her soul. She was *bien educada* until the very end.

Being *bien educada*, or well-educated of the heart, is about providing an environment where the soul can emerge, where love can reside and expand itself. My parents were always that—loving. This is not to say that they were saints. When either of them was not acting as a *bien educada* or *bien educado* person should, they would eventually apologize and then learn new ways to continue becoming even more well-educated of the heart.

Given my upbringing and my experiences, I assume that the soul has to be included in any healing process. In the depths of pain and sorrow, the soul can be felt and experienced if we stay present and mindful. That kind of vulnerability opens up the heart and lessens the suffering. We know there are connections between the mind, body, and soul. It is the "how" that is the mystery.

Trauma can disrupt our home, but never our hearth. So when

our mother's health declined rapidly in the last six weeks of her existence, we had to adjust to the awful change. We grew beyond what was familiar in order to keep our love strong and to be present enough to enjoy the gifts she was leaving us, as well as the gifts we were unfolding in ourselves as a consequence of her departure. The range of grief and the joy of togetherness mixed in our bodies. Despite the range of emotions, the touch of love and faith carried us through.

There is no difference between societal trauma affecting our groups and traumas affecting us individually. Societal- and individual-based traumas can stop us and kill us, or they can be used to transform us and force us to grow beyond the grief in order to keep our love for each other and ourselves alive. Trauma, if approached with a heart for living, can be transformative and healing.

I invite you to explore some of the various ways that trauma affects the souls of all of us; the ways that we look at the world; and, just as importantly, our dreams and life aspirations for not only what we want to do but also for who we are. As long as traumas touch and rule our hearts, our hearts will never sing their songs, our bodies will not know peace, nor will our souls soar in freedom.

Chapter 2

REALIZATION OF TRAUMA: IDENTITY AND GRIEF PROCESS OF INDIVIDUALS AND GROUPS

I developed a diagram to help me understand the process that I was observing. I originally called it "Realization of Societal Trauma: Identity and Grief Process of Individuals and Groups." It integrates the concepts of grief with fight, flight, or freeze responses, as well as other elements. Since then, I have dropped the *societal* term because any trauma—no matter whether it comes from the macro or the micro or both—affects individuals and groups (regardless of *which* group) in a similar fashion.

With ongoing triggers and life-threatening events, our healing process can be a difficult journey, spiraling upward from the areas of denial to victimization to surviving to finally thriving. During the course of our lives, we may revisit all or some of these areas whenever there are new kinds of triggers or if there is an increase in frequency of the triggers. As individuals and as groups, we undergo this process, with groups taking longer to go through it.

While we go about our healing, some members and some groups may revisit one or more areas if they are "triggered" again. Healing is a spiral affair, not a linear one. Just when we think we have learned and moved on from one chapter of our lives to another, something always seems to happen to get us to go back and review that other chapter again. We may review with "old" emotions but with the gained knowledge and understanding of what had occurred. The triggers no longer hold us as long, until, eventually, they finally leave us, as we develop healthier ways and gather a growing number of healthier supportive people and groups.

In a spiral form, we proceed onward to the next period in our lives, with the old emotions giving way to ones that serve us in our present.

Realization of Trauma: Identity and Grief Process of Individuals and Groups

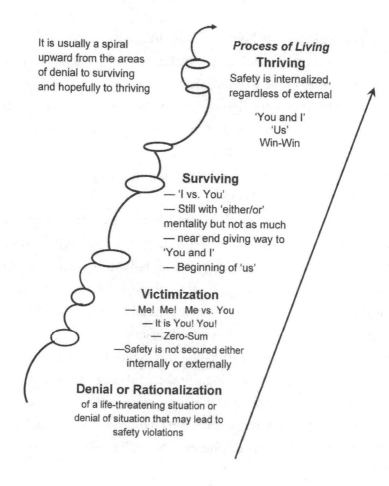

It is usually a spiral upward from the areas of denial to surviving and hopefully to thriving

Process of Living Thriving
Safety is internalized, regardless of external

'You and I'
'Us'
Win-Win

Surviving
— 'I vs. You'
— Still with 'either/or' mentality but not as much
— near end giving way to 'You and I'
— Beginning of 'us'

Victimization
— Me! Me! Me vs. You
— It is You! You!
— Zero-Sum
—Safety is not secured either internally or externally

Denial or Rationalization
of a life-threatening situation or denial of situation that may lead to safety violations

The Denier: Traumas Do Not Exist

. . . remember, all of us, in some capacity,
we are judged for the sole fact that we are women.
You might not notice it, and ignorance is bliss.
But it's out there and it is holding us back. . .
even times we have good experiences and forge ahead.

The point is,
we have to forge past sexism and racism and all the other isms that are inherent—
so inherent sometimes we don't even notice them so we forget they exist.
Whereas those not affected don't have to forge past the obstacles,
because certain obstacles don't exist for certain people.
(I think we all have obstacles, just not always the same ones.)
Spike Gillespie, *writer*

Denial is the way we avoid looking at situations and feelings that are too overwhelming for our bodies' systems to integrate all at once. Yet when denial becomes a way of life or a coping skill, who is benefiting and who continues to get hurt? If denial is a way of life, your whole being will find ways, even to the point of distorting itself, to accommodate that need of yours.

You and I will tune out words, turn a blind eye to situations, or avoid—at a subconscious level—anything that might penetrate our shields of denial. Ultimately, denial does not serve us in being totally who we are. Nor does it allow us to go beyond our comfort zone so that we, as individuals or as groups, may explore the world.

When such denial is caused by societal trauma, we initially blame the victim. If we did not, then we would be faced with the notion that it could happen to us, or that we live in a society that is not really safe for our group members. Denial can also occur on the part of the abuser or perpetrator. Many books have been written about government participation in genocidal practices.

At this time, the perpetrators are still in denial
of the enormity of their genocidal actions and oppression. ... The
descendants of the colonists prefer to stay in denial about the Holocaust
that they have perpetrated.
Eduardo Duran

If there truly were remorse and social justice, there would be no current "isms." There would be no ongoing seeds of societal traumas. There would be no group scapegoats (the "problem child") in times of national crisis or war. Those in power would not overtly or covertly encourage one segment of society to turn against another segment. The perpetrators in many ways are still in denial. The question is, is it convenient for them to stay in denial? Or is something else at work?

When there is denial on the part of the perpetrators for whatever reason, those who perceive themselves as victims may resort to extreme measures in order to break through that denial. People who have experienced individual traumas from family members or from trusted adults or friends know all too well that the abusers — pedophiles, for example — will deny or actually be in denial of how their actions have affected those people and their loved ones. It is no different at the societal level when systems have been put in place to help with that denial or to minimize the impact that policies and laws have had on segments of the population.

At the family level, a person may go to therapy or attend AA or CoDA or other kinds of meetings to address, in a group setting, the impact of behaviors such as taking alcohol or drugs, which they thought would buffer them from the memories of trauma. Other individuals may act out, or get into trouble with the law, seeking coping skills in whatever fashion may work for them, the victims, in the short term and possibly also in the long term.

Yet if the body is not looped into healing but instead is used as a buffer by means of cutting, doing drugs, developing and maintaining "aholics"-type behavior (alcoholics, causaholics, workaholics, etc.), then inadvertently the person keeps the stories of trauma and self-victimization alive.

At the societal level, it can mean many things—from civil rights, social justice movements, and advocacy for those who have been disenfranchised, to destructive ways of disrupting the normal patterns of society to gain attention and hopefully change those aspects of a status quo that harm rather than elevate. Those of us on the receiving end of the societal traumas cannot afford to stay in denial for too long. The same holds true for individuals: Denial has to be a *stage* in the growth toward freedom. Denial cannot be a lifestyle or a manner of living.

Otherwise, the abuse, the pain, the grief, and the frustration can affect all of society in various ways, from a failing economy and an upsurge in crime (including sexual assaults and domestic violence), to low morale, societal upheaval, and terrorist attacks.

Attitudes of a Person or Group in Denial

Someone in a denial stage will make comments such as the following:

> "It wasn't that big a deal."
> "It didn't happen."
> "It's my fault for putting myself in that situation."
> "She should have known better." [usually referring to

the victim and denying that the perpetrator is at fault]

"That's just how human nature is."

"It happened to my group. Why should it be any different with yours? You just have to 'suck it up.'"

"It wasn't traumatic." [despite the tone of voice reflecting shame]

When pressed to realize that an event might have been traumatizing, the person becomes defensive, "moves away," or "checks out" mentally or literally. If there is any assignment of blame, it is the victim's fault.

Many times society and individuals will collaborate in maintaining a denial state. Yael Danieli calls it a "conspiracy of silence," especially if we include mental and medical health providers that we trust to assist us in our empowerment. By participating in this conspiracy of silence, we deprive ourselves, and eventually our descendants, of the avenues for healing.

When we are in denial, it may not be out of malice but rather out of a fear that we cannot prevail in a particular situation. Or it can be the shock of knowing that the horrific actions have been done in our names. If we are in denial, then how can we address the problem? How can we ask for help? How can we mend if we do not allow ourselves to feel the gaping wounds in our hearts?

If society is in denial, our healing challenges are compounded. There is no mirroring from the very institutions that supposedly were constructed to take care of all its citizenry. Dispelling the denial state, therefore, takes on the form of the individual's and his or her group's struggles to regain reality.

When we are confronted for the first time with some expression of an "ism," spurred by disbelief we quickly check our hearing or sight. Could such a thing be happening? If that "ism" develops into a trauma, that denial soon leads to the reality of the situation. In the areas of loss, denial is seen as part of the grieving process.

When trauma occurs, normally the initial shock is indeed denial because the trauma shakes the belief of our reality. Our senses reel as we try to make sense of our new reality brought forward by trauma. Usually denial is a phase, not a lifestyle or a set worldview. If denial is experienced as a phase, the next area to experience will be victimization.

Victim—Ground Zero of Pain

As in any other kind of therapy or healing, there first needs to be awareness of the trauma before any long-term healing can occur.
Eduardo Duran, *Native American Postcolonial Psychology*

After the initial shock wears off, reality usually sets in. You look around and see a different world through the new lens given to you by trauma. People in the victimization area might make comments such as these:

"Wow, this really happened!"
"Look at what happened to me!"
"I'm hurt and angry!"
"I still feel helpless and not in control."
"I have to watch out!"
"I was victimized."
"The perpetrator is at fault. Can't you see that?! Why aren't you doing something about it?!"
"I want revenge!"
"They're the ones who have to change, not me. They owe me. I want to be acknowledged for what they did!"

"Get away from me. You don't understand what it's like."

"How can I trust you if you take their side?"

"You're telling me to forget it? Forget it? It may be history for you, but it's the present for me!"

Issues of safety arise. Trust is low, if it exists at all. Justice is sought. If there is no justice, revenge or retaliation may take its place. Hypervigilance and hypersensitivity are active all the time, it seems. Why? Because one has to scan for triggers in order to feel safe.

Trauma mechanisms and the development of trauma coping skills become paramount. At this stage, emotions and feelings kick in as the gravity of the situation settles into the human body. Inability to distinguish between memory of abuse and the possibility of impending abuse occurs.

Fight, flight, or freeze reactions are activated beyond their time, still scanning and searching for the return of the threatening situation. Trauma sets in, as the sympathetic nervous system of scanning becomes a way of existing for the body.

The victim may not want to get close enough to the perceived threat to find out if it is truly a threat or only a reminder of what happened. A physical and an emotional distancing may occur between the perceived offending person or group members and the person being victimized.

Attitudes of a Person or Group in Victim Mode

Feeling victimized, the victim is in safety mode: "They must earn my trust, especially if they remind me of the perpetrators. I would be a fool to do otherwise." The body and brain are in survival mode, pumping adrenaline as the sympathetic nervous system continues to be on alert for incoming triggers and their traumas. The identity and affiliation are those of a victim: "The perpetrators have wronged me. They're never to be trusted."

The victim is self-focused to the extent that everything is seen through the lens of safety and the need for some measure of peace.

Let's say that we continue to stay in a victim mode. Eventually, our health will be adversely affected. If anger or rage becomes part of our lives, homocysteine is secreted. Coronary heart disease may occur. If anger, covertly or overtly, becomes a way of life or the primary tool for any stress or crisis that comes our way, the body starts to be negatively affected. Blood pressure is affected. The involuntary or autonomic nervous system gets stuck on the sympathetic system end—that is, the fight, flight, or freeze mode of that system. If left on too long, the organs become impacted.

In terms of Chinese medicine, the liver may start to act up, to get resentful. If the liver gets taxed, blood circulation becomes affected; the so-called "bad" cholesterol (LDL) increases as the body believes it is needed to convert to various components, including serving the fight, flight, or freeze mode. If the LDL is not used up, the body becomes negatively affected as the LDL is stacked up in the form of plaque in the arteries. Think of it as not having enough storage space in the usual areas—and now you have to store objects in hallways where there are many people coming and going. Eventually, the plaque gets in the way of the flow.

Adrenaline and other needed hormones will continue to increase, even if they tax out other vital hormones and elements necessary for good health.

Safety, the priority, is at risk. If the liver continues to experience the stress of fight, flight, or freeze reactions as well as anger and/or prolonged fear, then other organs become involved, such as the kidneys. And the list goes on. Staying in victim mode is hazardous to the health of the individual's whole being. On the societal scale, production rates are lowered, mental health issues and medical costs increase, and the ability to communicate is disrupted (with increased cases of misunderstandings when communication *is* attempted).

The intimacy and love that we seek might become twisted or distorted toward seeking safety and wanting to be rescued. If sadness turns to depression and hopelessness, the body's systems slow down. We narrow our views of our abilities to dispel the clouds of sadness. We feel our energy being easily zapped or depleted.

Like walking through molasses on a cold winter night, the effort to move on becomes a struggle. Long-term stress stemming from unresolved traumas increases the possibilities of domestic violence, violence at the workplace, and other possible violent reactions if people reach a point of "what's the use?"

If stress becomes systemic in our society, *suicide by cop* may increase. This term is used for people who want to commit suicide but at the hands of law enforcement. You can well imagine the trauma of the officers forced to kill someone who wants to die. As unresolved stresses mount up, so does the probability of various kinds of traumas. The identification with being a victim takes many shapes.

Conversely, we may seek high-risk situations. Daring death, we glimpse the excitement of life through adrenaline-pumping activities. Constantly seeking movement, living at a quick pace, keeping the mind occupied and the body under its oppressive control, we use speed to avoid and deny what must be addressed.

Who we had hoped to be is shunted aside as we become the object of adrenaline-oriented activities. We become addicted to *doing* as a way of dealing with feelings of having been victimized. Still others see taking big risks as surviving and as demonstrating control over life threats. Addiction to such behaviors and ways of thinking may follow.

Being a victim becomes who we are and not a role that can be tossed away. The "I" becomes the casualty of the trauma. I lose myself. We lose ourselves because we hide ourselves deep inside of us, securely away from any more threats and harm.

It is important to acknowledge the victimization, but *not* to attach to it our identity and our dreams—*not* to lose our hopes to any trauma that inadvertently freezes us in time and place. If trauma permeates our minds and our perceptions of the world, then it will take up residence in our bodies.

If we are able to see ourselves, in terms of our identities, as human beings being victimized or abused (rather than as *the* victims or *the* abused), then we can proceed to the next step toward reclaiming our lives. If we allow curiosity to become an active player, we can detach from the label of "victim" and move forward.

Survivor—Learning to Cope, Learning to Breathe

As we look around, we realize that we are not alone. Others have experienced what we have undergone. We seek help. We want to survive this trauma. We do not want our transgressors to dictate our worldview. What we experience as individuals and as a group(s) need not lead us to trauma.

We accept what has happened. We want the transgressors to make amends. We want to educate them about what they did to us and to others like us. Forgiveness enters the picture for the first time.

We start to reflect. The exploration of healing and its maintenance are deepening.

"It wasn't our fault."

"Maybe not all of them [members of the offending group] are to blame. Instead, they need to be educated on how they perpetuate the traumas that come from discrimination and bigotry."

"Maybe my family can't comprehend that such a horrible thing has been done to one member of our own family by another. I need to give them time to absorb what happened to me. But if they don't understand or don't want to, that's not going to stop me from getting the help I need from outside the family."

"It isn't my fault. It's theirs [the offender's]. My job is to focus on my healing. Also, I have to educate them … make them aware of how much pain they've caused me."

Our TMCS are not our only primary line of defense. We develop other coping strategies that do not tax us physiologically or psychologically. Our faith deepens and expands. We can distinguish between memory of abuse and genuine impending abuse. We look at the meaning we had given to the traumas. We examine what the meaning of abuse holds for us as individuals and as group members. Does the meaning serve my group and me now? How do I define myself as an individual? As a member of my group?

Part of healing is naming ourselves. We establish our identities in our own way. The civil rights movements were not only about social justice for the particular groups, but also about the right to name ourselves in a positive way.

As individuals, we start to breathe again. As groups, we allow our breath to expand our view of the world as well. You and I continue to reflect. We continue to question how we want to lead our lives.

How do we want to lead our story from this point on? An understanding deepens of how a traumatic situation can, in fact, have an unseen benefit, or a silver lining. We take into account the skills we have developed, and we marvel at our survival instincts. Taking that which had to be borne in order to cope with the traumas, we transform them to serve us, to help us live.

We realize that we matter.

As we delve further into this stage, we start to look at patterns and cycles of societal abuse in a nonjudgmental way. Still, at this stage, we may continue to see social justice primarily for me and you and our groups only.

Slowly, and then at an even quicker pace, as we find ourselves feeling safer and further along in our realization that we have survived, we may turn our heads and our hearts to wanting to live. Surviving is simply not enough anymore. Wanting our hearts to sing and our breaths to exhale with ease and peace, we move on to the next step.

Thriver—On Becoming Human Again, or Maybe for the First Time

Having gone from denying what has happened, to acknowledging that we were victimized, to surviving our ordeals with skills and new meanings, the next part of our journey is to find life meaningful again and to live our lives with joy being a frequent visitor. We reframe and give new meaning to our lives and to life's situations, including traumatic ones. There is a continuing effort to break the cycle of abuse in society via social justice activities (macro) and individual healing (micro).

We seek social justice for all groups. We seek forgiveness for all, while not excusing their behaviors, institutions, or attitudes. Love the soul, but object to behaviors and attitudes that are not *bien educados* (i.e., not loving and respectful, not demonstrating expressions that are of God).

TMCS are rarely used now, as we are rarely in truly immediate life-threatening situations. We may still keep a few TMCS in our toolboxes for reasons of safety, since discrimination and bigotry still exist. We seek loving and healthy people in our lives and communities who make us flourish. We disengage from individuals who perpetuate old patterns that no longer serve us. Safety and trust are integrated. Support systems have been set in motion. I see my group and other groups as being different but equal.

My pride and honor for my identity (race, ethnicity, gender, religion, economic status, sexual orientation, etc.) are not at the expense of other groups. I stop the cycle of abused/abuser, non-power/power.

Collaboration among groups is sought and integrated, but only if other groups (e.g., the dominant group or the perceived abuser group) want it too. I do not seek to educate those members of the abuser group(s) who do not wish to be educated. My healing is not based on other people's healing process. I see life as an adventure, not as a series of challenges and burdens.

It is important to understand how racism, sexism, classism, and other "isms" affect our realities and how these societal stories detain us. Until this point, the vast majority of trauma recipients have bought into believing that their societal ailments are fully of their own making, thus absolving society's role in the creation of the "isms" and possible subsequent traumas. Any individual healing, through any modality, has to include the awareness that we may be also healing from societal wounds.

We come to the realization that healing starts at the individual level, with ourselves, as well as at the macro level through coalitions, social justice work, and role modeling to others in our groups. If we are to maintain our health, then our healing has to include our environment. Part of our healing process is to understand the macro influences on our health, including our perception of ourselves, our sense of identity, and our value as human beings.

Deborah Hunt, Bonnie and Eduardo Duran, and others who have worked with First Nations people concur on the impact of oppression on self-identity, as well as on group identity. I have observed the legacy of oppression in myself and in others. Any abuse negatively affects the identity of the abused. Given the impact of abuse on individuals and their groups, it would behoove those who are fighting for social justice to have done some recovery work themselves, so that they do not inadvertently continue the cycle of abuse.

Wounded Leaders Perpetuate Cycles of Suffering

If leaders were courageous enough to do their own healing and to role model their journeys of healing, then social justice work would be more effective. Is it any wonder that in some parts of the world ongoing traumas and violence between groups continue because the leaders are themselves in the middle of their own trauma and grief? These leaders are highly prone to reactive forces created by the ongoing fight, flight, or freeze responses of their own bodies and are restimulated by the ongoing experiencing of death and conflict.

If any permanent conflict resolution is to occur, the conflict inside leaders' bodies must be addressed as a major priority. Psychological violence and sporadic ongoing threats of trauma to groups and individuals eat away in bites and in chunks. Leaders and influential individuals of nondominant groups must be role models by addressing their own health and well-being. Within that healing, leaders and the rest of the group membership must understand the impact of trauma on grief and identity formation.

I have witnessed social service agencies and advocacy groups involved in totally or partially dysfunctional behavior patterns. Some of the very agencies that espoused humanitarian concerns for their clients at times treated their own staff in an abusive manner, pushing healthier employees to quit if they could, while other employees were forced to stay due to financial reasons. In some cases, the employees themselves were in an abuse cycle pattern and did not notice how they were being treated.

I will describe an example. The executive director of one social service agency, herself a battered wife, verbally battered her staff. She was in denial of her domestic situation; and, unfortunately, because she was in denial instead of in recovery, she passed on the battering dynamics and her workaholic desire to employees at the agency.

Staff members had to prove to her their loyalty to the mission of the agency by putting in long hours, which were not compensated. The mission statement became a cause and a way of life that she expected her staff to embrace beyond the normal forty hours per week. An expectation of regular weekend work with no compensation was the norm for herself. She expected others to do as she did.

As happens in the case of battering, there would be a honeymoon period of rewards and support, followed by tension buildup, and eventually the caustic, sarcastic comments that led to yelling and shaming employees on the spot, followed by half-hearted apologies. Then the cycle would start again.

Some employees were moved to tears because of the director's anger and inappropriate behaviors. Others learned what appeased her. Some tried their best to become invisible, quietly doing their work, staying out of her way. One staff member made excuses and rationalized away the inappropriate behaviors as that of a highly stressed person. Eventually, all the Latinx quit. A few others, who were non-Latinx, eventually resigned as well.

The director did not view herself as racist. Nor did she comprehend that she was projecting her internalized sexism onto the women on her staff. She was a wounded person in a position of authority, setting the tone and dynamics of an abusive cycle.

Fortunately, I witnessed other agencies that thrived. In these, there were policies and protocols in place, as well as activities and events that supported the health and nurturing of their staff. For example, one agency in Stockton, California, was growing in leaps and bounds. It had a low resignation rate and employee morale was high. The number of employee positions was increasing, and the agency had attracted increased funding within two years' time.

When leaders at the helm of an agency, a cause, or a group are willing to heal themselves and provide avenues for their employees, followers, or group members to also heal, that is when social justice flourishes and expands to everyone involved. Healing is not a linear progression but a spiral upward.

Our hearts have to soar. If we do it at the expense of someone else's heart, we will plummet back to the cycle of the abused-abuser and the never-ending cycle of violence and revenge.

It need not be the case. We can, despite the whirling winds of trauma and changes, find ourselves living our lives through the courage of embracing others and ourselves. By stepping upward, we help our descendants. We stop passing on the legacy of traumas. This is what we must do if we are to thrive.

Chapter 3

A WHOLISTIC HEALING APPROACH FOR THOSE EXPERIENCING TRAUMAS

On the following pages are paradigms. The first one describes the influence of trauma on our being. The second one provides possible options for healing from trauma. Neither of them addresses all areas, by any means. Rather, they should serve to get you started in thinking about the possible roads you have taken and about new roads you might want to consider.

For some of us, it will be difficult to disentangle ourselves from the influence of trauma. Trauma's influence will have seeped into the ways we do things and how we view ourselves. We create customs out of our coping ways. Those customs that are passed down from generation to generation, whether through groups or families, become how life has been and will always be. We acquiesce, even when we know in our hearts that there has to be a better way to love and be loved.

The other paradigm points out possible areas for exploring different ways of getting your body and your mind to sync with your healing. See which one moves you to action.

Be your own writer of your own life. Explore what you have collected along the way. Examine which areas continue to serve you. Are those tools of coping, those beliefs, attitudes, and behaviors helping you to unfold the loving soul and human being that you have always been? Who you are need not be the traumatic story. What you can do is transform that story into an adventure in which you are the hero who moves beyond trauma and into life.

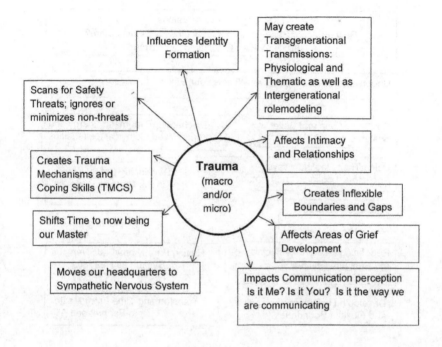

©1999, 2001, 2003 and revised 2019
Darling G. Villena-Mata

How do we address the components in our lives that have been redirected to fight, flight, or freeze responses? How do we transform the dynamics to that of living and not just surviving? How do we transform traumas into adventures for our souls?

**A Healing Approach
for Groups and Individuals Experiencing Trauma**

Below is a summary of areas touched in this book. For many, we prefer tables,
diagrams, and summations in addition to or instead of narrative approach. This too is
part of understanding ourselves and others.

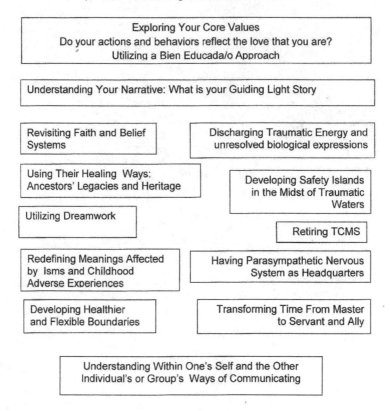

Exploring Your Core Values
Do your actions and behaviors reflect the love that you are?
Utilizing a Bien Educada/o Approach

Understanding Your Narrative: What is your Guiding Light Story

Revisiting Faith and Belief
Systems

Discharging Traumatic Energy and
unresolved biological expressions

Using Their Healing Ways:
Ancestors' Legacies and Heritage

Developing Safety Islands
in the Midst of Traumatic
Waters

Utilizing Dreamwork

Retiring TCMS

Redefining Meanings Affected
by Isms and Childhood
Adverse Experiences

Having Parasympathetic Nervous
System as Headquarters

Developing Healthier
and Flexible Boundaries

Transforming Time From Master
to Servant and Ally

Understanding Within One's Self and the Other
Individual's or Group's Ways of Communicating

©1999, 2001, 2003 and revised 2019
Darling G. Villena-Mata

How Trauma Can Influence Grief and Identity

Grief affects our bodies, our minds, our way of being, and our souls.
Yet it also heals and provides opportunities for us to be reborn
again. It is wholistic in that it requires us to look inward, to delve

into areas where we might not have delved, had it not been for the loss in our life.

Grief affects how we relate to the world, both as members of groups and as individuals. We play both of these roles: the individual, but also very much the member of various groups (although often a society might prefer not to address the grief inflicted on members of groups and on the groups themselves). Healing both as individuals and as members of groups is needed if we are to fully heal.

For those who experience individual traumas, in times of grief and mourning the world can be surrealistic, not real. The world is around me but I do not feel part of it. The meaning that the world once gave me—or, rather, what I once gave to it—now seems oddly unreal.

Death is as valid as life. Depending on where I am in my grieving process, death may seem like a kind stranger waiting to help me cross the street to its realm. I can appreciate why some people, when overwhelmed with grief, might want to die themselves. The pain is so great, so profound.

Some do die, including in a slow death—through acts of self-mutilation, through sabotaging their own lives, through violence, through martyrdom, in quiet desperation, or by simply giving up. Their immune system is taxed because grief tells it that the status quo has been disrupted. Many people fall ill or develop health challenges stemming from unresolved grief, anywhere from the time of the loss to years later.

Grief questions our being, as well as our relationship with others and ourselves. How important are things? What priorities do we give to people? Do we as individuals matter? Suddenly everything takes on new meanings—or no meaning at all. We feel stuck in a rushing world with no anchor to steady our ship of life.

Winds of change come blowing our way, confusing our minds and our hearts. If what we lost had provided some core identity of who we were, then now we feel rudderless, having nothing with which to steer our ship. Those gentle winds seem not to be guiding us onward.

Some people have anger that may lead to revenge as salvation for their human bodies not to give up. It gives them a sense of heaviness that is mistaken for grounding and purpose. They use anger or revenge to continue forward, to feel that they matter, to fill the void they sense. However, to fill that void with action does not serve these people (or groups) well in the long run.

As witnesses for those who have passed on before us, we may feel obligated not to stand down, to remain vigilant to justice denied. How many times have we heard that their loved ones did not die in vain (even though deep in their hearts they sense the conflict as a mistake)? Death must have value. For some, it means rationalizing revenge or the continuation of conflicts and more deaths. That then becomes their meaning. That then becomes their new identities cemented in anger or, for some, in revenge. For others, the identities that are created serve to isolate them from having to become close to someone again, thereby avoiding future losses.

Grief impacts us in obvious ways, deeply and quickly. Grief impacts us surreptitiously and slowly as part of rituals and cultural expressions passed on from generation to generation. It can ask of us to appreciate what was lost, or it can pull us to dwell in the past without hope for a future that promises the joy of life.

Grief in itself is the human being's struggle to make sense of the new reality, when what we cherished has departed. If we allow grief to "be" with us, if we acknowledge its presence and integrate it into our souls, ultimately grief can act as a passage to mend our spirits and to provide a doorway to a new reality.

The Two Griefs

There are many kinds of grief, two of which I will address. One is "common" (but, nevertheless, painful) grief that we as individuals experience by simply being on this planet as human beings, caused by events such as changes in our job or residence, divorces, separations, and death. The other is the grief arising from societal and individual adverse trauma, which in turn arises from discrimination that we, as members of nondominant groups, may experience by virtue of our membership, as well as any kind of abuse, neglect, or traumatic event (e.g., rape, incest, betrayal) in our individual lives, regardless of group membership.

Common to both these kinds of grief are our reactions to changes due to loss. Whenever I experience some sort of loss, all kinds of emotions and body sensations emerge.

My first reaction is disbelief. *Did that really happen?* There is an element of surprise. My body may even experience shock. I gulp or hold my breath. I feel a bit "separate" from the rest of me. My environment feels surreal, as though I am in a dream. *This can't be happening.*

I may ask for more information. Or I may feel too stunned to say anything. My body sensations and my mind are trying to cope with the loss. This disbelief might last a few seconds, minutes, hours, or even days. Kübler-Ross refers to it as part of the "stages of grief" in her book *On Death and Dying*. While she writes about grief in the context of terminal loss through death, there are other living "deaths" that we as human beings experience.

I would argue that we go through such stages as areas not only with a physical death, but also with any significant loss. It can be the loss of a job that was our "identity," a friendship, a spouse through divorce or death, a precious item, or the "loss of face."

If we have emotionally invested in and provided meaning to the lost item, person, or situation, then grief follows. The depth and duration of the grief depend on the investment of emotions and meaning, as well as on any spiritual belief we may have.

Areas of loss also happen in the context of societal trauma. Grief can be due to the loss of civil rights, loss of a cultural identity due to forced assimilation, loss of being respected, or the loss of being seen as an "equal" to another human being.

Language

The grieving process follows any loss in which we have an emotional investment, including the loss of the language through which we describe our world and world beliefs—our identities. The deeper the investment, the deeper the felt loss is experienced.

I will explore the example of language. I recall thinking to myself that there are more ways to express "I love you" in Spanish than in English. Being the romantic that I am, it would be a great loss for me not to have access to more ways of saying how much I care for someone. Another example is a particular word in one of the dialects of the Quechua language (found in Argentina, Colombia, Bolivia, Ecuador, and Peru) that combines the feeling of odd, strange, weird, humorous, and ironic. It is the word *chuzco*.

The loss of one's language is significant, because it is through language that we make ourselves known to ourselves and to each other. Language describes how we experience our world. Rather than being confined to one language, I was raised to know more than one, and I could therefore expand my worldview and deepen my appreciation of other people's worldviews.

Young people create their own language to communicate their feelings, their emotions, their thoughts. We create languages to help explain the worldviews of groups or peoples—even fictional ones.

As an example, the Klingon language was actually created for the television series *Star Trek. Why?* To have viewers understand Klingons' identity as a warrior race and the culture that stems from their perspective. The youth of every generation coin their own words and expressions, which, with time, may get integrated into the speech of older generations. (Example: *Cool!*)

The yearning is to understand—to be understood and to share with another soul. I want you to see me and understand me. I want to see you and understand you. Language—both verbal and nonverbal—creates those bridges we walk upon. Or we may bomb those bridges, or allow those bridges to deteriorate through time, therefore losing the richness of what we both could have shared with each other. Yet for some, they see no richness in the "other"— only in their own culture and identity.

Is it therefore a coincidence that language can be the first casualty of assimilation? Is it any wonder that some groups struggle so fiercely to keep their language intact? And why others, as part of reclaiming their identities, try to revive their language after decades or generations of disuse? Is it any wonder that conquering nations have made threats or enacted laws to deny conquered people their native language? Three examples from history are Native Americans and First Nations people being sent to boarding schools; African slaves in the colonial and post-colonial eras; and Mexican Americans and the school system in the 1940s through the 1960s.

Deny me or you our group's language(s) and you deny us our worldview of life and our emotional expressions of our heritage. At least, this is the belief of the dominant group—whether their dominance is based on age, gender, or power.

People who have been oppressed or conquered ultimately find ways to keep that part of themselves alive. Yet there are others who do lose their languages forever. With that loss, how they experience their environment is gone. These losses impact the descendants of all groups.

When humanity loses a language, we also lose the potential for greater diversity in art, music, literature, and oral traditions.
Would Cervantes have written the same stories had he been forced to write in a language other than Spanish?
—Daniel Bogre Udell of Wikitongues

Languages are the repository of thousands of years of a people's science and art – from observations of ecological patterns to creation myths. The disappearance of a language is not only a loss for the community of speakers itself, but for our common human knowledge of mathematics, biology, geography, philosophy, agriculture, and linguistics. In this century, we are facing a massive erosion of the human knowledge base.
K. David Harrison,
When Languages Die: The Extinction of the World's Languages and the Erosion of Human Knowledge

We are discovering that there are many thousands of plants that are medicinal, which would benefit all of us. Think of the plants that have given us pain-killing medicines such as aspirin. Many of them are found in rainforests and in other lands where the indigenous peoples have in their language the means to identify these beneficial types of plants. As their languages disappear, so too does that knowledge.

What Do You Keep? What Do You Fear?

There are individuals who have maintained their heritage and culture, as in the case of the dominant group, as well as members of nondominant groups who are traditional or acculturated.

Some of the comments I used to hear from White supremacists and nativists were related to their fear of losing their own culture, their way of living, their identity. Among traditional and acculturated nondominant group members, the comments are similar. Many members of all these groups feel forced to give up something that they wish to maintain. None of these people want to lose their sense of group identity and worldview. Some are scared that their language will cease to exist as they know it to be. They are afraid of what is called language contact or contact linguistics: languages that influence each other when they come together for a certain period of time in cultural exchanges. Instead of their viewing multi-languages as expanding their horizons, their fear comes from the conquered/conqueror mindset or the mentality of "either-or." Some people forget that there are words in their own language that stem from other languages or have been directly borrowed from another language.

Assimilate or maintain tradition. There is no middle ground for those living in hierarchical-leaning societies. The fear is too great for anyone to believe that acculturation (selecting the best from the cultures) may, in fact, honor both parties' cultures and their cultural identities.

Some people forget that all cultures undergo a natural organic transformation. Old English spoken in the Middle Ages was very different from the English that is spoken in the twenty-first century. Iberians, who later became Portuguese and Spaniards, developed their own languages with similar roots from the past. Languages change through time and, because of this, knowledge transfer is better maintained.

The fear is based on the speed and the quantity of the changes, I believe. "Too much, too overwhelming" are the feelings of the people already established in a place. "Like a tidal wave, too many of 'them' come to our shores." Those already established may not be prepared, especially if there is very little diversity of cultures in their own neighborhoods or towns, or if they interact only with others of their own culture and class.

In some countries, the people already established welcome the newcomers. Host families are part of the welcome package. In other countries, it is left to volunteer organizations to provide host families or some other type of outreach to help the new arrivals get situated. There is a sense of openness and of wanting to help them, in some fashion, to understand the culture they are soon to be part of.

Welcome or Beware

I remember my mother sharing one experience of confusion she had in 1958. A woman from our church took my mum to the supermarket. She told her that in the aisles where there were canned and bottled goods, the picture of what was in the container would be shown on the can or bottle. Cans of peas would show a picture of peas. Cans of tomatoes would show a picture of tomatoes. Easy to grasp and understand. No problem. Until my mother went to the aisle where there were glass jars with pictures of babies' faces. Now she was totally confused. She knew that North Americans were not cannibals. The surprised expression on my mother's face drew smiles and then chuckles from the woman from our church. "There are exceptions to everything!" she told my mum. "These are showing who the food is supposed to feed." They both laughed.

People who choose to immigrate to a particular country come prepared to let go of some of their cultural values—and sometimes even their language. In my family, we kept our language and learned English. For some of my cousins, they were not encouraged to keep their mother tongue but to speak primarily in English.

What newcomers are *not* prepared for is being seen as "less than" and being the recipients of disrespect and the victims of stereotyping. Sometimes differences are viewed with fear, sometimes even with hatred. "Who are these people? Will their ways supplant ours?" These are a few of the questions that I have heard. The underlying fear is this: "Will they do to us as our ancestors have done (and, in some cases, currently are doing) to others?" Again, the hierarchical notion is echoed: Would the newcomers pull them off the rungs of economic and cultural ladders where they are presently positioned?

For refugees, loss of language is like tearing at the flesh or the heart, adding to the many losses they suffered during their escape to freedom and safety. They did not want to leave. They had to leave. Forced from their homes, their culture, their homelands, and their ancestors, they fled for their lives. They were barely able to bring anything with them except for the clothes on their backs and currency to pay people to either help them or to look the other way as they escaped brutal wars, violence, or dictatorships.

Mass migrations have occurred throughout history, including relatively recently: the fall of Saigon, those escaping the Khmer Rouge, those fleeing Nazi-held countries, those escaping drought conditions, those fleeing Central America, families struggling to escape the wars in the Middle East, and so on. What legacy can these people give their children if all they have are the few items they have managed to hang on to during their long trek to freedom? How would they convey their dreams and stories of love and home? If their language is suppressed, a part of them dies too.

With pain, suffering, and desperation, they seek a haven in any land that would be safe for them. Many of them are not prepared.

Culture shock. Economic shock. Gender roles that are different. The list goes on.

For displaced peoples, such as First Nations, Native Americans, and other indigenous cultures, the transgenerational and intergenerational TMCS stay active. Why is this, if the displacement takes place within their same country? In many areas, there may exist violence toward them; at the very least, they may face discrimination and bigotry. Prove to me that I am safe and I can exhale with smiles. Then TMCS may finally take a breather and deactivate or at least stand down.

Aside from language or cultural expressions, another major fear of loss concerns religion. There can be a fear that one's religion or one's connection to God or Spirit will be undermined, threatened, or systematically destroyed so that the conquering group's religion can take its place. This fear is well founded, as evidenced by multitudes of examples throughout history, for those who have been displaced, conquered, or pushed out in mass exodus from their lands they love.

For displaced people, if signs begin to appear that their religion may be undermined, threatened, or destroyed again—or perhaps these things actually *are* happening again—the TMCS become activated. Here is an example. Currently, there is a fear between some Christians and Muslims that the one group wishes to destroy the other's religion. Whether that is true or not, it does not matter. What does matter is the perception and the subsequent activation of behaviors, attitudes, and actions that will arise from such a perception toward each other's groups and their members.

Yet for those nondominant members that have assimilated, they may not see a value in retaining or maintaining their language or core areas of their culture. They may not consider it important.

Now let's look at the individual level where loss has occurred.

Loss leaves a void, depending on the significance we have given to that loss. What is my attachment to having that person in my life? What is my attachment or investment to having an idea, situation, and way of life still be part of who I am? What kind of identity and worth did I assign to myself and others before the loss? And what is it now? The meaning and attachment we give to the loss affect how deeply and how much time we undergo when we enter each of the areas of loss.

What am I, now that my child has died? Who am I, now that I have moved away from my family home? Who am I, now that I have been laid off as an aerospace engineer or any other profession with which I have identified as an integral part of my being? Who am I? What in my environment and relationships will help me see my Self?

I am reminded of the time when I was speaking to a young person who was in a gang. His role in the gang gave him meaning—more meaning than his biological family gave him. He was willing to die for his group because that group provided him with an identity that said he made a difference. For him, his actions or inactions mattered to the group and to the group's well-being.

How often have little children come to us wanting to help? There is something in all of us that makes us wish to participate and to feel good, that makes us want to contribute to something, someone, some family, some kind of group. If individuals experience the feeling that they matter, that they are significant, then they will fight to keep the status quo that makes them feel this way.

Children want to be needed, whether it is for the good of the family or community or the society at large—or for the "bad," as in violent gangs and drug cartels. Consider child soldiers. Often they are kidnapped or recruited and then indoctrinated by their captors or armed forces. They find themselves in roles that they eventually view as their only identity, especially if they are trapped and have no escape. The younger they are, the more vulnerable they are in coming to believe that their identity is based on the role they serve in their armed forces group. This is no different from adults or people of any age who are in transition or feeling loss of some sort. They are vulnerable to those who would prey upon them and mold their identity to the leaders' liking.

For these reasons and others, it is important to win the gang members, the child soldiers, the freedom fighters or terrorists (depending on your view) over to peace—to promise and then give them better roles that grant them significance and self-worth. Their roles must also be considered in any conflict resolution if healing is to take place for them as individuals and for the larger community. Different role models, ones who promote healthy relationships and peace, are important. Otherwise, these individuals can be the carriers of trauma and of the cycle of violence.

If people are raised in a household in which domestic violence has taken place, their identities are formed by what they see and feel. These individuals' primary goal is to keep safe and out of the way of the abuser.

Grief is a wholistic attempt by the mind, body, and spirit to grasp and integrate the changes and emotional loss. The "Areas of Loss" approach, which I developed as part of my dissertation, is a way of understanding that the whole person is grieving the loss of someone or something. These are areas, *not* stages.

Mind-Body Reactions: Areas of Loss

Reaction By	In the Form of
Mind	**Disbelief.** The mind goes into a 'void' of not understanding the new input from the reality it thought it knew. Denial, shock as a way of coping and minimizing the change of reality and the loss. For example, the shock once again of being discriminated.
Body	**Emotional deluge.** The body reacts with an array of emotions as the new information becomes embedded within the body. "Fight, flight, or freeze" may get activated within this time. Sadness--ranging from tears, sobs, sadness, to depression and back again is experience. Anger--ranging from being frustrated to being angry to blind rage can occur. From a physiological perspective, the 'molecules of emotions,' as Candace Pert as coined it, will cascade as the body reacts to the loss. Stress of what next fuels the reaction as the immune systems try to make sense of how to respond.
Mind and Body	**Beseeching** or pleading is experienced as the mind and body revisit past decisions and steps, which led up to the loss. What could have been done differently? Was I to blame? Were you to blame? Them? Bargaining to blaming (self and/or others) may be a way of coping and trying to "corral" the feelings and pain into a box. Negotiation and 'quarter-back' hindsight may help propel the person forward. Or it may keep the person stuck in the past in a loop of judgment.
Mind, Body, and Spirit	= **To finally Letting go.** "It is as it is." "Asi es." It is an acknowledgement of the happening. It is a time of reframing the loss and the event/person. New meaning is created to help you grow and go forward in life

Four things emerge from the grief process and its impact on human beings:

1. Grief is a wholistic attempt by the mind, body, and spirit to grasp and integrate the changes and emotional loss.

2. The greater the meaning attached to the loss, the greater the emotional investment.

3. Some groups may emphasize certain aspects of the grieving process more than other groups.

4. The longer the person is in grief, the more it affects the mindbody's abilities to go forward. Conversely, if the person tries to short-circuit the grieving process, the longer it will take to get over it. That approach will suppress and add to the pile of prior griefs that have not been fully addressed—until the day when one grief will be the last straw and will bring to the surface all the submerged griefs.

If we allow the areas of loss to be visited, eventually we will get across that bridge onto new ground and accept our new reality.

It is important to understand that grief is inherent in societal trauma. Expressions of grief can be passed down from generation to generation if the trauma has not been satisfactorily healed. If I do not realize that part of my legacy is about grief, I may continue to carry it. Or I will subconsciously assume that how I cope with grief is the *only* way to handle the loss.

How are grief and loss handled among members of my family, my culture, my religion, or my gender? I may feel uncomfortable if my way of dealing with my loss is different from the way my group deals with it. Or I may be judged by members of my group as not honoring the loss (whatever it is) in an appropriate fashion. Members of other groups may judge the way I grieve. Or I may judge them in how they grieve.

Reality changes, as do anchors of familiar paths, familiar ways of being and behaving. These areas of loss include any perceived significant loss to the person.

It can be very difficult at times to get to the final part, which is acceptance. Is it betraying the need for justice if I accept the existence of an "ism" or the societal traumas that are created by it? Some people have a tendency to stay angry as a form of witnessing or as a way of keeping the loss alive. It may be a way to prevent what or whom we cared about from disappearing. Anger can also be used as a fuel for movement. Anger can be the driving force for initial dissension and for maintaining a crisis-oriented perspective as a way of life.

This holds true for any area of loss, whether it is tears or bargaining or denial. Any area can be used as an initial reaction to help gain attention to an abusive situation. Healing requires that we go through all these areas and that we not use any of them as a way of life or as a final form to maintain attention. Maintaining such a stance taxes us physiologically and psychologically.

Crises, Addiction, and Grief

I remember reading an article in *Newsweek* magazine that was almost totally devoted to the different perspectives held by African Americans with regard to their civil rights progress during the last forty years. What struck me was a quote from Ellis Cose's article "The Good News of Black America":

> How can civil rights leaders acknowledge the real and evident progress without encouraging complacency? How can they keep the pressure on to 'move the glass from half-full to three-quarters full' [in (Hugh) Price's words], if they give up the language of crisis and damnation?

Anyone who has interacted with addicts knows that the only way to get their attention is to disrupt the focus between the addict and the object of addiction. Giving up "the language of crisis and damnation," as Cose said, would mean giving up a tool that has thus far been useful in breaking the focus between addict and object of addiction. Society primarily changes the status quo only when it is threatened or in a crisis. The same may be true at the micro level: family. Does a child have to crash a car in front of the police station in order to get the family's attention? (This scenario is based on a true account.) If the abuser has designated one of her or his family members as the troublemaker, is it because that person is creating a crisis to get help from somewhere, anywhere, outside the affected family?

If society is not proactive in resolving and healing wounds, then it becomes difficult for those who have been the recipients of trauma to give up TMCS—if these tools are the only ways to get the attention of those in power.

Crises can be a form of addiction as well. Violence can be another. Both can keep individuals in unsuccessful physiological and psychological fight, flight, or freeze responses. In a society that thrives on addictions (e.g., crises, violence, mind-altering substances), it would make sense that many civil rights leaders would continue with crisis-oriented words in order to get the addict's attention.

Yet is it *healthy* for us to continue using TMCS as primary attention-getters? If we live in an addiction-oriented society, do we not perpetuate the dysfunction? Is not our well-being affected by playing by those rules of addiction? Are not our identities affected and formed around these rules?

Living with addicts impacts how we grieve and how we express that grief. It affects our overall well-being. For those of us who struggle with personal addiction, living in an addiction-oriented society presents a challenge for us to stay sober. It challenges all of us to honor our personal grief as well as any societal-inflicted grief. It is therefore important to understand the relationship between addiction and the grieving process, both at the individual and societal levels.

Society's behaviors and attitudes can reflect those of an addict. "Macro and micro expressions of addiction and dysfunctional behaviors are more than mirrors of each other: they are one and the same," according to Anne Wilson Schaef and Diane Tassel, as they discuss the impact of addictive persons in management and leadership positions.

Individuals and families make up society. Individuals in positions of power set policies and mission statements, which then impact implementation and enforcement. If we have wounded leaders, then would it not make sense that their world perceptions would be filtered through unresolved wounds? Being a causaholic is no different from being the addict at the societal helm.

Is it the perceived abuser group's advantage to have "walking wounded" people? What if it benefits them to have people being preoccupied with existence and survival? If people are so tired and in need of distraction from a cycle of work, sleep, work, then their having a variety of addictions would benefit those not wanting a populace that can question the status quo and become activists for living fairly.

Authoritarian or totalitarian governments know whom to target and whom they can placate. They also know that the latter will not question them. Yet groups do react in some form. The actions may not necessarily be healthy: revenge, martyrdom, terrorism, to name a few. People who are under ongoing stress have higher rates of poor physical and psychological health. Poor health and increased medical costs have an adverse impact on a society's economy, not to mention the individual's pocketbook and budget.

People preoccupied with their daily survival have more of a tendency to fault those around them who are different, rather than question authority figures and systems. Much like individuals in a dysfunctional family, authority figures can play one sibling against another. A populace in a survival mode may be encouraged to react, rather than reflect. They can be easily manipulated and given disinformation and misinformation by emotionally and psychologically wounded leaders and others who have vested interests, as well as addiction-oriented systems. Totalitarian, authoritarian, and oligarchic governments throughout history have utilized ways to keep traumas, even minor traumas, alive—and with that, transgenerational and intergenerational ways of coping are passed from one generation to the next.

Often, unresolved grief invites addictions. Addictions act as buffers against feeling pain, loss, and helplessness. Addictions are distractions and forms of escape. Yet the trauma is still there inside the body, affecting our perceptions and limiting our emotional growth. Paradoxically, avoiding the feeling of the grief actually keeps the grief alive and, therefore, the trauma alive.

Knowing *why* I allow trauma to remain the focal point of my life by keeping certain areas of grief alive beyond their time will help me become more conscious of how I am limiting myself and preventing healing from taking place. Chronic grief can keep us in a loop in which there is no growth, no insights, no real advancement for our communities and ourselves.

Understanding *why* I stay in a particular area of loss will help me look up and expand my horizons for other kinds of strategies and expressions that can assist me in transforming my environment. If, for example, I continue to use anger or continue to stay in only one part of the grief process or refuse to follow through, I am at risk of hurting myself physiologically, as well as impacting my ability to let go of my TMCS. I am not allowing myself to heal. Ultimately, if healing is to take place, acceptance of the situation has to take place.

Acceptance does not mean surrender. It means acknowledging what has transpired. It acknowledges the impact that the loss and subsequent changes have had on my life. By allowing the areas of loss to go through me, I can be free to pursue my activities—not with tears or anger, which come from the trauma, but with the passion of my heart, which does not deplete me nor take me away from all of who I am or from the full life I wish to lead.

By being more of who I am, I am able to lead a balanced life of family, friends, and heart.

Meaning, Loss, and Investment

The greater the meaning attached to the loss, the greater the emotional investment. The deeper my attachment had been to what was lost, the deeper and longer I may stay in one or more of the areas of loss.

Two kinds of meaning take place: my overall meaning and beliefs about my life, and the specific meaning attached to what was lost. For example, if I have "faith or hope" as part of my overall meaning of life, my visits to those areas of loss might be shortened. Instead of viewing the loss as a loss, I might now see it as a transformation or step toward something else. The overall meaning of my life could well then supersede the meaning I had assigned to the particular loss.

Once my whole being understands that acceptance is simply an acknowledgment of "what is," and not a surrender or betrayal or belief in hopelessness, then I can view my present situation with the tools and resources that are currently at hand. I can then be free to reframe or find a new context of what had occurred in order to help me grow today and in the future.

I am reminded of the organization called Mothers Against Drunk Driving (MADD). The founder, Candy Lightner, had lost a daughter to a habitual drunk driver. As part of her regaining herself through the grieving or mourning process, she reframed the meaning of the deaths: *Never again.* She lobbied until laws were enacted to help reduce the incidence of driving while intoxicated. She did not want other parents to go through what she had experienced. She took her grief, she explored what her loss meant to her, and then she reframed it to empower herself and help others.

Some groups may emphasize certain areas in the grieving process more than others. I saw the macro implication of grief on groups. As a trainer and mediator, I witnessed heated debates and conversations among people concerning the issue of racism.

Member of Group One:

"It happened already! Can't you get on with it?! Why are you still dwelling on it? Why are you crying over 'spilled milk'?"

Member of Group Two:

"You're trying to gloss things over! You don't care. You don't want to discuss what happened. You just want to get on with it, as though nothing has happened."

Member of Group Three:

[to Group Two] "You're always so angry!"

[to Group One] "If only you would have done what you promised, but you never do. We shouldn't have taken you people's word. As long as you people don't show remorse, how can we believe you?"

Might there be a possibility that groups develop their own ways of expressing grief? Might a group favor one area of grief over another? Might a group that has been and continues to feel ongoing trauma choose parts of the grief process as ways to witness the loss? If so, then conflicts may arise from perceptions that grief is not being "appropriately" demonstrated by the other group.

Of course, the culturation spectrum would need to be considered to avoid the possible stereotyping of members of groups. There are differences in expressing grief within groups if factors relating to socioeconomic level, past generational pain, gender, and religion are included.

I offer an example. In my household, emotions are expressed, as are feelings. Or so I thought. When I was about fifteen years old, a friend of the family died in a tragic car accident. I remember crying and feeling upset. All my family members were upset. I recall hugging my father with tears streaming down my face. He consoled me. Yet after a few minutes he started to pat my back and more or less told me, both in words and in energy, *"Ya pasó."* It already happened. The phrase meant to me that "It's over and done with and there is nothing we can do about it." That was the subtext of the expression.

As a young adult, I found myself using the coping mechanism with my relationships that my father had used a decade earlier. *"Ya pasó."* With that concept, I would start to problem-solve with a person who was clearly not ready for it. It was not until a good friend told me I was hurrying her up with her grieving that I understood I had been passing down an intergenerational behavior. I was surprised. I had no idea.

There are enough anecdotes of racial- or group-based conflict to make me wonder whether we are missing the mark if we do not consider the grief process.

Understanding how and when I grieve and understanding that you may grieve differently from me will help me to avoid getting so "triggered" during discussions of "isms" (classism, sexism, racism, etc.). Whenever I have addressed this in my workshops and classes, the shift from anger to understanding occurs. People suddenly see the "other" as another human being with pain and loss. Compassion has a chance to grow. Comprehension takes place. We start to see each other as individuals.

Understanding how grief plays a role in how we feel and behave is part of understanding how it may affect our sense of identity. If grief becomes chronic, it influences the way you and I feel toward others and ourselves. Depression shuts out the world. A person or a group can retreat inwardly, emotionally, and psychologically. Becoming a "rage-aholic" pushes people away.

Living in the water of tears creates isolated islands from ourselves and others. It creates so much space that intimacy and trust cannot be developed.

Or in the guise of being an "enabler" type or a "mediator-rescuer," a person may *become* the role, losing one's identity and thereby avoiding healthy conflict and healthy discussions.

The identity molded by trauma, the identity that is formed by unresolved fight, flight, or freeze reactions and by "stuck" grief will know no other guiding stories. One of the first steps to take then is to loosen the grief, to unclamp its hold on our bodies and make internal inroads toward regaining ourselves. Into creating new stories that honor ourselves and others. Into rewriting the trajectory of our autobiographies.

Chapter 4

GETTING THE TRAUMATIC ENERGY OUT OF THE BODY

In recent years, the idea of wholistic healing has emerged in trauma studies. More psychotherapists are delving into the body and the body's responses. The field of psychoneuroimmunology (PNI) has gained increased prominence. Neurosciences have gained traction. Interdisciplinary sharing and discoveries are taking place. Traditional psychotherapy is integrating or giving way to the impact of power or lack thereof regarding their clients. Furthermore, energy modalities touch on the understanding that if trauma is to be dissipated, the whole mind and body need to be addressed.

The Violence Within Us

Neuroscientists such as Debra Niehoff argue that as long as society does not include the neurobiology of human beings when addressing how to resolve violence, we miss half the story. Stress, fight and flight responses, and repetitive exposure of those responses to the body's systems affect the person's behaviors and attitudes. Among her suggestions are pharmacological answers to contain or normalize memories that hold intense emotional and biological reactions to trauma. One drug, propranolol, caught my eye. In her words, this drug "accomplished something far more subtle: it prevented emotions from tagging the memory with survival labels, so that the story was logged in as if it were a commonplace event."

What would be the ethical ramifications of a drug such as propranolol, which can dampen the emotional impact of a trauma? Two factors concerned me: the medical side effects, and the people providing the treatment. Propranolol's side effects include the increased possibility of congestive heart failure and the masking of hyperthyroidism and diabetes. In ethical terms, if such a drug were in the wrong hands, then a traumatized person given it might have his or her moral outrage of injustice be dampened or taken away. Might that occur?

On the other hand, if such a drug were in the hands of true healers, the rewards of no longer being plagued by flashbacks and fight, flight, or freeze reactions would greatly assist in the healing process of the individual. The bottom line would be, in whose hands would the drug be?

Aside from the standard response of traditional psychotherapy and allopathic medicines (i.e., Western drugs) to trauma, clients and therapists alike are no longer satisfied with simply containing or "living with" trauma's aftermath. Clients no longer wish to develop further coping mechanisms to handle the aftermath. They want the trauma to be gone from their bodies, minds, and hearts.

Even though the body harbors the trauma, many psychotherapists deal only with the intellectual and psychological impacts. This may account for why it requires many years for individuals to get a handle on trauma, contain it, and then develop ways to push the traumatic memories into the memory stacks of their minds. Addressing trauma need not be this way.

SE and SER: Helping the Body Let Go

Peter Levine has an answer for dispelling the traumatic energy. He has written extensively on this subject, as well as produced tapes and conducted workshops to train others in the use of Somatic Experiencing (SE). By assisting the client to recall the events leading up to the life-threatening situation, Levine verbally facilitates the person into a body position that the body would have taken during the fight, flight, or freeze response. The "extra" energy is created by the bodymind for the fight, flight, or freeze as a response to a perceived life threat. It does not matter if the perception is based on belief or actuality. The bodymind responds.

Levine discovers what the body position is by observing the client's body language, any subtle movements, tone of voice, inflections, and gestures. Once the person finds herself or himself naturally getting into that body position, the biological discharge can take place. It does not require the person to remember the actual traumatic event, only the memories leading to the trauma.

By allowing the body to follow through the motions it had originally wanted to make, the biological discharge of the existing trauma energy is released through that "exit" posture created by the body. For Levine, trauma is an unprocessed short-spurt energy that was created by the body to deal with a perceived life-threatening situation.

Similarly, John Upledger created SomatoEmotional Release (SER), a procedure to assist the body in letting go of the traumatic energy, or "energy cysts," which have come from the outside into the body. This SomatoEmotional Release procedure helps the body to realign itself into the body position the person had taken at the time of the traumatic impact.

Longitudinal case studies on Vietnam War veterans by the Upledger Foundation were conducted to determine whether the discharge or release of these biological reactions dissipated post-traumatic stress symptoms. The results have been promising. No full reliving of the trauma, nor any return to any post-traumatic symptoms, have thus far been reported by the clients. In addition, there was a reduction in the most serious symptoms, such as violence, anxiety, and depression.

By doing craniosacral work, that is, by using gentle acupressure manipulation on key points on the body, notably the cranium and sacrum areas, the practitioner facilitates the flow of the cerebral spinal fluid (CSF). It is the renewed flowing of this fluid that dislodges the energy "cysts" and activates their departure. Upledger suggests that trauma creates havoc on the CSF and the neuroendocrine systems. If wartime trauma is successfully dislodged, then societal traumas can certainly be, as can individualized traumas from childhood or other life stages.

Both Levine and Upledger have observed that once the energy is discharged from the body, any secondary ailments, such as fibromyalgia, rheumatoid arthritis, and other kinds of autoimmune illnesses, as well as eating disorders, have dissipated with time.

EFT: A Gift from Gary Craig

In recent decades, other tools have been developed along the concept of energy, meridian lines, light to deep hypnosis, and neurolinguistic programming. I will highlight one technique, EFT, although several other healing modalities exist, such as Callahan's Thought Field Therapy and TAT. It should be noted that many of these techniques take their lead from Chinese medicine's view of *chi*, or life energy, as well as the meridians that Chinese medicine practitioners use for acupuncture.

In simplest terms, in Gary Craig's Emotional Freedom

Techniques, or EFT, clients tap with their fingertips on their bodies to stimulate certain meridian points, while they are "tuned in" to the problem through focus and a form of neurolinguistic programming (NLP) is being used. "The cause of all negative emotions is a disruption in the body's energy system," according to Craig.

> To some newcomers, this may seem strange. To others, it hits the bull's eye and represents a missing piece to the healing puzzle. The subtle energies that circulate throughout the body have been largely ignored (until recently) by western scientists.
>
> As a result, our use of them for emotional and spiritual healing has been sparse at best. With EFT, however, we consider these subtle energies to be the front-running cause of emotional upsets.

What makes Craig's approach special is that he originally gave away his techniques to anyone who was willing to learn and who had some type of counseling background. Many thousands of practitioners took advantage of his generosity to learn his methods, which were derived from Callahan's Thought Field Therapy. Because of his generosity, his EFT approach has been used extensively and globally. Feedback and case examples have been pouring into his professional listserv, website, and conferences around the world.

Clinical studies, such as those by Pratt and Lambrou and by Andrade and Feinstein, have shown the high success rate of this modality, as well as other meridian-tap approaches. The studies by Andrade and Feinstein found that EFT was effective in lessening, if not eliminating, such issues as post-traumatic stress, anxiety, guilt, shame, painful memories, anger, and phobias.

Many international organizations have included EFT among their modalities. One of them, the United Kingdom Association for Meridian Therapies, has been very encouraged by EFT's success. In one of their publications, Chris Hardisty has observed that a component of EFT, "psychological reversal," may account for why some persons are unable to let go of trauma.

> The concept that EFT brings is that of 'Psychological Reversal.' This suggests that if the natural energy flow becomes reversed due to shock, stress or trauma, healing (which is the body's natural function) cannot take place easily as the body is fighting against the natural healing process. ... In other cases, where therapy is unaccountably not producing results, or only producing results very slowly, psychological reversal must be suspected. ... EFT seeks to correct psychological reversal. As the patient gently taps or presses on an acupoint, neural receptors under the skin convert this pressure to an electrical impulse that is transmitted to the brain and it is these signals that are intended to correct the psychological reversal.

Up to this point, EFT has been largely used for non-societally-induced problems. EFT coupled with hypnosis has shown anecdotal successes in resolving micro issues. Craig has encouraged practitioners to use EFT to address societal-based traumas.

Hypnosis: Getting to the "Bottom Line"—the Unconscious

From a hypnotherapy perspective, the unconscious is accessed in order to address "out-of-date commands." Old ways of dealing with racism or sexism, for instance, may now be counterproductive.

By bypassing the subconscious part of the mind, the directives and needs of the client are forwarded and stated directly to the unconscious via the alpha brain wave. When we are awake, we are in the beta wave.

The prime directives of the unconscious in preserving the body are optimal health, safety, and peace. Therefore, a hypnotherapist can facilitate the request of the client to recalibrate and expand on them.

When there is societal trauma, the person develops coping mechanisms and skills that "preserve the body," given the level of safety and resources the person had at the time. Over a period of years, that command may continue to be running in the background, especially when it comes to safety and trusting people, as well as to using one's judgment to assess situations and persons.

One of my clients used anger and hypervigilance to keep her safe from racist remarks and potential harm to her physical, emotional, and financial well-being. Years later, those tools of anger and hypervigilance were getting in her way of moving forward in life, in particular at workplace situations. She and others like her were tired of being angry and being "triggered." Their health was being negatively affected. Bouts of depression and low energy were not uncommon.

Through hypnosis, the unconscious was able to recalibrate what was truly a life-threatening situation to her body and which situations were not. If it were truly a physically life-threatening situation, the appropriate response would be "fight, flight, or freeze." Preservation of the body is imperative and time is seen as an enemy. Everything must be done quickly—in nanoseconds.

However, if the situation were not life-threatening, then time would be a friend and ally. Therefore, there is time to access other tools that are not fight-, flight-, or freeze-based. Space created by curiosity and by being *bien educada* replaces the space that was once created by anger. The assumption changes from viewing the person as a racist or sexist out to do harm, to the assumption that a person may have made a racist or sexist (or whatever "ist") comment, yet we do not know their intention and meaning without doing some type of follow-up.

It is part of being *bien educado* to separate soul from behaviors so that curiosity and exploration can occur. Furthermore, it creates possibilities for dialog, creates space for reflection, and fosters an environment of safety.

Below are examples of questions that can be asked from the heart—that is, if the person experiences a sense of security inside and can see time as an ally—so as to take the time needed to investigate and to explore.

"That's interesting. Can you expand on that comment so I can understand your intention or meaning behind it?"

"This is what I'm hearing you say: ____. ... Do I have it correct?"

"That word [or term] has historical or emotional meaning to me. It reminds me of ____. I'm feeling hurt, scared, or concerned because of that."

"When I hear that word [or statement], I get a vision of ____. Is that what you intended or what your purpose was?"

"I'm curious. I heard you say ____. Is that correct? Is that what were you trying to say?"

The ability to breathe, give pause, and reflect can occur only if the person is not in the fight, flight, or freeze mode. We may find out that the person is indeed a racist or sexist. We may discover that the person is "clueless" or is someone who is passing down subconscious training with no thought of harm. It does not matter what we discover, in the sense that *now* we are in control of how we choose to react or reflect. We can react with anger, with fright, or with some other emotion that taxes our health and dampens our spirits. Or, we can now respond in the safety of our bodies.

We may disagree with the person. We may clear up a misunderstanding or miscommunication. We may not choose to be around that person in the future. Or, we may learn to strategize how to relate with that person who is a colleague, or someone in an authority position so as to have our needs met.

The conflict may even become an opportunity for all concerned to explore the dynamics of the "ism." We may even choose to become active in politics or social justice because of that person and others like her or him. But we will do it from our hearts and loving passion in order to make our world safer and healthier for all.

We will not tax ourselves and hurt ourselves as a way of dealing with the "isms." We will not get traumatized or continue on that cycle. We will not let other people's "isms" control how we respond and how we treat our own bodies in the process.

After utilizing hypnosis and coaching based on the principles of this book, the lives of my societally traumatized clients have improved, both at the workplace and at home. For one client, work improved to the point that her supervisors and colleagues happily noticed. She no longer uses the "fight" mode but, rather, tools that promote conversation and exploration.

Consequently, there has been increased insight among everyone concerned, and the White staff members now better understand their transmission of racism, which was affecting their African American colleagues.

Unfortunately, my client's situation, along with that of other clients, is not unusual. Racism is pervasive, but how we deal with it can be different. Our tools need not tax us but, instead, can nourish our identities and ourselves.

Optimism: Letting Your Heart Sing Its Songs

Martin Seligman has observed that another way of healing is magnifying the good within the person or helping the person to "learn optimism." What we say to ourselves has an impact on our well-being and how we view life. Seligman challenges us to examine our "automatic thoughts" and change the scripts we give ourselves. He has documented the impact that optimism, depression, and pessimism have on the immune system.

Seligman points out that when a person has been in a state of helplessness for a prolonged period, the immune system is compromised. Furthermore, the person will attract additional examples of life situations that validate a negative or pessimistic view of life. The repetition of loss and traumas, in one form or another, throughout one's life will increase the probability of the immune system's being impacted. A vicious cycle is born.

These findings are important for those of us affected by societal traumas and those affected by individual adverse experiences for two reasons: accessibility and cost. For many of us, accessibility and cost have been obstacles to getting the help we need for our healing. With accessible and affordable tools such as those described, we can also help empower our own groups in their healing process. We can help others and ourselves.

An additional reason is that we often believe that the "ism" we experience is a "part of life" over which we have absolutely no control. We accept that the best we can do is to either ignore societal effects (i.e., be in denial) or be consumed by its effects (i.e., accept the feeling and be a victim). Such attitudes and beliefs affect our overall health.

If the traumas stem from our family, we do not have a safety place at home. For those who have both societal and family traumas, there are no areas where we can relax, and remember who we are, and touch our joy. If the major part of our waking and sleep life is not safe, then there may be increases in high cholesterol rates, abnormal blood pressure rates, and certain autoimmune illnesses.

The healing modalities used for micro traumas can be used for macro trauma healing. By using somatic-oriented approaches to help our bodies experience well-being, we start on the road of freeing ourselves of the trauma stories. One of these steps is having a sense of optimism, which creates hope, desire, and the persistence to continue forward.

I do want to clarify something. While there may be life circumstances that we cannot control, by consciously walking on a healing and spiritual journey, we will give ourselves tools to discern what we cannot change from what we can change or transform in our lives. Trauma, whether micro or macro, can all too often cloud our minds and hearts as to what we are able to do. Life-threatening situations may create pain, but they need not create suffering.

Pain and Suffering: Separating the Twins

Pain may be part of our life's journey, but suffering need not be. Suffering can be confused with pain. People may avoid pain in order to avoid suffering, which has no real set limits or boundaries. Avoiding this blending of pain and suffering may be the case with many members of the dominant groups. Suffering, as I define it, is an emotional relationship component of the meaning we give to the pain (physical, emotional, spiritual, etc.). Suffering may include feelings of shame, blame, survivor's guilt, hopelessness, "stuck" grief, and so on. Suffering becomes our master.

Pain, on the other hand, is our "servant" that tells us something is wrong. An example: I hurt my finger. Pain is the messenger to let me know that a cut has occurred and that my finger needs medical attention. Once the cut is treated, the pain eventually leaves. It has done its job of letting me know that my finger was injured.

Suffering is an emotional component. Let's say that the finger belongs to a right-handed person who writes. Because of the injury, the person finds writing painful and cannot write. And yet her work depends on writing. She becomes angry and frustrated because of the inconvenience and the interruption. She has to wait for the healing to finish. She blames herself. She gets into a foul mood and projects her anger onto others, especially her closest loved ones. She is suffering.

Had she not suffered, she might have found other ways to compensate. (Suffering narrows our vision and our thinking.) A tape recorder could have helped her. She could have asked someone to help her by doing the typing. She could have acquired a computer software program for dictating directly into the computer, with the computer typing the text for her. If there was no deadline, she could have taken that time to rest and do other things. If there *was* a deadline, she could have asked the person who imposed it for a postponement. The point is that there are many options and avenues she could have taken had she not chosen suffering to be the master companion of the pain.

Societal trauma can induce suffering, keeping it a companion to pain. Suffering distracts us from seeing alternatives and opportunities. Pain is the messenger to show us what has been injured. By listening to our pain, we can find different paths to healing. By listening to suffering, we get caught in a loop of chronic unhealthy grief, cutting off our paths to move onward. Suffering invites an unending grief if the suffering is chronic. Suffering may skew our perceptions of ourselves and of others.

In order to let go of traumatic energies, we need to differentiate the roles of pain and suffering. We can unhitch these elements from each other. We can let go of the suffering along with the traumatic energies.

The reality of "isms" will continue until there are shifts in consciousness or until there is the perception of mutual benefit by the groups concerned to address and take actual societal steps to heal the perceptions and dynamics between groups and within groups. Remember, we are all in some way members of both dominant and nondominant groups. Classism, sexism, ageism, racism, heterosexism, as well as favoring one religion over another in practice, body shaming ... and the list goes on. The legacy of "isms" includes the deteriorating health effects of all people involved. But we can change that as we breathe in hope—and change our bodies' chemistry while doing so.

Breathing Life into Your Story

Trauma can capture our breath and hold it still. Or trauma can hurry our breath and keep us from taking life fully into our core. How can our hearts sing when the hand of trauma muzzles our dreams? Breathing is essential. Without breath, we die. Yet how many of us have forgotten how to truly breathe? When we are frightened, we may hold our breath, then suddenly gulp or gasp as the body pushes us to get air into our bodies. When we are in a fight, flight, or freeze mode, our rhythm of breathing becomes erratic and shallow. Deep breathing is out of the question if we feel threatened in some manner.

Yet it is deep breathing that will give us peace. Deep rhythmic breathing helps our bodies shift from the sympathetic system, where the fight, flight, or freeze reaction resides, to the parasympathetic system, where non-crisis, peace, and relaxation occur. In a healthy body, both systems are experienced in a balanced way to move and relax the body on a daily basis.

When there is an extreme use of the sympathetic system, the body suffers. The whole person suffers. Our judgment narrows. We focus on life-threatening and safety issues to the point that we ignore areas in which we are already safe. The beauty around us sinks back to the grey shadows. Issues of safety expand, grabbing a panoramic view of our vision, diminishing from our sight, sound, smell, touch, and mind any beauty and any non-crisis vistas.

Part of letting go of trauma is to learn how to breathe again and to find your own rhythm, literally and figuratively. Many people turn to yoga and its various forms to not only get their bodies and minds in tune, but also to breathe.

There are many kinds of breathing and breaths: Fire-breathing (rapid breathing), alternating-nostril breathing, deep sighs and exhalation through the mouth, belly breathing, and certain kinds of breathing as different body postures are adopted. People who have gone to Lamaze training in preparation for childbirth are well acquainted with the essential need to breathe a certain way so that the delivery can be easier for the mother and baby. Marathon runners know how to breathe in order to pace themselves for the long haul. Singers learn how to breathe. Certain body postures elicit certain kinds of breathing and—this is important—emotions.

Try breathing when your shoulders are slumped and your head

down as you shuffle in your walk. What type of breathing happens when you adopt that posture and movement? What emotions seem to predominate? Now try taking a Wonder Woman or Superman stance: standing erect with hands on the hips, looking up toward the sky or directly in front of you as though you are witnessing something far away, and with feet spread apart. How is your breath now? Are there any breathing constrictions occurring? What emotions do you seem to experience?

Breathing is automatically done by the body; however, we can also influence how we consciously breathe. By slowing our breaths when we are "triggered," we not only give ourselves additional oxygen, but we also help ourselves stay in the parasympathetic mode, where we can better access our critical thinking and assess the situation at hand more fully.

We can keep or regain control over what our life stories can be. Be with breath; work with breath; have fun doing different kinds of breathing and take in that lush air that gives life to your lungs, to your bodies. Breathing is so essential in getting over trauma. Doing breath work can help to transform our stories into the kinds we wish for ourselves and for our loved ones. Without breath, healing cannot be complete.

Enhancing Well-Being: The Normal State of Living

While Levine, Upledger, and others have focused on releasing the trauma, there are others, such as Patricia Deer, who have been focusing on enhancing our existing well-being. Deer has compiled not only an impressive literature review of healing modalities and their effects on conflict resolution, but has also conducted extensive somatic experiments. These tests explored whether somatic practices would have significant effects on the person's ability to resolve conflict.

Deer argued that if a person is in a state of well-being, conflict will naturally dissolve. Her approaches focus on enhancing well-being, not on containing or omitting trauma or its effects. She expands the concept of what is wellness, with the expectation that the wellness will flourish. As a side effect, the trauma will resolve itself.

Her observation is that conflict comes from fear. Fear is the driving force of conflict. What she discovered through her experiments is that, indeed, if people are able to be in a state of well-being, conflict is easier to address and resolve. Well-being can be a "prevention" to conflict if individuals are in touch with their body's sensations and in touch with others around them. A better understanding can occur and, with that, more effective communication to address any concerns—before those concerns become negatively conflictual and adversarial.

If well-being is prevention, then should we not focus on watering that plant of well-being at the societal level as well? At the societal level, is it any wonder that conflict grows where weeds of poverty exist, civil rights are denied, advancement on the societal ladder is prevented, poor health is the norm, and terror-ridden environments exist? With these weeds that decay the mind, body, and soul, how can well-being grow? Fertile ground for conflict and societal trauma may occur.

There are many modalities of healing that people can use to get the traumatic energy out—or simply to become reacquainted with their bodies. I became interested in bodywork therapy because of the observations I had made when I was a masseuse eons ago. I noticed that people held their muscles in certain ways, just as they held their bodies in certain postures. I also noticed that the body area that had been abused was tight or needed massage. As that body area released the tightness, it was not unusual for the client to get flashes of memories or to become emotional as the body relaxed. Before I knew of Levine's or Upledger's work, I saw the shaking and the sighing that accompanied the discharges that followed certain kinds of massaging.

I decided to focus on the approaches discussed earlier since they are on the cutting edge of releasing traumatic energy. Also to consider is the method of EMDR (Eye Movement Desensitization and Reprocessing) treatments, offered by Francine Shapiro. Many research studies have duplicated its high success rate. EMDR is taught internationally, as are the other modalities that I have mentioned. It should be noted that, whereas EMDR can create retraumatization, especially in the hands of the novice therapist, the other modalities described above have, so far, had no such record of retraumatizing clients.

¿Cómo Te Sientes?: The Value of Body Positions

Life can give us multiple answers in one. How we sit may tell us how we feel. How we stand up (for ourselves) may tell us how we feel. Our posture gives us away if we say something to the contrary.

Virginia Satir has spoken of body positions and how each type of position elicits certain kinds of emotions and perspectives. I used Satir's methods and incorporated my own when I was a psychotherapy intern. The results were truly amazing. A depressed female client exhibited a body position of her head down, hunched or slumped shoulders, poor posture, and a barely audible voice. I invited her do a Wonder Woman stance of walking with head up high, chin in, straight posture, and hands on hips, and say, "I am Wonder Woman."

Changes in attitudes and self-image were noted. More assertive words and boundary readjustments became apparent. I have integrated Satir's methods into my workshops, gatherings, and in coaching with wonderful results. While this is anecdotal evidence, it would be interesting if recent research would include the dispelling of traumatic influences vis-a-vis the use of these postures.

Whereas Satir was a psychologist focusing on body postures, the anthropologist Felicitas Goodman explored international archetypal body postures and breathing, which elicited visions and connections with the "otherworld," or spirit world. Altered states of consciousness were achieved. Indigenous healers, *curanderos* or *curanderas* (as they are known in Latin America), and wise men and wise women, have known this for generations and have used certain body postures to connect with ethereal spirits, to connect with their patients, and to help them in "soul retrievals." The notion of using body positions is nothing new.

What *is* new is Western researchers' and practitioners' understanding of the importance of body positions from the other end of the telescope, so to speak. They have observed the outcome: Clients go into certain body positions as the trauma energy makes its way out of their bodies. In indigenous cultures, healers know that in order to get the trauma energy out, they have to guide or position the body in postures to elicit such outcomes.

It seems that indigenous cultures, East, and West are coming together. For generations, indigenous healers have been using practices that Western practitioners are now discovering for themselves. However, many Westerners use the essence of the modalities (e.g., Shapiro's EMDR) in an individual manner with their client, whereas indigenous healers often invite or have in mind the participation of the whole community as part of the healing process. In societal trauma, perhaps having many members of the group participate in the healing may provide more levels of healing and support. Having whole groups participate in the healing process from what is essentially a group trauma would have tremendous benefits.

The Media: Leader in Healing, or Provider of Secondary Traumas?

No discussion of societal healing would be complete without mentioning the media's involvement. "The media determines what people will see and knows how to use the power of suggestion," according to Gina Ross, an author on the roles that the media can take in the healing of trauma. I have had many discussions with her concerning this aspect of the media. As a therapist and international consultant and trainer, Ross has witnessed the effects of the media's ability to magnify secondary traumas for its viewing and reading public. Yet, as she pointed out, the media has the potential to be leaders in healing. The media can provide needed information on trauma and on curtailing the effects of trauma on the population. The media plays a major role in disseminating images of violence, stereotypes, and traumas. By providing healing tools rather than sensationalism, the media can play a critical role in educating viewers and readers about the effects of violence and trauma.

This is the question I then need to ask: Is the media courageous enough to break this cycle of creating secondary trauma regardless of rating standings? The ongoing repetition of showing a gruesome scene or verbal anguish throughout the day or week adds to the stress nervous system and, consequently, to an increasing desensitization, which leads to further repetitions. This is much like an addictive drug: One needs to up the dosage to get the same effect. Those who are addicted to adrenaline and violence will not want to have their "drugs" taken away from them.

The media, such as the entertainment sector, will have to be creative in producing nonviolent shows and films that do not perpetuate "isms" or societal traumas. Yet the bottom line for the media is, of course, ratings and advertisers.

Is the media willing to expand on nonviolent themes in the name of long-term gain? In the name of short-term benefits, is it responsible enough to show the truth about violence and how to survive it in a realistic manner? Will short-term profits win out over the media's long-term responsibility to its audience? During times of war and internal domestic conflicts, will it add to the stress and trauma of society, or will it be part of a collaboration to assist in healing and in the promotion of well-being?

Another factor is the reporters that are on the front line, out in the thick of things. Secondary traumas can occur. Are these reporters, as well as others who face and engage in the reporting and dissemination of the news, debriefed? If not, will they—the same as a body's defense—numb themselves, or desensitize themselves?

I have presented a smattering of modalities to invite your curiosity. From what I have observed, it is essential to remove the traumatic energy from our bodies if we are going to go forward in our lives, as individuals, as leaders of movements, as governments, as members of groups, and as whole groups. Members of the media who do the reporting and entertaining are also subjected to traumatic energy, and they may steel themselves or learn to become numb to what they are reporting on and entertaining us with.

There are many kinds of people and many kinds of healing. Each of us will choose whatever healing modalities seem appropriate for us. Societal trauma affects us in many ways. One of them is energetically and physiologically. Another way is how we view our heritage, our ways and our groups' or ancestors' ways of healing, and our comfort with our own groups and with other groups. As we explore our own heritage, we discover that the roots we need for our healing have been next to the roots that caused us pain.

To heal as individuals from families that have hurt us, so too must a person realize that within our own families there are healing methods that have been used successfully and methods that may have worked. It is up to you to be the explorer that you are meant to be in your own life and to expand your comfort zone to adventures that will make your heart smile.

Chapter 5

ANCESTORS' LEGACY: HERITAGE AND HEALING

Each group has its own ways of healing. The healing ways may have been interrupted or suppressed by the abuser or oppressor groups historically or in the present. Cultural considerations and the legacy of trauma are part of the healing. Part of the healing often involves revisiting history as portrayed by the dominant or oppressor group and by the oppressed groups.

As part of a group's healing, the members may come together to talk about what happened, what legacies were left, how identities and self-worth were affected by the oppressor groups, and so forth. Part of the healing is to take the group and its members out of denial. Denial often occurs when the severity of the impact is such that to confront it may mean shame, blame, loss, grief, and the belief that group members may not be able to survive if they allow themselves to experience the loss, the shift in reality, the facts. By understanding that our present may be carrying past dictates and experiences, members of nondominant groups, as well as the groups themselves, can then be in a better position to choose what coping tools to keep and what tools to develop.

I am reminded of a former colleague. She is a fifth-generation Irish American. At the time of my writing this, she had been a

Buddhist by choice for more than twenty years. She spent time with Thich Nhat Hanh, a Buddhist monk and noted author. Following her stay in Southeast Asia, she told me that Thich Nhat Hanh told her and other Westerners that complete healing comes when they include their own heritage. According to him, people cannot truly feel whole without having explored the influence of their heritage on their present lives. For my former colleague, it meant visiting Ireland, her ancestors' home. How could heritage have that much of an impact on her present life? She was about to find out.

She spoke with healers and learned more about the folklore, legends, and old religions. She traced her family lineage. She increased her knowledge of Irish history, in particular the various invasions faced by the Irish. She learned of the coping skills and attitudes her people were forced to develop if they were to survive the changes brought by the various invasions.

She learned about the effects of unabated trauma. She began to realize how much her ancestry and its intergenerational transmissions have indeed affected her. She returned to California a changed person. She incorporated what Thich Nhat Hanh had told the Westerners. She had her clients explore their ancestry as part of the healing process by using the analogy of the tree. Some of the tree roots may be rotten and therefore have not nurtured the tree. However, there are other roots that have nourished it. Otherwise, the tree would have been completely dead.

It is through seeking those healthy roots near the rotten roots and then nourishing the healthy ones that the tree can continue to grow and expand. Many people avoid exploring the roots because of the pain caused by the rotten or rotting roots nearby. When we are "triggered," we shun or avoid being anywhere close to those roots. Yet near the pain lies the "antidote"—the other roots.

For those of us who are acculturated, not fully belonging to one group nor the other, or for those of us who are a product of many cultures and groups, healing is not that easy if we use the tree analogy of one heritage. Healing can come from our heritage tree as well as from other trees' cultural roots.

Many times people are reluctant to explore their own roots because of the pain, especially if their cultural healing ways have been ridiculed, shamed, or taken apart and reassembled in the ways of the dominant culture (e.g., the way drumming becomes part of a weekend "shamanic" workshop). For those of us who have assimilated, a visit down memory lane might be painful but still prove beneficial. For those of us who have acculturated, we can have the benefit of exploring the healing ways of various cultures, as long as there is respect for the creators of such ways and their descendants, and as long as we delve deeply into the roots and not just pick at the leaves. For those of us who are traditional, it is important to expand our knowledge and understanding that, whether we like it or not, we do live in a polycultural world. Using traditional ways of healing as the focal point, along with tools from other cultures that have entered our lives, our avenues for healing will be increased.

If we are to heal totally from traumas, it will be through ourselves and our communities. Societal trauma happens to a group, not just to the individuals in that group. Societal as well as individual traumas affect society and its members. Healing, therefore, must include both levels. Two of the major victims of trauma are our societal beliefs and our sense of self as a people, as members of a group.

Healing has to come from many sources. Included in the healing process is our need to reexamine our beliefs and our expectations of ourselves and of our world.

Some First Nations writers have examined the need to explore the core beliefs and the effects of oppression on identity formation. For some of us, even the notion of how we look at life and how we lead our lives may not even be part of our vocabulary. If that is the case, then the healing starts there—to identify the core values and beliefs that we want to happily have and then launch ourselves with those values and beliefs into the world. What are the core values I hold? What are the core values and beliefs that my family and prior generations have? That my community and society have?

As I stated previously, I attended meetings with local representatives from Northern Ireland. We talked about our core beliefs and values. They spoke of how they (Unionists and Republicans) viewed each other and what they held dear to them. They told stories of death and frustration. According to the Republicans, the practices of apartheid had affected their resolve to maintain their identity and heritage. (They heard no dissenting comments from the Unionist representatives present.)

The greater the insistence on assimilating and on accepting the majority's cultural ways of looking at life, the more the minority groups became adamant about holding on to what little they could call their own. Listening to them was like listening to my American colleagues and students. Listening to them was like hearing the anger and frustration of people who were civil rights activists. What is at the heart of any group is to avoid becoming obsolete or to suddenly become an ancient culture or civilization that is read about in history or anthropology books. Groups, like individuals, want to survive and thrive.

If the nondominant groups are not destroyed, not forced to be assimilated, or not vilified by the dominant groups, then these groups and their members would naturally transform as well—acculturating as time went by. All cultures concerned would learn from each other and eventually acculturate. Yet with the introduction of societal trauma via "isms" — and history is replete with them — time is used as a weapon to wipe out cultures and to institute only the cultural ways of those in power. If time is used this way as a weapon, issues of safety and trust for all the groups in that society cannot be guaranteed.

Transforming Time from Master to Servant

Time as a servant allows people to while away their time, to breathe, to take pause, and to observe. As a weapon, time becomes a master in a situation in which speed and efficiency are to be valued over the concept of time being a servant. Time may give us space to critically think and respond, rather than abdicate our thoughts and decision-making to others, such as those in authority and power. When time is used as a weapon, it hurries; it promotes unthinking reactions and a quick perusal of situations and people.

Stereotyping and categorization blossom under time being the master. Under this master called *time*, it becomes easier for people and institutions to vilify, since there is no time available for scrutiny. For individuals in survivor mode, they prioritize their attention to their immediate needs, forgoing their attention to their community and societal responsibilities. When this kind of attitude is pervasive, it is easy for authoritarian governments to hoodwink the public and promote their own agendas, without fear that the public (i.e., you and I) will scrutinize or even mobilize for action, should the situation warrant. It may be advantageous for such governments to promote time as a master. By setting this tone, general feelings of anxiety and anticipation are sustained. An environment for assimilation can be easily created when there is a perpetuation of addictive distractions and societal practices that allow "isms" — racism, classism, ageism, or any other kind.

These distractions and practices then affect our overall well-being, taxing and stressing our physiology (e.g., the adrenals and endocrine system in general) and hastening our breath (literally).

Crisis and trauma reek of time speeding by, taking no hostages, and creating slaves of us all. If time continues to be our master, and if we continue to let time be used against us, we will be kept in a life not of our own making. To free ourselves, time needs to be seen as a human right. If we start to have time to think and feel, we may want to be treated as human beings.

The Fear of the Oppressed: Honoring Differences

Is this perhaps why those who misuse their power fear the anger and retaliation of the oppressed? Do they, the oppressors, fear that if the tables were turned, the groups they had been oppressing would want to destroy them and their culture? In some cases, though not all, this has occurred because the issue of trauma and its effects had not been taken into consideration in terms of conflict resolution and healing.

In these cases, treaties were made without regard to terminating the cycle of violence, the addiction to violence, and the effects of trauma on the whole person. Additionally, diversity was not secured within the legal language with proper enforcement of such liberty.

In democratic countries, many members of the dominant groups may not be fearful of physical revolt or retaliation by nondominant groups in that manner. But there may be a psychic fear, a fear of the emotional, a fear of being overwhelmed by "them." Sometimes fear exists whenever there is a language other their own being spoken — or when there is a perception that their own way of life will disappear. It may be the fear of the unknown coming to stay, changing their familiar terrain.

[The stranger] had to be absorbed, meaning—assimilated. Disarmed, undressed, transformed. He would be welcome to stay, but only after giving up his name, his past, his memories, his bonds with his own people; a Jew, for example, had to become Christian, or Moslem, or Communist—or whatever. He would be offered the possibility of living, and living happily, provided he paid the inevitable rite de passage, *which was a kind of metamorphosis or transsubstantiation. You wish to be with us? Be one of us.*

Elie Wiesel, *From the Kingdom of Memory*

Wiesel talks about accepting the stranger. What *is* a stranger? What meaning does the stranger give us and induce us to consider? Wiesel argues that there is value in allowing what the stranger wishes to offer us: "not what we already have—or whatever we may have given him—but that which he has and we don't."

Being with a stranger invites us to look within and outside ourselves. We come to realize that part of healing is accepting others for who they are and looking for the gifts they may give us by simply being who they are.

Does the stranger have to "make sense" to our heads and emotions? Will our hearts not do? If there is societal trauma and if we are in the victim and/or possibly the survival mode, we may not know how to "be" with a stranger, with someone unfamiliar.

I know what some of you will say: "You can't trust all strangers. And there are people and groups out to destroy us in some form." Yet if we allow fear to be our guide, then that fear will make everyone seem like the "enemy" to us. If we allow time to become a friend, to do critical thinking, and to trust our heart, then it is easier to discern between "enemy" and "not-enemy."

I am reminded of the film titled *Men in Black.* There is a shooting gallery scene filled with cardboard people of all sorts. An agency is screening recruits who wish to join. The recruits are given guns and told to shoot the bad alien that is among the good guys. The recruits, except for a guy named Edwards (played by Will Smith), "kill" the obvious aliens to save the "pretty little eight-year-old girl" human, who is in the middle of the aliens. These recruits are dismissed. They have failed. Then it comes to the hero of the film: Edwards. He sizes up the situation and quickly shoots the girl. Why? She was out of place, among all the different kinds of aliens. As the character Edwards states it, "She was the only one who actually seemed dangerous. At the time." He is accepted and joins the "Men in Black."

The worst thing of all, Elie Wiesel warns, is being a stranger to oneself. By getting to know ourselves, we are better able to discern about others and their worldviews. We are able to see what matters and what to let go.

With this I wholeheartedly am in agreement. If I do not know myself, who will? If I do not embrace all of me, why then do I righteously expect that others will? If there is self-hatred, fear, embarrassment about my own differences, what right do I have to expect others to understand and support such differences? Notice that I say *expect*. This is because expectations and perceptions lead us into misunderstandings, neediness, conflict, and wanting to be saved.

By becoming authentic, by accepting who we are and also understanding our groups, we begin to give ourselves choices about how we want to lead our lives, despite the "isms" that exist in society.

As we look inward, we find that in order to go beyond survival, we need to address not just our bodies and our emotions, but also how we present ourselves to the world and how the world receives us—namely, how do we communicate? Many areas in our lives have been affected by trauma, including our communication with one another.

Chapter 6

IS IT ME? IS IT YOU?
IS IT THE WAY WE COMMUNICATE?

When you are in a life-threatening situation, there is no time to look for details. There is no time to reflect. Quick judgment based on prior experience and the body's sensations of impending threat necessitate quick actions in nanoseconds. Later, after the threat has left, you can then breathe more easily, take time to reflect on what just happened, and determine what future actions to take should that threat or similar threats occur again.

As we move toward responding rather than reacting, we start to realize that we have more time than we thought to make a proper decision and to take a more appropriate action. One tool for doing this is a method that a friend of mine shared with me. It had been passed down to her by another friend. It is a method to help a person distinguish the origin of a potential or actual conflict or threat.

I call it "Is It Me? Is It You? Is It the Way We Communicate?" Time is a valuable ally in this method. With practice, this method can be carried out in milliseconds. It includes listening to your body, paying attention to other individuals' nonverbal reactions, and assessing their communication styles. The underlying assumption of this method is to doubt what you are actually hearing and experiencing.

Is It Me? Is the Trigger in Me?

When you sense a conflict—in yourself, between you and another person, or simply coming from that person—pause, breathe, and say to yourself with love:

How am I feeling?

Am I hearing *all* the words being said, or am I tuning in and out of the person's words?

Is my heart quickening?

Do I find myself holding my breath, breathing faster, or gulping?

Has my body temperature changed at all (i.e., suddenly feeling cold or hot)?

Am I suddenly getting physically uncomfortable?

Am I suddenly feeling moody? Irritable?

Do I want to disappear?

Do I want to cry?

Am I feeling angry?

Do I want to hit someone or something?

If any of the above is occurring, it is probably because you are being "triggered." Fight, flight, or freeze reactions may start to emerge, along with their physiological sensations. Your body is telling you that something has "triggered" its defenses. You have an opportunity, if you are in tune with your body, to stop the fight, flight, or freeze response from fully occurring while you still have your ability to discern.

You continue on with your assessment by asking yourself these questions: Does this situation remind me of something or someone? Am I still seeing the individual before me, or is that person reminding me of someone else? Depending on the situation and/or how safe you are feeling about the person in front of you, you may choose to do the following:

Tell the person that you think you are being "triggered" and that you need time to sort things out. You can work together in figuring out what caused the trigger. Or you can take time for yourself, away from the other person, to do this.

If you do the latter, then tell the person that you need to figure out what the communication problem is on your own. Let the person know that you will return and that you intend to complete the conversation. Give a time frame for when you will be returning. Do *not* just leave. Otherwise, that action might cause a trigger of abandonment for the other person if he or she has issues in that area. Make sure the person realizes that you simply need a "time-out."

Please keep in mind that at this point you do not need to know exactly what it is that is causing the trigger for you.

If, in your assessment, you believe that the core of the communication problem is not stemming from you, the next step would be as follows:

Is It You? Are You Projecting onto Me?

Is the other person being "triggered"? If so, that person may not be aware of it. Depending on how the person is reacting—for example, being angry, or crying, or threatening to leave in some way—you may choose to do the following:

If the person is angry, she or he will not be able to hear you. Let the person speak. Do not try to correct impressions unless asked to do so. Listen, even if you are thinking that you are in strong disagreement. Listen, even if you know you are being misunderstood. Role model regular breathing. Make yourself softer and gentler in appearance through your demeanor; do this in a genuine manner.

Keep in mind that the person is outputting or venting. Inputting or listening on his or her part is not going to happen at this time.

Give the person physical space. Do not approach the person, unless you know that he or she will respond positively to that action. Many angry people when approached feel more threatened and defensive. For many people, anger is a way to create space. Honor that.

When someone is scared and you are expressing passionate opinions, that person may misunderstand and think you are angry and about to physically strike. I have seen this misunderstanding take place, especially when the person who was scared had a history of abuse. Such people may confuse passion with anger. (By the way, a wonderful book for exploring these kinds of misunderstandings is Thomas Kochman's *Black and White Styles in Conflict.*)

Some cultures confine passionate feelings to certain areas of their lives (e.g., sexual interplay, sports competitions, politics, fights). In the situation I am describing, passionate feelings get mistaken for wanting sexual intercourse. When you say "no," then the other person may get angry and say you are leading him or her on.

After the person has calmed down enough (sometimes a sigh is heard or seen, or a "deflation" of some sort occurs), very gently and with a firm but normal tone of voice agree with any of the points that he or she may have raised. For example:

> "I could see why you're angry if you felt that I said x or y."
>
> "If you heard x or y, I can appreciate why that bothered you."

Remember: You are validating the perception, not that he or she is right and that you are wrong.

If the person is crying or on the verge of tears, stop whatever you are saying. Let your silence and a sympathetic expression on your face speak for you. Wait for a sigh or an obvious indication that the person is now ready to hear you.

Very gently ask the person if what he or she felt or heard was what brought about the tears. Let the person take his or her time to respond, even if it requires a long silence.

Check your own comfort level about silence and tears. Are there any triggers from them? If so, take care of yourself without faulting the person. If you need to go away, let the person know that you too are being "triggered" and that maybe it is best to take a mutual "time-out" to figure out what is happening.

Depending on what kind of relationship you have, you may want to approach the person. Do not automatically hug or touch the shoulders, unless you have a history with that person and you know it is all right to do this. You can get closer and maybe touch his or her hand. Ask and approach slowly.

You can elicit dialog once the person is in a listening mode. Some examples follow that you could say in a gentle, calm voice, and with regular breathing:

"May I ask you something? What was it about my saying x that made you think that I meant y? ... Oh, I see. ... Well, what I was thinking when I said x was [restate it in a different way]."

"I can see why you got upset. I didn't realize [because you really did not know] that x meant y to you. I'm sorry that you're hurting/angry/crying."

Breathe; give a silent pause, in case he or she wishes to add some more thoughts. Sympathize or empathize if you can.

Sometimes the problem in communication may not be about you or about the other person; it may be about *how* you are communicating.

Is It the Way We Communicate? Are Our Words Interfering?

I may be talking in a storytelling form, maybe appearing as if I am "beating around the bush," while you may be talking in a linear, to-the-point, businesslike fashion, appearing to me that you are in a hurry and do not want to be bothered. We may be saying the same thing, yet our different styles of talking prevent us from hearing each other. Or the communication pattern may "trigger" a cultural miscommunication. Perhaps what may ensue is a conflict or a fight, flight, or freeze reaction.

Let me give you a concrete example of a conflict and its resolution. I was working for a social service agency whose clientele were recent Southeast Asian refugees. During my first week on the job, I accidentally insulted a person without even knowing it. Fortunately, for me, the person let me know in her own way. Having been raised polyculturally, I understood that cultural "goofs" can happen, and I am open to learning. I have no ego or pride in wanting my ways to be the norm for all, or for them to be the only ways of doing things. Being *bien educada* supersedes that.

A family for whom we were providing services needed a staff person who spoke Chinese. The program I was coordinating had no Chinese-speaking staff member at that time, but the other program in our agency did. I approached the coordinator of that program. Judy (fictitious name) was an Anglo European American. She said it was fine for us to have her staff member help us. Judy then went to her staff member and told her that she, the staff member, would be helping me out the next day. The staff member was polite but cold to me.

Later that afternoon, one of my Vietnamese staff members came to me to say that I had offended the Chinese staff member by not talking to her directly before going to her boss. I was to go and apologize to her for this offense. I was truly surprised. My staff person told me that it is the custom to ask the person directly if she wants to help. It was insulting to the Chinese staff member that I had asked her boss as though she, the staff member, were an object, like a typewriter to be used. Of course, in any other agency, had I approached the staff member prior to her boss, the boss would have been upset and would have thought that I was undermining her authority.

So who was right? It did not matter. That was not the goal. Understanding was the goal. Here was a case of a classic cultural conflict, exacerbated by the staff member's experience of "isms" (in this case, classism) and some of those effects in the form of trauma.

What mattered to me was that someone had been hurt due to a misunderstanding. I did tell my staff member, who was acting as an intermediary, to state the American custom I was used to and to clarify my intent. I also said I was very sorry and that I respected the Chinese staff member and her work. Had I not, I would not be asking for her assistance and expertise. My staff member took that message back to her. After an hour, I went to her and directly apologized for my lack of courtesy in the manner she was accustomed to receiving.

Now let's apply the tool: Was it me? No. Was it her? Yes. Was it the way we communicated? Also yes—my manner of communicating had "triggered" her on several levels. Her trigger, as I found out from her later, was that she had experienced people treating her without respect. On top of that, she had been an object of classism and educational snobbery. The cultural misunderstanding had magnified this, especially coming from a non-Asian person in authority.

Had I allowed my pride or ego or my own triggers to get in the way of wanting to understand her point of view, including her emotions, I would have missed the opportunity to know a fine human being and for her to know me. I did not allow my role as a coordinator to interfere with finding a way to honor a staff member. I was open to resolving a conflict. She approached me in a traditional way, using a mutual colleague as an informal mediator.

The use of an intermediary helped both of us not to "lose face," that is, lose dignity. Since she did not know me, or what level of real power I had, she asked someone who knew both of us. Later, whenever there was any kind of misunderstanding or even an honest difference of opinions, she and I could speak directly to each other. Safety and trust had developed.

I used time and I followed my core belief (to be *bien educada*) to mend our relationship. While in the beginning it may have seemed to be "wasting time" when other job duties arose that should have taken priority, in the end, honoring her and myself also helped the workplace and the clients we were serving in our respective departments.

The tool "Is It Me? Is It You? Is It the Way We Communicate?" helped me on several fronts: not to make snap judgments about other people's intentions, nor misunderstand what is being said; and it allowed me to breathe and access the higher part of my brain. This tool slowed me down so that if there were any triggers, I would not automatically react. Instead, I responded. I will always be grateful for this tool because it has served me and others well, especially when dealing with "isms." With practice, this assessment part of the tool can be done in seconds. The tool prevented some traumas from being created. Utilizing time as a friend helped me to see others and myself as human beings.

A caveat here. If your body or mind believes you are going to get physically hurt, molested, sexually assaulted—then leave and go to a safe place. You can find out later if your perceptions were valid or if, in fact, your triggers stemmed from memory—and not from a warning sign. If it is from memory, then you can, if you so wish—and depending on what the nature of the relationship is or was—share with that person why you had to leave and ask what she or he meant by their tone, words, movement, etc.

Chapter 7

TIME: REGAINING MORE OF OUR HUMANITY

As part of becoming my own autobiographer, I have learned to appreciate that time is an ally, not a master whom we serve nor an enemy to defeat. Time is to be used as a servant or a beloved friend. It is a way for us to breathe and appreciate the present and those around us. In life-threatening situations, time is used efficiently. There is no time to waste. However, if we are to live in a non-crisis fashion, then one tool we need to learn is time.

By using time as our tool, it teaches us how to discern what truly is a trigger and what is a misunderstanding. If we experience time as a servant, then we can slow down to explore who we are: our "beingness." Who are we? Are we defined by how much we produce, accumulate, or move around (literally and figuratively)? If we slow down to appreciate nature, to contemplate, to meditate, to "smell the roses," are we concerned that people will see us as stereotypically lazy, shiftless—perhaps a beggar? Do the stereotypes prevent us from taking in life? Whose values and beliefs are we honoring—theirs or ours?

If I do this [making money as a primary focus], most [people] will commend me as an industrious and hard-working man; but if I choose to devote myself to certain labors which yield more real profit, though but little money, they may be inclined to look on me as an idler. ... If a man walk [sic] in the woods for love of them half of each day, he is in danger of being regarded as a loafer; but if he spends his whole day as a speculator, shearing off those woods and making earth bald before her time, he is esteemed an industrious and enterprising citizen.

Henry David Thoreau

Thoreau might have been seen as a member of a counterculture. He argued that life was more than producing, and that the worth of a person was not based on how much money or possessions he (or she) accrued. A person's worth was how much his (or her) labors enhanced the souls in a society.

Time was given by God so that we can experience ourselves and others—not as a master to reign over us, inadvertently remaking ourselves into robots to produce, or functioning like rabbits reacting to traumas (real and unreal). There is an illusion that by moving, doing, and working all the time, real production occurs and our quality of life will increase. However, has that happened? Our country may produce more, but are we any happier? How do we Americans compare to the rest of the world in terms of time off for vacation and sick leave? A one-week or two-week paid vacation? How about thirty days? How many days for sick leave? And what happens if you need more than those days? How do countries such as ours compare to others that give workers much more? Do we have more time for our loved ones and time to enjoy the beautiful homes our money has bought?

Are we producing more at the workplace but producing less for living?

I am reminded of a saying of Lao Tzu, which is translated and quoted in Ram Dass and Paul Gorman's book *How Can I Help?* "The sage does nothing, but nothing is left undone." I found this saying true in my life. As I meditated more, slowed down more, paid attention to my whole being more, not only did I nourish myself, but I also became more aware of what mattered and how to get things done. By slowing down, more things came into clearer focus. By inhaling and exhaling more deeply, literally and figuratively, perspectives changed. I found myself finishing more of my projects in half the time and enjoying the newfound time with myself, with people I cared about, and with the world around me.

By being, everything got done. Becoming more aware of myself allowed me to reflect how I wanted my life to be, how I wanted to lead my own life.

If we don't allow time to serve us, then play, imagination, and spending quality time with family and friends may not occur. Instead, many of us embrace distractions and addictions. We let other people imagine for us (e.g., video games, increasingly violent sports, and films that leave nothing to our imagination). We turn over our imagination and creativity to others. Unfortunately, many guardians and parents are training their children to do the same. As a consequence, we inadvertently train ourselves and those we love to be followers of other people's visions, not our own. With that, we also lessen our skills and abilities to do critical thinking, to question and be curious of what is told to us as "truth."

Instead, increasingly we find ourselves being dictated to by day planners and appointment books, as we quickly chat on our cellphones. We zip from here to there. This subject itself could fill an entire book. The point is that when we are harried and when we are struggling to make ends meet, trauma can easily become a permanent resident in our homes. Trauma need not be a giant creature. It can be small, or a series of small ones, that many individuals will become accustomed to experiencing, since they have known no other way of going through life.

There is no time for healing and loving ourselves and others.

Intimacy becomes an infrequent guest. Living in trauma robs us of our time and our presence with others. Yet in today's society, there appears to be a push to do just that.

For many of us, to contemplate how we use our time becomes a political question as well as an economic one. Do we dare ask those questions in a serious way and take steps to regain our lives? Are we seeing the return of nineteenth-century child labor and the sixty-hour work week? Do we need to revisit what we thought we had won in the past for our children and ourselves? Time has to be included as part of the social justice agenda. It is not to our benefit to let time be used against our well-being. Time can be manipulated, or used in a deliberate or an inadvertent way to keep us from existing and surviving.

Is it any wonder that those of us who come from cultures that use time as a servant try to resist assimilation?

If we are to heal and actually live lives and not just survive, having time work for us (rather than the other way around) becomes a political and human necessity. Requesting, or in fact demanding, that time be used once more as an ally, and not just as a time clock for productivity, is a dangerous undertaking. Why? If injustices are indeed deliberate and if there is merit in the belief that it behooves a totalitarian or authoritarian society to have traumatized, survival-oriented, and addiction-oriented citizens, then asking for time becomes a dangerous request.

Ordinary man is, in fact, a totally conditioned machine, but he does not see it, and if he is told so he does not wish to believe it. The play of associations proceeds in him unceasingly, almost always without his knowledge, in the form of automatic reactions to the situations with which life confronts him. ... It is quite obvious that no hope of change or of transformation is open to man as long as he is such a prisoner of his masks and his habits. And if he becomes aware of this, the question arises for him of how to escape.

Jean Vaysse, *Toward Awakening: An Approach to the Teaching Left by Gurdjieff*

By using time as an ally or servant, and not a master, we give ourselves opportunities to witness a new side of existence that leads us to living in the way we had hoped.

We give ourselves time to breathe, to enjoy life, to spend time with ourselves, our families and friends, and other loved ones. We also give ourselves time to become more aware of our environments, how we wish to live and by what principles, ethics, and beliefs. By using time to nurture ourselves—body, mind, and soul—we are then in a better position to determine which trauma mechanisms and coping skills are still needed to keep us physically safe and which ones can be retired.

Chapter 8

Retiring the TMCS: When Peace Becomes
"Familia"

May the Great Winds
sweeping across our world
sweep away what we no longer need,
and bring us to ourselves and All That Is.
Brooke Medicine Eagle,
"Spirit of the Winds" from *A Gift of Song*

In America, when we say 'that's History' we mean that is of no
consequence. In Europe, when they say 'that's History' they mean that it
is the crux of the matter.
Hughes, observer in Albania during the Kosovo-Serbia war, May 1999

For Albanians, Kosovars, and other cultures whose worldview is past-present oriented (other cultures may be present-future oriented), history is not a dead issue. The fruits of the present come from the seeds of the past. When trauma has visited their lands, it has become integrated and part of the intergenerational passage of worldview beliefs, family beliefs and values, and individuals' legacies to carry forward. This includes trauma mechanisms and coping skills (TMCS).

Brooke Medicine Eagle's view of life is to let go of what is no longer needed. It is about going forward to where the wind of time and of Great Spirit moves us, knowing that wherever we go, we go to find ourselves.

I begin with the belief that we come from God. I believe there is an inherent desire to be loved, to be acknowledged for being who we are, to be safe, to exist, and to share our love with other souls. Consequently, our behaviors and attitudes develop along those lines. Not all behaviors and attitudes are healthy, but the *intent* of these behaviors and attitudes is to help somehow. When there are life-threatening situations, many elements come into play to keep us safe and to help us continue to exist.

Previously, I discussed the TMCS that are developed as the result of fight, flight, or freeze reactions. They were developed to help us in some manner. Yet we have often pathologized them, making them, to a certain degree, enemies to overcome. I have come to believe that they are, instead, friends that have, in their own way, tried to help the individual. Eventually the time comes to let them know that their efforts, while needed during the actual crisis or trauma, do not serve in a non-crisis environment.

I let go of the TMCS that no longer serve a purpose of protection. I start with the ones that are obvious to me. In my case, it was clothes and makeup. Many decades ago, every time I left the house, my mother would comment, "Where is your makeup? What will people think?" and "You should dress up more, even if you *are* just going to the drugstore and coming back." While on the surface some women can relate to this story, for me it took on a deeper meaning because of other comments that were made. *What will they say about Ecuadorian women? What will they say about Latinas? What will they say ...?*

It was not about being presentable; it was about being a

representative. No longer an individual, I was a representative of my family and my culture. If I did not look good, then a negative stereotype might emerge and hurt my group and me.

Since that time, many things have changed, including social standards and how I view myself. I no longer carry that extra weight on my back. If I want to go out wearing jeans, a casual top, and no makeup, I do. Prejudiced people will find any excuse to validate their stereotypes. Their opinions do not matter to me. *I* matter to me.

Another coping skill was my need to know "everything." It started in grammar school when a few teachers expected me to know the history of all of Latin America and what "my people" thought about a multitude of subjects. All eyes upon me, I felt the embarrassment of not knowing, of looking like a fool, especially when students would snicker and the teacher would say, "Oh. Okay. Let's turn our attention then to ...." In order to appease and to be on the good side of those in authority (usually Anglo European Americans, as they were called then), I decided that I needed to know more—or at least know something, so that negative stereotyping could be avoided. I became a good "codependent," as those who are familiar with childhood familial abuse could appreciate.

Anne Wilson Schaef and Diane Fassel define *codependence* as "a constellation of behaviors that emerge in relation to the addictive system and dysfunctional family patterns." In my case, it was dysfunctional societal patterns. My family was my haven, a place of heart. To come back to the story, I ended up being a generalist—knowing a bit about "everything." For me, it was not acceptable *not* to know. It invited more than embarrassment; at times it invited validation that "those people" (meaning my group) were not bright.

Of course, later I allowed myself to unfold more. I let go of

having to know. I realized it was acceptable to say, "'I don't know."
I let go of being the representative. If people are prone to judge a
group's worth based on an individual, so be it. I have no control
over what they think or do. However, if they were to behave in
discriminatory or life-threatening manners, I would have to act
accordingly to keep myself safe and to address whatever I could
with others regarding the situation. I found myself through those
childhood years being a quiet person in school. I tried to keep a low
profile and not volunteer in the classes in which the teachers'
behaviors toward "minority" people made me feel distrustful.

It was not until I joined a sorority in my first year at UCLA that
I started to shed my wallflower image and behaviors, of trying to
hide and "blend into the walls." I started to socially blossom again.
My sorority sisters treated me as an individual.

In college I learned that it was all right to say I did not know
something, and that there was no reason to feel shame for doing it.
I learned to say, "I don't know" from teachers who did not pretend
to know everything either. I learned that I was bright, intelligent,
and that my sense of humor in those college years could be wicked.
Being with people from different cultures and subgroups, as well as
getting in touch with other Latinas and Latinos in college, helped
me blossom.

I also learned from them that I was not alone in my experiences.
They too had had similar situations of being seen as the
representatives of their cultures and expected to know everything.
They too had known what it was like to be shamed by teachers who
should have known better.

For some students, it was quite a culture shock to be at such a
large university such as UCLA. Some had come from the barrios, as
the inner cities were called then. Others had come from rural areas.
Yet others were Vietnam War veterans returning to school.

It was from making friends with the Vietnam War veterans that I came to realize the effects of trauma. Strangely enough, we were similar in our ways of coping and in being hypersensitive. Years later, I would introduce the concept of post-traumatic stress and concurrent traumatic stress and their similar symptoms as a shared bridge between seemingly different groups.

Racism and all the other "isms" which have generated so much trauma for me and others in the United States had to be "de-toothed." By embracing and expressing my total self with love and respect, I was invalidating the power of such "isms," which used weapons like fear, intimidation, disrespect, hatred, shame, manipulation, and inequality.

There may be discrimination, but I need not be traumatized by that. Discrimination presents us with the challenge to transform it into avenues that all people can use to find their own love, health, and peace. Part of any healing is to reclaim our voices, both figuratively and, at times, literally.

For me, the way to make traumas of any sort ineffective was to let go of the *majority* of the TMCS generated by them. A person would be foolish to let go of all the TMCS if they did not feel completely safe and secure.

Unhitching the Physical from the Trigger and Embracing the Dream

One of my life passions was to be a speaker in front of large crowds. However, my body would not cooperate. I would get laryngitis, strep throat, or both. Job assignments that included some degree of public speaking went to other staff members, since I would get sick on those days. It was frustrating. I did not have the awareness to realize that my beloved body was trying to keep me safe from ridicule. It remembered how I had felt when I was younger and a few teachers had embarrassed me in front of their class. They had mocked my accent or my understanding of things. My body remembered even though I had consciously forgotten.

I could not understand why I got ill when I so much wanted to do public speaking. I did not want my body's fears through illness to stop me from realizing my dream. I was determined to embrace my dream into reality.

In my late twenties, I would daydream. I would see myself speaking before large crowds. At night, I would program myself before going to sleep that I was talking to a large audience—and with positive results. Then I had a chance to break the hold the TMCS had on me in that regard. I deliberately accepted a job as a health educator. The job required a great deal of public speaking. So every time I was about to speak, I would get stage fright—nausea, lower back pain, hyperventilating, and raspy throat. But I led my body forward.

My desired dream was stronger than my fear. I was determined to realize that dream, and I did. I eventually got over my bodily symptoms, including dry mouth, fast heartbeat, and cold hands, which are indicative of fight, flight, or freeze reactions.

Eventually I found a job that, to an even greater degree, sparked my passion and concerns: child abuse, refugee work, and living fully. I recall going to a statewide child abuse conference. The keynote speaker was Eliana Gil. I found out that she had been born in Ecuador, just like me! I heard her message and listened to her body language and general communication style. I saw the audience members' reactions and said to myself, "Someday, I too will be in front of this audience."

This time when I daydreamed, I became very detailed as to what I was envisioning. I used all my senses, repeating many times the same scene of public speaking. It worked because I had passion in my heart and the desire to be of service by sharing what I knew. One year later I was speaking at the statewide conference—not as a main speaker but as part of a plenary group. Later I was a recurring panelist and workshop presenter for a number of years with the organization that sponsored the conferences, and with other groups as well. Years later, I was one of the major speakers at conferences.

I had a desired goal and I achieved it. I used imagination and detail visualization. I used self-hypnosis. I wanted it so badly that I could literally experience the reality in my body. I used lucid dreaming to manipulate my dreams. I essentially reprogrammed my subconscious, which then addressed the unconscious and, consequently, my body's reactions.

I gave my TMCS eyes and ears to the present so that they would not be listening to the past as though it were the present. I told them, in effect, that public speaking was part of my health and joy. The TMCS services were no longer needed in that regard. They were dismissed with love and appreciation for the work they had done on my behalf during the years that I did not have the necessary skills and self-love. Now that I did, they eventually left with no resistance.

I succeeded because I had the founding support of my parents' words echoing in my body. My beloved mother and father had both said, in Spanish and in so many words, the following:

Follow your heart. Question authority figures—they are human beings, after all. Question even your own internal authority, and question us. We may be your parents, but we are human and we can and do make mistakes for which apologies and corrective actions are signs of love. God will support you if your heart is to be of service. Follow what makes you sing and love.

I had and still have wonderful support from them (from beyond this world). Through their examples of role modeling, patience, humor, storytelling, and love, they helped me to let go of TMCS that no longer worked. For those of us who did not have such parents or guardians or family members, we do have ourselves. We matter enough to live with joy and peace. We matter enough to write our own autobiographies and to choose which coping skills still work for our continued growth and which ones we need to escort out of our hearts and bodies.

Yet some TMCS may need eyeglasses and hearing aids to discern when new traumas are forthcoming, and when they are simply the echoes of old ones whispering in one's ears. I may hear comments that are racist, sexist, classist, homophobic, or against a certain religion without getting angry or feeling a need to immediately educate the person who has said them. I open my heart more, rather than close it. I breathe in deeply and regularly and I look at the person—look into their eyes and observe their body language. Is it worth my time to say something, other than "I'm offended by that remark" or "I don't care for those kinds of jokes" or "I know you have a good heart, and it surprises me to hear such a comment"?

Whatever I do, my responses are not automatic; they come with thought and caring, even if it means walking away or spending time listening and dialoguing. I am not in a fight, flight, or freeze mode anymore when it comes to verbal comments, unless I see an accompanied physical movement that appears life-threatening. Grief is not activated. Neither anger nor sadness is engaged, but only breathing, caring, and reflecting.

My parents reminded me that often it is the small pebbles in one's shoes that will impede a great journey, not the boulders before us. Little TMCS matter. As I said earlier, I started getting rid of the small ones first. When I did, my body felt it and recalibrated down from red-alert status to one of peace.

Everything helps, and ultimately when the larger TMCS need tackling, we have the reserve in our immune system, in our confidence about ourselves, and we literally rest to draw energy and a sense of well-being we can utilize. It can be the subtle expressions of triggers of traumatic memories or the fear of additional ones coming down the road that may tear or erode at our well-being, not necessarily the blatant ones.

Without our knowledge, the covert expressions slither their way into our bodies and minds. We find ourselves being like a frog that is put into a pot of water. Slowly, the temperature increases and the frog acclimatizes to the heat, not realizing that it is being cooked to death. On the other hand, the overt expressions are easily recognizable and we have opportunities to see how we want to handle them. In that case, when the frog is put into boiling water it immediately jumps out.

By letting go of what no longer serves me, I embrace life more. By being more in the present, I allow myself to be more of who I have always been—a loving person. I also give myself the opportunity to have the other person be more of who he or she is. This does not mean that I forget about past events and/or current discriminatory and traumatic practices. It means that, by being in the present, I can use the skills that I select for today. Furthermore, I leave myself open to acquiring other skills in the future, without closing my heart to intimacy and exploration.

I embrace the TMCS then let them go into retirement, thanking them for the love they gave. In the name of friendship and love, I say goodbye. I learn to detach and to breathe. I use analogies and metaphors to help me let go of them. For example, when they try to take control of the steering wheel of my vehicle, I put them in the back seat or get them out of my car. It is an internal dialog of love and caring.

Releasing old TMCS is not enough, but it is an important beginning to opening a space in which new coping skills and new mechanisms better suited to the present can be created and developed.

For those of us who come from cultures that are past-present oriented, it is important to frame the letting go as honoring the past and our ancestors by having a present that holds the best of the past and all who came before us. We then become the creators of the past for our descendants. The future's fruits have the seeds in our present, in our hands. In this way we honor our ancestors, ourselves, and the generations to come. I end this chapter, as I began it, with the words of Medicine Eagle.

Bones

We call upon
our ancestors for their wisdom
and, in return,
we pledge to them that we will live out our sacred purpose as
a promise to seven generations of our grandchildren.
We pledge to release disruptive family and cultural patterns,
and to carry forward the good, true, and beautiful
of the ancient lineages.
This Maori song calls
to those bones, those ancestors.
—Brooke Medicine Eagle, from *A Gift of Song*

Chapter 9

REVISITING FAITH AND BELIEFS:
FINDING A BRIDGE TO OUR HEARTS

The only way to have faith
is to be thoroughly grounded in reality.
Stephen Sachs, Pipe Holder, writer and poet

Our religion is practiced not studied.
For this reason, I do not understand your book [the Bible].
It is like a chant that one only knows the words to.
And I tell you,
it's the rhythms that are the most important thing.
Kalweit, *Shamans, Healers, and Medicine Men*

When trauma washes upon our shores after a major natural disaster, we look toward faith to carry us through. Faith sometimes invites us to create new meaning out of these disruptions to our lives. What does faith tell us about the effects the disruptions have on our souls and our sense of self? What do I mean by faith? Can I live without faith?

How does faith interact with healing, with our bodies? There are no scientific studies that directly test the power of faith to heal the human body. Indirectly, there have been many studies on prayer and focus concentration, popularly made available through the writings and work of Larry Dossey and others. It is not the intent of my writing to delve into these studies. Prayer can be a product of faith or of a belief in something that may not necessarily be about God. It can be a belief that something will work, or that what it is carries with it the power to heal. A strong belief, even as a placebo, can heal the person or create an environment where healing can take place.

Yet what is faith? *Tenga fé.* Have faith. Listening to those words, taking them into my body, I discover how I automatically take a deep breath, my mind quiets, and my body relaxes. I let go. I cease to worry. I hand over my worries to God and trust. In this process, my physiology changes. I get out of my fight, flight, or freeze mode and I signal to my body to go to a non-alert status.

Faith can affect my physiology. In *Timeless Healing*, Herbert Benson presents anecdotal incidents, case studies, and scientific explorations of how believing in faith can relax the body, thereby stopping the physiological process of fight, flight, or freeze. In his book, Benson shares one client's experience:

But when she lay down and recited 'The Lord is my shepherd' or 'Give me peace' to herself, her heart stopped beating as hard as it used to and she could drop off to sleep. …

Mrs. Frank called upon the power of the top-down capacity of her brain to make her belief real to her.

Then she applied her belief to a mental focusing mechanism that brings forth the physical relaxation she described.

Benson, a physician and professor at Harvard Medical School, noted that people who activate faith (whatever that is for the person) send signals to the body to let go, to release and turn over to God the idea that everything will be all right. Having faith and being able to use faith on a consistent basis for actually healing the body remains to be scientifically validated on a consistent basis. What is significant is that faith affects our way of looking at life—how we literally take in our breaths and give signals to our bodies, as well as our hope for a better tomorrow.

Not all cultures use the terms *hope* and *faith* in the same manner or with the same definition as Westerners do. Nor are these terms used only in religious contexts. For example, civil rights movements have used these terms to forward their causes and beliefs for brighter futures. I am reminded of my own family. We say *tenga fé* (have faith) more often than we say *tenga esperanza* (have hope). For without the springboard of some form of faith, hope cannot take flight.

The feeling of faith and the power of its tools—hope, prayers, patience, and letting go—can affect our bodies. We experience changes in heart rate, pulse rate, and in our biochemistry before and after the shift from nonbeliever to believer.

For the purposes of this book, I wish to focus now on faith as it relates to its development, its effect on our outlook and our ability to go forward.

For me, faith aids us in developing our humanity, our ability to take risks with ourselves and with our world. Faith reminds me of time and the temporary nature of life. Faith reminds me how to relate and connect to my abilities to proceed or to be still. It reminds me to experience my vulnerability as strengths to touch and to be gentled by them. Faith tells me that I am not alone, that I am part of God, and that we are all related. We are part of the beauty that is God, and therefore we *are* beauty—of heart, of soul, of love. No matter what occurs, God is within me, around me, through me—everywhere. Faith is more than a bridge. It is active and dynamic.

Faith can die or be thwarted in its growth when societal trauma interrupts our own growth, especially in the forms of conquests, oppressions, wars, denial of civil rights, lynchings, hate-bashing, and harassment. Historically, it has not been uncommon to have the conquerors squelch the souls of the conquered, to use their bodies but stifle their souls and hearts. In many cases the conqueror would forbid the conquered to speak their own languages.

For example, in boarding schools many Native Americans were beaten or shamed when they spoke their own languages. Instead, the conqueror's language was imposed. The conqueror's religion was imposed as well. The community rituals of the conquered were shamed or forbidden, and the conqueror's cultural practices were held as the norm and as something to aspire to. The list goes on. In cases such as these, the original faith in all its manifestations and avenues is slowly and systematically destroyed, or, at the least, the conquered individuals are made to feel abnormal if they continue to practice it.

What better way than to destroy faith. Destroy the means by which faith can be interactive. Destroy the social structures of the oppressed. Set land mines on the bridge of faith, and the explosions will affect our hearts and our way to life.

Is faith a component of basic human rights? I believe it is, for it speaks to the very heart of how we view life and how we conduct ourselves. While faith can be religious in nature, it can also center on a career, a country, an institution, a cause, the scientific method, or even oneself. In different cultures and different religions, the expressions of faith are as unalike as night and day. Yet a thread exists common to all expressions: meaning. Humans, it seems, cannot live without meaning.

Specifically, faith is about creating meaning, or making sense of our lives. It is a context in which we fill in our beliefs, attitudes, and our confidence to take risks when tangible experiences would tell us nothing. Faith in some way implies miracles—something unexpected and divine to assist us in our life journeys.

Faith is relational, as are trust, love, and grace. Meaning is relational. When dealing with trauma, meaning and faith are of paramount importance in helping a person go from being a victim, to surviving, and to finally living a creative life. Without faith and imagination to soar and persevere, we lose that bridge from the known to the unknown. In the world of "isms" and potential societal traumas, that internal bridge to better ways is needed.

Faith comes from the inside. When I question my story, my life, in a way I am questioning my faith, especially if there have been changes. I look inside me to explore. Who am I? Do I matter? Do I matter to myself anymore? Is life worth living? Does God exist? Is there a Plan? Why? If there has been trauma, faith is questioned. Will I be able to leave that land of darkness to cross over to the land of love and safety? How will faith help construct the transforming story? Will the existing faith help in the transformation of that story?

A crisis of faith is not unusual after overwhelming events have seemingly tested it.

We can speak of faith as a living, ongoing process with one single principle overriding everything: We are part of God. We are part of the womb and of creation. Knowing this gives us stability.

My friends who are Native Americans say, "We are all related. We are part of each other. We are part of Spirit." I agree with that. I agree that life cannot be savored if we are living in fear of each other or in fear of ourselves.

If we are part of God, then we are of love and beauty. Therefore, the most logical thing to do is to let go of the veils that keep us from seeing who we are and our connection with each other. "Isms," as well as childhood and adult adverse experiences and their consequences, seek to veil not only us but also others. We are all veiled. With some form of faith, those veils can be thrown away, shed away.

I do not find it a coincidence that in many encounters I have had with people who have been traumatized, those who were successful in crossing from existence to life have been spiritual and have had some form of faith. The faith may be animistic, Buddhist, Islamic, Judaic, Hindu, Christian, Baha'i, or any other set of beliefs. These people have been able to transform their stories of tragedies into stories of adventures for their souls.

Faith is a way of life, of looking at ourselves and others. It is a way of being, of how we carry ourselves and how we honor others' souls. Faith is standing up for our rights despite great odds coming against us from the outside or from within ourselves. Faith is an invisible bridge taking us to soon-to-be familiar lands.

If we are oppressed, it is faith that carries us. Faith nurtures our dreams of living freely and equally. Without faith of some kind, would hope soon disappear? When everything appears helpless and stagnant, it is our faith that delivers us from stagnation into movement.

When I had been preparing to teach a class on faith development, the following came to me in a dream.

That which makes life a joy and a wonderment
cannot be seen or smelled.
It is not concrete and cannot be touched.
Yet it affects our hearts, our beliefs about ourselves and about others.
It can enchain us or set us free to fly.
It can make our hearts sing
when what we see before us is darkness.
It is what I call faith.
Faith reminds us of our souls
and our connection to love,
our beingness.

Faith is a living bridge that needs nurturing and cultivation. It requires us to use our imaginations, to question our realities of how we see ourselves. A leap of faith means to me that we jump into the unknown, knowing in our hearts (even if our brains do not know) that we will land—for we are always in God's hands. With faith as the bridge, new meanings can flourish and old ones can be let go.

Redefining the Meaning and Traumas

If we see ourselves as victims, then concepts of helplessness, vindication, revenge, need of safety, and distrust all start to permeate the way we view ourselves and others. Concepts such as prayer, faith, forgiveness, and spirituality will be colored or transformed into the world vision of victimhood. The same as the process for writing a book, we will go through many revisions, many "working" meanings along the way.

Caroline Myss states that often people get stuck in being a victim. Myss suggests that many people who realize they have been victimized often stay in that realm. These people start to develop a way of speaking and looking at life through the lens of being a victim. As Myss puts it, "victimology," or victim language, creates a world of its own. It creates its own meaning and purpose.

What, then, transforms us? What shifts us from a victim-oriented perspective to one of empowerment? Earlier I discussed identity and grief process. Yet what *motivates* a person to move from one area to another?

Perhaps our bodies "hitting rock bottom" (to borrow a phrase from the recovery movement) would draw our attention. Often hitting rock bottom means health challenges, or life changes that are out of our control, or shocks to our "reality," which become opportunities for us to expand our horizons and our way of treating others and ourselves. Or it can be epiphanies that arise during momentous times that draw our attention.

To develop our own understanding of who we are in relation to race, gender, sexual orientation, gender roles, class, age, and other aspects of ourselves, we need to look at what we, you, and I have accepted at this point.

Ask yourself these questions: Do I use my imagination as a storyteller and my curiosity to go beyond my perspectives? Do I question and delve further into a subject? Have the meanings that I use to define my world been given to me by any societal institutions (e.g., law enforcement, education, courts, the media)? Are my meanings coming from generations long gone—and, along with them, old realities? Do they help me be a better person to myself and to my communities at the present time? Do they help me see the reality of what is before me as it is *now* and not then? Do I let the meaning of trauma enchain me, or do I let it give me the opportunity to expand my worldview and myself? Or, as a colleague and friend, Stephanie Rothman, would say, "If the belief doesn't serve you, fire it! And if the belief serves you well, promote it!"

Traumas can be portals we step through. They can take us into a landscape that can expand our awareness, or they can act as negative effects, collapsing our desires and diminishing our well-being. How we treat societal traumas and "isms," as well as individual adverse traumas, can become a catalyst for tearing down the veils of ordinary reality and social norms that do not promote health and peace. We can have an opportunity to face the fears induced by traumas. Transforming the meanings of traumas can lead us to expanding our consciousness and being.

Let me give you an example. Every year of my adult life, my New Year's resolution prayer has been to be of service to others and to God. Each year my prayer is answered in particular ways. Each year I have learned more about myself and others, coming from the context of that prayer.

As I have mentioned, there have been times that I faced discrimination, occasions when societal traumas affected me and my well-being. However, most of the time I have chosen not to let those occasions traumatize me or make me a cynical, angry person. I have been able to use faith and have created new meanings to help me continue forward in my life. The airplane situation I described in the fifth chapter of Section Two is an example that I used to help me explore grief and coping skills, as well as power and non-power dynamics. When I was a child, an administrator and a few teachers shamed me. I developed TMCS because I could not fight, flee, or even freeze successfully. Curiosity and self-love drove my need to understand.

My starting point was my parents' belief that such folks are "ignorant of their own hearts, so how can they be educated about other people's hearts?"

My parents passed on the belief that all human beings are innately good. They believed that because we are God's children we are made of love. When we become strangers to our hearts and foreigners to our Creator, we forget the love that we are and the love that others are. I was and am blessed to have José Alberto and Graciela Elisa as my parents, for they gave tangible proof of the meaning they were trying to convey to their children: to share unconditional love and to be aware that not all people are aware of their own hearts.

This vital message they role modeled in our family helped buoy us during stormy and transitional times. They did not have to be, nor were they, saints in parenting or in being human. Instead, they were angels reminding us to remember our humanity and our connection to each other. Love as an active role in my life helped me weather traumatic events.

Remember this: Trauma is frozen energy derived from fear. It is an energy yearning to thaw, be transformed, and allowed to go back to God. What is left behind when this happens? Space for us mortals to create adventures for our souls, where we are the heroes and authors of our own lives once again—or maybe for the first time.

If I am in the midst of traumatic reactions, and if I realize what this internal energy symbolizes, I can then have an opportunity to acutely experience myself. I can experience sensations and allow them to depart, provided I stay out of the way of analyzing them. Gendlin, Levine, and Deer speak of this felt sensation. I call it getting to know myself beyond words, to know more of my beloved body through the body's own language of sensations without attributing feelings or emotions or thoughts.

If I am left with traumatic side effects, such as body illnesses, what can I learn from them? For example, do I notice that my lower back tends to spasm whenever a certain person is in my life, or that my throat tends to close up whenever I am asked to speak, or that my stomach tends to churn whenever I enter a particular place? What are these body sensations telling me? I take the time to breathe into that affected area, assigning no meaning, but simply to experience the body sensation. I take time and love to find out. I have learned, and those "teachers" (the body illnesses) have gone away.

Yet for some of us the illnesses may be lifelong companions for reasons we may never know in this lifetime. So how do we make peace with something that literally gives us pain? What meanings do we ascribe to the pain so that our quality of life and our hearts can sing or continue to write new songs? The answers within the stories we live by are unique to each of us. When trauma knocks at our door, it may be an opportunity for us to help ourselves and others.

If I consciously create or choose meanings that are more life-affirming, despite my pain or illnesses or life's circumstances, then I will be more successful in establishing and maintaining well-being in my life. I can look at trauma as transforming and expanding my love for myself and others. By redefining the meanings I have attached to my life stories, I can contextualize my stories in a manner that helps me lead my life more fully—no matter what "storms" or "tornadoes" head my way. I may not be able to change the reality that existence has given me, but I can change how I approach it. For many, reality is no "bed of roses.

Looking Below the Trauma Layers

A poor family in Ecuador reminded me through their actions and approach to living that trauma need not be the guiding story of one's life—or that trauma need not be created, despite one's life circumstances.

I had gone to visit my relatives when I was in my early twenties. I was younger than my numerical age in terms of being naïve. As I walked down certain streets in Quito, I saw poor people struggling to survive. There was something different about them compared to people I had seen living in poverty in the United States. What was it? I could not put my finger on it. I went to visit the countryside. As I was walking through an area near my cousin's farmland, I came upon a shack of a home. Their only door was open. I saw that the shack had a dirt floor and a thatched roof. One big room for a family of five.

For me, it seemed like abject poverty. No running water, no sanitary conditions. The whole family came out to see who was walking near their home. I introduced myself. Then, there it was again. Something was different. It was more than their being very gracious and hospitable. They asked me to come share their food with them. I was touched to see them offering whatever meager food and drink they had with me, a traveler. But it was something more than that.

Suddenly, I realized what I had been sensing and seeing. It was their love and the gleam in their eyes. We spoke for some time. Eventually, I asked them very politely how they could appear joyful. Looking back, I see now that this could have been a rude question; yet given the circumstances and how we were interacting, there was a sense of intimacy, of having known each other for a while. This is what they said, translated into English:

Tenemos Dios. "We have God. God has blessed us with the love that we have for each other and for the love of our family. Each day is a good day when we remember that. That is not to say that sorrow does not appear at our doors. It does all too often, but it does not rob us of knowing that we are part of God. Who knows what tomorrow will bring? What we do know is that we have each other and the good fortune to meet such nice people as yourself."

I have never forgotten their answer. This is not to be misconstrued that poor people in Ecuador feel blessed and are happy about being poor. Who in their right mind would be happy about being poor, especially in classist-oriented societies that equate material gain with human worth? However, people can feel blessed regardless of economic factors and traumas. Those whom I happened to meet approached in the best way they knew how — through their faith, and creating, whenever possible, avenues to experience love for each other and those they encountered. They moved my heart.

As in any country, the dominant group tends to move slowly

when it comes to the concerns of nondominant groups. Being in Ecuador, I felt strange to be considered a member of the dominant group there. I was not used to being on the other side. From a couple of my cousins who were wealthy, I heard the same kind of talk I would hear from some wealthy and middle-class friends in the United States and in many parts of western Europe I had visited.

Regardless of the language, regardless of the country, the tone used and the comments made by some people of higher economic and/or educational levels were the same when they addressed or discussed individuals of lower economic levels:

"They're lazy. They don't want to succeed. There are resources available. Why don't they use them?"

"They want us to care for them, when it's apparent that their lot [read: group] hasn't tried for generations. They're still in the same economic situation they've always been in."

"Why can't they be like us and have a decent work ethic?"

Whether people are poor, rich, in poor health, in good health ... whether their lives seem to be a constant battle for survival or everything comes very easily, I believe we are each other's keeper. No one can become successful without receiving some form of help or encouragement from someone. Part of my healing and the foundation that I developed came from being *bien educada*. By opening my heart to myself and by extending that heart, I became blessed by meeting wonderful people from all walks of life.

I also met difficult people, bigoted people, and others who were simply prejudiced in a "clueless," unknowing way. Some of them affected my employment and others my housing, and one even slashed my four perfectly good tires in a neighborhood that was becoming turf-oriented. Yet my core was never broken. My heart retained its flexibility. I may have sighed, even cried. But I let grief pass. I kept my eyes on the prize of becoming more of who I am, of being *bien educada*, which also meant doing social justice work—being of service to nurture existence into life.

Getting back to my story of when I was a young woman visiting Ecuador, when I came back to the States, I started to feel that something was missing in my life. I felt a hole in my stomach and a yearning that I was not *cumpliendo*, or accomplishing, something. It was a promise that I had given myself when I was five years old. I had forgotten it until after my experience with that family.

When I was five years old, my mother and I went on a vacation to Quito, Ecuador, to visit her side of the family. She gave me money for the whole summer to spend. I was thrilled! I felt like a grown-up. She had even bought me a little purse to carry all those coins. One day, she and I were walking down a cobblestone street. There were vendors on it shouting their wares. People above them, hanging out from windows, shouted back what they wanted and threw down money to the vendors. Then the vendors would throw up, with excellent aim, the food or whatever else had been bought, to the people in the windows.

There were children playing and people walking to their destinations. I was enjoying it all. (I can remember that day as though it were yesterday.) Then I saw a little boy urinating on the side of the street! I asked my mother why he did not go home to use the bathroom.

My mother replied that not all children had homes, that he might be homeless. I continued staring at him. Suddenly I pulled my hand away from my mother's gentle hold and ran to him. I told him in Spanish, "*Toma.*" I thrust my purse with all my coins into his hands. He had a surprised look. I ran back to my mother and took her hand. We continued walking. My head was down, looking at the cobblestone street, thinking of the poor boy. My mother asked me why I had given him all the money. I told her that he probably could use it, and who knew what he did not have. "Besides," I said as I raised my face to my mum's eyes, "I have you and your love. I don't need any money." I swore that day that when I grew up I would do something to help children and their parents not be homeless. I made a promise to try to change what I could and to help others.

Decades later, when I was back in Ecuador, that family reminded me that we are all in this existence together. They also gave me a gift with regard to approaching hardships. As existence would have it, I have experienced many of them, such as the loss of my dear parents and the loss of dear friends. I cannot change reality, but I can learn how to approach those kinds of events and circumstances. I can continue to love myself, love others, honor travelers who come my way, and make loving differences. I can take what existence gives me and position myself to lead my life. I can be *bien educada*.

Bien Educado—A Way of Living

Bien educado is a home where other values and beliefs reside. It is an umbrella that shades us from the blistering heat of anger and one that protects us from the tears of undue grief. By choosing to keep this part of my heritage, I have helped myself have a better life. We can choose to be well-educated of the heart—to be *bien educada* (if one is female) or *bien educado* (if one is male). Each culture has something comparable to this concept. We do have access to living this way. Not that existence is easy. Challenges and obstacles are experienced, as is the grief that at times the winds of change bring us, simply because we are human beings. Yet by being *bien educados*, we can weather the storms and appreciate the rainbows more fully.

To be *bien educados*, we must separate soul from behavior so that the soul will have "elbow room" to move about and let go of the behaviors that do not honor it. Mindfulness and being present are essential. How can we value ourselves and others if we do not experience the person before us in the present tense? Sometimes it may mean walking away to allow space to occur and reflection to take place. Walking away temporarily but not abandoning the person altogether is also part of being *bien educados.* It is in the demeanor and intent that we leave behind with the person that sets the tone. It means using time as an ally, breathing regularly and sometimes deeply, and exhaling and letting go of what no longer serves our highest good.

Letting go of behaviors that have been encrusted upon our soul takes care, so that the soul will not fear that you are going to tear away parts of it. For those of us who have been abused, we may mistakenly interpret our behaviors as being who we are. An abuser may tell us so often that we *are* the behaviors that we forget it is a lie. We have a choice to let go of attitudes and behaviors that act as veils, covering up who we are and covering our dreams to be treated with dignity, respect, and basic kindness.

Those of us who have separated our souls from behaviors, so that we can explore and see if the behaviors still serve us, can then help others to do the same by creating an environment of respect, civility, and time. It means looking into the person's eyes with kindness and remembering that the person before us, even though she or he is being discourteous, rude, hurtful, or bigoted, is a human being with feelings and emotions.

This does not mean that we become "doormats," allowing someone to trample us. That would not be a *bien educado* thing to do. Allowing someone to be *maleducado* or *maleducada* (i.e., showing ill behavior) does not serve that person or us. By allowing *maleducado* behavior to occur, we condone a manner that veils the beauty of the person before us. The best we can do is to provide a supportive environment where that person can unfold who he or she is without our shaming or embarrassing or threatening the person. Because if we do shame or embarrass or threaten, we become the abuser and we activate the person's trauma mechanisms and coping skills. We become the triggers for him or her. His or her walls of defense will go up, and the possibility of entering into an offense mode will be increased.

Bien educado is a gentle approach, yet it can be very powerful. Often we think of strength in terms of having to be hard, or physically strong, or harsh. Yet in the gentleness of a voice and a manner that speaks of caring and compassion, the other person will pause to reflect, and perhaps touch their heart. They will see your eyes and your heart. And it may also give you time to defend yourself or help someone else.

"I don't think so!" you say. "How naïve," you think. Let me tell you a story about how being *bien educada* helped in the recovery of a stolen wallet.

One day, my cousins and I were in San Francisco at Fisherman's Wharf. Tourists abounded, and we moved slowly down the street. Vendors were selling their wares by shouting out what they had. My cousins were ahead of me, single file, as we made our way through the crowd. In front of me was one cousin with her handbag, swung over her shoulder and facing toward me. As we walked along, a young man quickly put his hand in the handbag, relieving it of my cousin's wallet. As quickly as his hand had been in her bag, it was now starting to tuck the wallet under his jacket.

"Excuse me, sir," I addressed him.

Startled, he looked at me and paused. At that moment, I reached out and took the wallet. "Sir, that doesn't belong to you."

Frozen, he did not know what to make of my demeanor.

"Attention, everyone! There is a thief here! Be aware of your belongings!" I shouted, while also calling out for police. He had been so taken aback with my initial politeness, he had not moved. Suddenly, he reacted and ran away.

Had I done otherwise, such as immediately saying, "Hey, you. Stop, thief!" or something else he would have been used to hearing, I might have lost the opportunity to retrieve my cousin's wallet.

Another example of being *bien educada* or *bien educado* is to bring time as a friend into a heated argument or any other situation in which your own triggers have riled you. Being polite, and even formal at times, will get the person's attention. People, unfortunately, are not used to being addressed in a polite way when in conflict.

At one job I had, I heard the director shouting and shaming the receptionist at the reception area—through the walls of my office. When I came out, I saw the receptionist crying and the director livid, pointing toward her in an aggressive stance. She was all of five-feet-five, but that anger and authoritative power from being the director made her seem like a giant. As a witness to such a horrible situation, I had a choice: to let it go or to say something. I could not speak for the receptionist, but I could speak as to how being a witness was affecting me.

From an "I" perspective, I went to the director and asked her politely if I could speak with her in her office. Once there, I stated how it felt for me to be a witness to such a situation. At first, she was very angry with me, stating that she could speak to anyone in any way she wanted, any place she wanted. I asked her with sincere curiosity if how she behaved was an acceptable thing to do. Did her behavior show who she was? Did her demeanor convey the message of helping to correct the mistakes that the receptionist had made, or was her intention to be angry and vent? The director grew even angrier and reiterated that she could do what she wanted anywhere with anyone. I said quite simply, "Okay." My voice became softer. Since she was angry, it would not have been a good idea to look directly at her. Instead, I glanced in her direction a few times. I reiterated, "Okay, if you truly believe it was all right to do what you did. Okay. I just wanted to share how it was to witness it, especially since I know you're a good heart." And I left the office.

Half an hour later, I heard her apologizing to the receptionist. I had said nothing else. Nothing more was needed. By being *bien educada*, I did not challenge her authority. Instead, I had shared how it felt to be a witness and asked her what her intentions were in a polite and loving manner, while reminding her that she was a good heart. I then reiterated her own conclusions to herself. The rest was up to her.

Of course, being *bien educada* does not always have the same effect on everyone. I have known disrespectful people who cling even tighter to their veils and robes of misbehavior and are determined to make others feel less than human. Being *bien educada* in those cases served *me* well, although it did not help the other person remember who she or he was. *Bien educada* reminds me of who *I* am.

As my mother would say sometimes with loving pity about the rude person, "*Pobrecito. No tiene sentido.*" (Poor person. He has no sense.") In this case *sentido* means no awareness of feeling of the heart. Clueless. Having said that, my mother would waste no energy on anger or hatred or frustration. It was as though she were commenting on a wounded bird—with love, doing the best you could, but then letting God take care of the rest, as you continue onward in your journey of living.

Yet the goal of *bien educado* is not for it to be used as a healing tool, which it can be; or to be an environment where people can laugh and enjoy themselves or remind themselves to be who they are—loving people both to themselves and others—which it *can* help to do. *Bien educado* is more than that. It is a way of living.

How do I honor myself? How do I respect myself? Do I have behaviors that illustrate who I am? Do I have attitudes that open up my vistas about life and people? Do my beliefs and values gentle my path? Do I matter to me to treat me with compassion? Am I polite to myself?

These questions start at home, with ourselves. With you and me looking inward and working our truths. It includes honoring our beloved companions who have been with us since birth and will continue to be with us until death's doors open for us to walk through. Those companions are our bodies.

Our bodies are our witnesses, and they are both companion and servant to our needs and desires. Our bodies are the vessels of where our souls reside. Whether we give our bodies conscious commands or subconscious ones, our bodies respond and react. It is therefore important to know our bodies—to learn the language and to see the signals transmitted long before a crisis occurs. How? By using our friend, time, to get ourselves acquainted in an intimate manner with ourselves. Paying attention to our bodies while they are healthy is as important as when they are ill or when we need our bodies to perform for us.

We cannot treat our bodies as slaves without expecting, at some point in time, a slave revolt to occur. Heart attacks, gastrointestinal disorders, sleep disorders, stress-related symptoms, depression, anxiety, weight disorders, and, increasingly, autoimmune illnesses—these are some of the health challenges our bodies will give us in order for us to pay attention to how we wholly treat ourselves. Using anger and fear as motivating factors to embrace or avoid off-balanced ways of dealing with traumas will, eventually, negatively affect our quality of life.

If we are truly to help heal ourselves from macro (group- and societal-induced) and micro (individual-induced) traumas and to help others, we must consider the totality of the effects of such traumas on ourselves and take the appropriate steps. Even if this means taking time and developing healthier boundaries that include the magic two-letter word, *no*. "No, thank you. I don't want to do that." "No, thanks. I have my plate full right now, and I can't do more."

Or that wonderful three-letter word, *yes*. "Yes, I want help, so I'm delegating these projects [or chores] to you." "Yes, I deserve to play and be creative in my own way." "Yes, I'm a human being." "Yes, I am from God and, therefore, I am part of that Love." "Yes, I honor my heart."

Being a *bien educada* or *bien educado* person and how to become one would require a full book. But I hope I have given you enough to start thinking and reflecting on how you are honoring yourself and others. *Honor* is a word that is not used very often anymore. And when it *is* used, it is usually in relation to the military or to a duty of some sort.

Es un honor de conocerla. "It is an honor to know you." *Honor* holds the elements of respect, pleasure, benefit, privilege, and admiration. Honor yourself and see what happens. New stories will appear—stories written by you, unfolding the beauty that you are.

Recreating Our Own Stories, Our Own Lives
... [you] cannot just balance checkbook,
see how much you got left.
Must balance life too.
Amy Tan, *The Hundred Secret Senses*

One does not need trauma to have an unbalanced life or to live in extremes. Life is not simply about survival; it is about living. Yet so often all a person does is exist, with life barely touched, if at all, only on weekends. When trauma enters the picture, life takes a back seat to existing. Trauma, if it is allowed, guarantees existence, but not life. That is, of course, if one does not utilize trauma as an opportunity to discover what really matters.

Brooke Medicine Eagle's prayer called "Bones" reflects Native Americans' worldview of group responsibility to their descendants through seven generations. Central to healing is the desire to take the gifts that our ancestors have given us and to stop passing down the ways that do not honor their memories nor serve our future generations or ourselves.

Using this desire to live a balanced and honoring life, we can develop new beliefs that can transform the impact of societal traumas on us and that can intercede in keeping an "ism" from becoming a trauma for us in the future. At this point, "isms" exist in our lives, but we can certainly affect how they influence our hearts, our joy, and how we view ourselves and others.

The questions are these: Whose story do I want to follow? Will I follow someone else's perception? The power of remaking perceptions helped me realize that I can create and recreate, develop and transform. When those epiphanies came to me, my perception shifted. I was no longer an outsider but rather a participant in my own environment. I became my own autobiographer.

I do acknowledge all the individuals who have helped me unfold, for I know I could not have done it alone. Analogous to the construction of our homes, the support beams in this process of unfolding are the other people in our lives, and we are the main beams of our own houses, our homes. If we do not have ourselves as the main beams, then our home falls, no matter how many support beams there are. All are needed in their proper places. We are interdependent.

Using the home in its proper way is also important. To continue with this analogy, all rooms must be used. If any room is not used or is rarely inhabited, a guest will know. Life is that way, too. The bedroom is a symbol for intimacy, the living room to entertain and be with friends and family members, the kitchen to nourish those who are there, the bathroom to literally let go of things no longer needed and to clean ourselves, and so on.

A balance and appreciation of all parts of our lives and of those who share our lives help to reduce trauma and its effects.

Recalibrating or realigning ourselves and our lives also helps. As Amy Tan's character in *The Hundred Secret Senses* essentially says, we need to balance life if life is to enter our breath and reside. By creating an environment of love for ourselves and by opening it up to others, we are expanding our environments. We will have more space to move about and will be in an environment of love.

Trauma also requires community healing, not just individual healing. How far will I get in healing only my body, mind, and what I consider my soul if I do not address the environment in which I live? Is my environment supportive of growth and health? I am reminded of the time I visited Spain. The country had a fascist government then and was ruled by a dictator, Francisco Franco. Secret police was the norm. I was twenty and somewhat clueless as to why people were cautious about talking to strangers on the topics of their government and of politics. They had no idea whether I was indeed a tourist or a member of the secret police. They could not feel the freedom that I took for granted. In terms of repression, Spain has changed since then for the better.

Or what good does it do for individuals to heal and expand when they have to return to a dysfunctional family that counteracts their new behaviors and feelings about themselves?

Whether it is on a much grander scale—such as a government

that does not advance its people in terms of freedom, healing, and expanding their vistas—or whether it is a family or neighborhood that stifles or places impediments not only for you but themselves, healing has to consider these scales.

As human beings, care must be given not to create a loop or a cycle of trauma as we venture forward writing our own autobiographies.

> ... *the oppressed must not in seeking to regain their humanity, become in turn oppressors of the oppressors, but rather restorers of the humanity of both.*

This statement by Paolo Freire held my attention. He is saying that it is *we* who have the responsibility. It is *we* who must stop the cycle of violence and oppression. If we are to become fully human and examples of what God aspired all of us to be, we need to let go of the "scorecard" of who did what to whom and how often and how lately. The revenge factor has to stop.

I was inspired to write the following after a meditation:

I Will Not Hate You
You took our land
and made it into your own image.

You poison our wells of hopes and dreams.
Yet, I will not hate you.

You bomb our streets.
But I will not hate you.

You murder my friends
in the name of a cause
in the name of a nation
in the name of something.

I will not hate you.

You kill members of my family.
You rob us of our jobs and our livelihood.
I will not hate you.
You may even kill my body.
And still,
I will not hate you.

You have hate in your heart
and in your actions,
no matter what you say it to be otherwise.

No enemy of yours could have achieved such great victory.
You have killed
your own humanity and soul.

But you will never kill mine.

Instead,
I will love you.

I will open my heart and help you
to Be again
the child of God.
God of Love.

That will be my sweetest revenge.
I will love you.

It takes no risk, no bravery to continue killing and maiming. It takes tremendous courage to stop even if the last headcount of deaths, tragedies, incidences of discrimination and humiliation "merit" our retaliation.

It is not enough to let go of fight, flight, or freeze reactions. It is not enough to let go of attitudes and TMCS that may have defined our perceptions. Do we actively want and seek ways to live and create a life that celebrates joy and peace? If we are to believe that we are all God's children, then relationships become important.

If we are all related, then what we do to others, we do to ourselves. "Do unto others as you would want them to do to you" takes on additional meaning and becomes clearer. We all matter, whether we realize it or not. It also means that we have to reflect how we treat ourselves. If you and I treat ourselves harshly and with anger, then "do unto others as you would want them to do to you" may mean more behaviors and attitudes of harshness and anger, because that is what you are used to—because that is your story you are following. By treating oneself with love and respect, the whole world opens up.

Everyone must be free, or no one is free. In any social justice movement, if humanity is the goal, then there can be no duality— no "us versus them." When we decide to look at our lives and the stories we follow, we can look for stories that affirm our being and our humanity, or we can perpetuate the "abused-abuser" cycle, the power/non-power dynamics, thus guaranteeing that the next generation will seek vengeance for having had its turn as the oppressed.

Traumas affect us all. Traumas affect us in ways that those who are in power may never comprehend, unless they are recipients of some aspect of those traumas and become aware of the effects they have on themselves and on others. Moreover, their understanding of their own traumas is not a guarantee that what they learn will translate to understanding other kinds of traumas and the effects those have on others. Whether or not they understand, whether or not they dismantle sources that lead to traumas, whether or not they are active partners in obtaining equal justice and respect for all—none of this must stop us, as individuals, from healing ourselves and our communities.

We can have open doors and open arms for the members of our perceived abuser groups to join us in healing and celebration. Yet whether or not they want to be part of the healing should not stop us from unfolding as loving human beings.

For those of you who have experienced familial childhood abuse, for those of you who have been raped, shamed, or battered—you know that your recovery cannot be dependent on whether your abusers acknowledge their awful deeds. Your recovery cannot be dependent on whether they go into therapy or actively repent with promised healthier behaviors on the way.

We heal because we have to. We heal because we have no choice. If we do not, we remain victims forever—forever replaying in our bodies and hearts the traumas of the past, as well as the potential traumas arising from society and from individuals in our lives. We stay in the grip of chronic grief, with anger and tears. We remain in the mentality of surviving, being able only to sleep, work, eat, and seek distractions that feed our fight, flight, or freeze reactions (that is, seeking adrenaline, melodrama, or numbing our pain and discomfort through addictions).

Trauma can be transformational. Difficult situations can become adventures of our souls. Trauma stops us in our tracks, making us catch and hold our breaths, magnifying our senses, then transforms our reality into an unknown landscape where safety and trust take on new meanings. Trauma can invite us to be trailblazers again, or it can lead us to stagnate, making us debilitated until all we do is react and blame.

We can take the raw material of the traumas we encounter and give them meaning in terms of hope, survival, and determination. Why did I survive emotionally when others succumbed and lost their way? I was curious and I was taught to question authority, even that of my parents. My parents knew they were human and told me so. My parents wanted us, their children, to see them and others as human beings, regardless of our roles in life. We all do the best we can, given what we have at hand.

"Storytelling" Our Own Lives

I have learned to use what my family does best: storytelling. What I did not know was that there were psychotherapeutic and mediation approaches based on what is called "narrative therapy" and "narrative mediation." Since childhood, I had been using them, with some variation, without knowing it. In fact, storytelling goes back a long way in many cultures; it is used to pass down a group's truths, morals, history, and the lessons to be learned from that history. My use of storytelling helped me survive.

In the case of societal trauma, we often see ourselves as being the problem because we are shamed or humiliated. In an abusive relationship, the abuser might call the abused person stupid, lazy, dumb, an animal, a whiner, or a sexual deviant. The abused oftentimes will integrate these remarks as though they were truths, so that even if the abuser goes away, that "tape" gets internalized and the abused subconsciously plays it back.

We end up with internalized racism, internalized classism, internalized sexism, internalized homophobia, internalized ageism, and the list goes on. Internalizing those words, those tones, those behaviors and making them our own—this limits us. We inadvertently believe it is who we are as a person, as a people. Part of unfolding more of who we are is to disconnect or detach ourselves from the behaviors and attitudes that we hold about others and ourselves.

Using "storying," we can separate our behaviors from who we are. By looking at our lives as stories, with us as its writers, actors, directors, choreographers, and producers, we can explore the problems as external problems, separate from us. We can identify small and large stories without shame or embarrassment. In trauma, as in melodramatic stories, what we think we are becomes who we are. The soul blends into behaviors and roles. By "storying," we can separate the soul from the behaviors and roles given to us.

We can then choose stories that honor our souls. In so doing, we can invite the concept of *bien educado* into our journey.

We can create an environment where our souls can be distinguished from our behaviors and attitudes. We can select an environment where we have opportunities and the space to select behaviors and attitudes that reflect our goodness. In narrative psychotherapy, as well as in the concept of *bien educado*, we externalize the problem away from the person. Using this approach with regards to "isms," we "un-brainwash" ourselves from the images and caricatures presented in the media.

It is about deprogramming ourselves from being our own abusers and our own "de-valuers" of who we are. We should not feed into the objectification of who we are. In particular, our beloved bodies are the first to be assaulted psychologically, spiritually, emotionally, sexually, and physically. Our bodies need to be honored and loved. I am reminded right now of the saying "united we stand, divided we fall." As long as we are kept at odds with our own bodies and how we perceive and treat that part of who we are, as long as we harbor conflict within ourselves, we are kept busy from truly attending to what really matters. If we berate and ridicule ourselves at our own expense, then we keep ourselves from the very things we truly want to experience: love, life, joy, passion, and peace.

It is through the language, the words, the tone, the nonverbal ways we communicate to ourselves about ourselves and others that define who we are and what our lives look like. What words do we choose to describe ourselves and our groups? A narrative psychotherapist or narrative mediator would explore the major or dominant story in the person's life. What or who in that story is defining his or her meanings, the way life is viewed, appreciated, and feared, as well as his or her dreams and hopes?

If the dominant story in our lives revolves around "isms" and their traumatic effects, then what are the other stories in our lives that are being overshadowed or "closeted" by that story? If the dominant story in your life is about betrayal by someone intimate, a loved one, a family member, or a person you held in high esteem, then what other stories that need to be in the limelight are being overshadowed?

What questions do we ask of ourselves? Have we taken time to "be"? Or are we too busy "doing," zipping from one place or thing to another? Do we make time to embrace and hug those we love? Do we utter words of love at any time, without waiting for a special situation to arise? What kind of legacy are we leaving children and our nieces, nephews, friends, and communities?

What is it that we want God to know us by? How do we want to be remembered?

Trauma cannot exist too long in an environment where we honor ourselves and others, where we take time to meditate and/or pray, where our focus is on living and not just existing. It cannot exist when we treat each other as *bien educados.*

Trauma need not be fatal to our hearts. It can remind us that we do have hearts and for us to sing our hearts' songs. It can help us recapture our dreams in a different way than what we expected. In fact, dreams can be a way for our traumas to transform and for us to gain new tools for living.

Chapter 10

DREAMS

When we reconstruct the fragments of our dreams, we bring an aliveness to the spirit that allows the imagination to go beyond basic human drives and the need to survive. Imagining a better world allows us to actively participate in creating our dreams, and when we take on that responsibility, we embrace the Remembering.
Jamie Sams, *Dancing the Dream: The Seven Sacred Paths of Human Transformation*, quoting Muriel Espinosa

Traditional psychodynamics includes dream interpretations, such as Jung's archetypal dreams and Freud's wish fulfillment. Yet dreams are more than that. In many cultures, dreams hold a sacred place. Through actual dreams, we let our imaginations fly. It is a land where we can heal and bring that healing back to our lives. Dreams can also be a place of stark terror, as flashbacks and nightmares of the past come to haunt us. Dreams are another form of communication in which our bodies convey their needs and alert us. Dreams can also be used by those who have passed on to come visit and share. How do we view sleep and dreams? A waste of time when we should be productively awake? Do we know how to fully utilize the dream worlds? Have we been taught about the various kinds of dreams and of dream questing?

In our dreams we can access our collective unconscious. We see ourselves represented in various forms. The dream is the dreamer, and the dreamer, the dream. Metaphors, sounds, sights—all are various aspects of the dreamer. Normally, when people think of dreams, they think of that Jungian interpretation of dreams. This is one kind of dream. It does not reflect the full array of dreams we may have.

Larry Dossey has written several books on dreams and prayer and their healing effects. He noticed that prayers are more powerful if done through dreams. He calls them dream prayers. For me, and for others from a range of cultures, dreams can also be a way in which our angels, spirit guides, or God communicate to us. Dreams are a place where we can feel at home, honoring that kind of reality and learning more of who we are in full awareness without needing to transform the terrain or the experiences in it.

Lucid dreaming is a place where we are aware that we are dreaming. Within that state we can, if we so choose, manipulate the dream. Dreams can be a place to work out issues in full awareness. Dreams can be a place where the effects of traumas can be addressed with hope and clarity. It is a place where we can remember who we are—part of God, the Great Spirit.

Choosing the path to becoming free and embracing life is not easy. Anyone who has chosen a healing path will tell you this. There is much pain when we let go of beliefs and storylines we may have followed all our years as though they were part of our being and our breath. Dreams serve not only as a purpose to relax and rejuvenate our bodies, but also as another avenue for communication with ourselves and our connection to God or Great Spirit.

My family always supported the remembering of dreams when we were children. I was particularly good at knowing my dreams and knowing which were "escape" dreams, which were Jungian dreams, and which were precognitive. I learned how to elicit lucid dreaming, a state in which I am fully aware that I am dreaming and able to manipulate the dreams within. In the state of lucid dreaming, I am able to communicate with others, especially my guides and God. I can be given messages from the Divine that relate to my so-called "waking" state—the one we call life. I could also dismantle any recurring nightmares in the lucid dreaming state.

For me, the dream world has been another place where any trauma can be seen for what it really is, for it is unclothed and bare to the winds of life. Dreams can also be a place for precognition, or they can be a realm of communication with who I call the ethereals/guides/angels.

Early in the morning of the day after Thanksgiving, while I was sleeping I knew I was dreaming. I was aware that I was in a dream and that it was a dream. In this dream, my mother was sleeping in the living room of their house. I could hear the siren of the ambulance as it passed by the home. She was showered with white light. My father was in the bedroom, frantic and unable to call 911. I tried to call, but I was receiving calls from people who thought they were calling the psychic helpline. Every time I would try to dial, there was another caller saying, "This is the psychic helpline?" I told each caller to get off so I could call 911. Then that voice said, "You do not understand. This *is* the psychic helpline." I knew what was happening. In God's way, a scenario was being presented to me so that all my senses were engaged, not just my intellect. My mother told me not to worry, that she did not know what all the fuss was about, that she was just going Home. She was a bit annoyed with my father's frantic behaviors.

Then a presence spoke to me. The voice said, "Your mother is in good hands. She will be fine. Take care of your father." And with that, the dream ended and I immediately awoke. I knew something had happened to my mother and that the dream was a message to me. My whole body was vibrating as though an electric current was passing through me, awakening me more than the normal state of being awake. I knew what that meant, as I have had those electric vibrations before in my life. It was a message dream from the outside.

I called my brother to find out what was going on. The logical thing would have been to call my parents' home, but I intuitively called him. He told me that Mami had been taken to the hospital and that Papi was staying with him. Later, on January 30, the day after my birthday, my mother died. She died at home. Hospice had been set up in the living room. She ultimately died peacefully in the bed in the living room facing the window to the front yard. Just like the setup in the dream. No one anticipated her death. But I did. Through that dream, I was given forewarning so as to lessen the grief.

That dream gave me solace and it prepared me. Yes, I went through grief. She was my best friend and a loving and good mother. She inspired me to be myself, even if she disagreed. Unconditional love. One night as she lay dying, I was angry. I went to the back yard and, with my anger and anguish of losing her, kicked down the side door to the garage. I was surprised and yet not surprised at the strength that it took to knock down the closed door. So, yes, I was experiencing an aspect of my grief on the poor door.

I miss her. But I also know—no, I *feel*—one major thing: She was and is fine. She is now more directly at one with God. As for Papi, I moved back home to stay and be with him until he died. I moved from Texas to be with my beloved father, who has always been there for me in various ways. I share this dream regarding my mother with you because that particular dream helped me through the grieving times of seeing her leave this existence. That dream was like a thread, reminding me that there is more than what we can actually see and physically touch.

We can use dreams to diffuse traumas or truncate their effects on us. Dreams can actually provide us with tools and guidance to go forward in our lives. Dreams can be used to help us transform our perception of our reality, as well as change our reality into avenues that take us to life.

Dreams are powerful, and they can help us to expand our sense of self, our consciousness, and our ability to live joyfully. Dreams can help us better understand the roles we play in society. It is up to us dreamers to be curious enough and open enough to explore, to blaze trails, and to delve into the dream state as we do in our "awake" lives.

The same as the awake state, the dream state requires that the person be anchored and grounded. In the beginning, a mentor or a "spot coach" for the dreamer would be good, until the person is well versed enough to be on his or her own for the more in-depth aspects of dreaming.

Dreams can indeed serve as an avenue to carry out healing work and to obtain a better understanding of the societal stories in our lives. I am inviting your curiosity to explore how you can use dreaming as an application for your own healing path.

Dreams and how we honor them are part of the heritage my parents passed down to me. I know that in other cultures, dreams are important and are used as ways to help us remember who we are and our purpose in this world.

Part of the damage that societal traumas can cause is the dissolution of healing ways that our groups have had for generations. In addition to the tradition of storytelling, the use of dream states is another avenue which has often been dismissed as a legitimate healing method (except within the confines of psychotherapy). We can regain our heritage of using dreams, or discover for the first time the value that sleep and dreams have in helping us transform our waking lives. As individuals, regardless of whether the traumas are macro or micro or both, we can seek and draw from dreams as ways for healing and peace.

DreamQuest Dreams

To dream and be real at the same time is one reality of many.
May you dream yourself real.
May your new reality re-awaken you to life, which is love.
Walk in beauty of Spirit.
Walk as Beauty, of which you are a part.
—what came to me in meditation

I now include a dream that relates to societal trauma, induced by "isms."

"An Act of Humanness," or "The Man"

The Man and his young son entered the apartment manager's office. The apartment building was huge. It contained many apartments, some of which were for rent.

Coming from Pakistan, he was aware that his attire and accent were not yet Americanized. His little boy was a talkative one and had to be told not to interrupt while the adults were speaking.

The Man was tired. He had been searching for an apartment that could accommodate him, his wife, and his seven children. He was all too aware of discrimination toward his kind: an immigrant, his ethnicity, and the size of his family. Yet he maintained his courteous ways and did not forget his manners, even when others would have

319

been muttering under their breath by now about the looks and the excuses given for not renting to them.

It was getting dark. He was hungry, as was his son. Inside the apartment manager's office, he looked around. Papers were strewn on the desks; unorganized filing cabinets caught his eye as he strained to look where he was walking. The room was dingy, not very well lit.

An African American greeted him. He was the manager here, the Man thought. They rode up the elevator to the seventh floor to see an apartment that seemed to have the specifications needed by the Man.

As he walked into the apartment with the manager, he knew. "Wonderful!" the Man said. "This is the apartment! It has so much space." Finally, he had found the home for his family. "Yes, yes, I will take this place. My wife will be so pleased. She will have plenty of closet space for all the children's clothing."

They went back to the office. The African American looked down at the rates for that particular apartment and then looked up at the Pakistani, with the boy wrapped around the Man's left leg and gazing at the manager.

"Oh. I made a mistake," said the manager. "The rent for that apartment isn't what I stated. It's been changed. I forgot. Let me look for the new rental sheet."

That was the last straw for the Man and his young son. He turned around and proceeded across the foyer to leave the apartment building. He was tired of the discrimination. Tired that people were bigoted.

His spirit was sad, and he was angry.

The African American was puzzled and ran after him. "Wait! Wait! The rent for that apartment is $100 less per month. Don't you want it?"

The Man stopped. He turned around, with disbelieving ears—and a grin so big that his whole face participated.

He looked at the African American, feeling grateful and a bit embarrassed for his abrupt departure. It was the one time he had forgotten his manners and courtesy.

"Look. I know how it is," the African American said to him. "I've been there. I know that look. And I understand why you left when you heard me say that the rent fee wasn't right."

They stood looking at each other: African American to Pakistani, Pakistani to African American. No words were exchanged. Yet a lot was said and understood.

The dream ends, other than that the wife goes to see the apartment. She is happy. All ends well.

Dreams can be powerful. They can frighten us. They can be nightmarish. They can be simply a state of rest, a time to regenerate, and then wake up. Dreams can serve many functions. In terms of traumas, dreams can serve as other avenues for comprehending, growing, and healing.

"An Act of Humanness," or "The Man," came to me on June 19, 2000. I was finishing my dissertation on societal trauma. For three nights I posed a question. What are some of the effects of ongoing discrimination? I wrote about this dream as it had come to me. I was the observer in the dream. I was witnessing with my full senses. I did not edit the dream. It is self-explanatory. Two titles came with the dream: "The Man" and "An Act of Humanness." The story is about two members from different nondominant groups and the effects of discrimination.

I woke up thinking about how often those of us who experience severe discrimination expect everyone to be a perpetrator toward us. Sometimes we expect this even from other "minority" groups because of the perceived competition for resources.

Our expectation to be hurt establishes in us a certain kind of attitude. We learn to walk in society with a type of "brace." We walk at times with a level of fight, flight, or freeze readiness—ready to go on the offensive, or ready to retreat or to brace ourselves. Our TMCS are ready to go into action at a moment's notice, at the moment there is a "sign."

In this dream, for the Man it took only one person to break that thinking, at least for the time being. If enough people show their humanity and understanding, then discrimination—as opposed to the human expression of kindness—will be the exception. When I looked back at this dream, the thought of retiring TMCS came to mind. Understanding how societal trauma affects our souls and our communication with members of other groups is the precursor to letting go of TMCS.

I shared this story with a friend of mine, Elissa Beach. She asked me when I dreamt this story.

"June 19th," I replied.

"June 19th? Why, that's Juneteenth!" she said. Puzzlement appeared on my face and then left. Of course. As I smiled and gave thanks to God and God's sense of humorous timing, I recalled with Elissa's help that June 19th is a famous date: In most parts of Texas, it was not until 1865, two years after the Emancipation Proclamation, that slaves were finally told they were free. There are many reasons cited as to why freedom was announced so late. Generations later, June 19th, or Juneteenth as it eventually came to be known, is celebrated nationally by many African Americans. On January 1, 1980, Texas law declared it an official holiday, as a courtesy to the struggle and efforts of an African American state legislator named Al Edwards. This is viewed as the first emancipation celebration granted official state recognition. It seems fitting that when the dream occurred, it was on Juneteenth.

Concluding Comments

While painful to undergo, grief can provide a passage for healing and for new meanings to develop for the new reality now being faced. New meanings often arise when the status quo has changed. Part of healing is redefining old meanings and revitalizing our faith, exploring our imagination and creativity, and daring to be trailblazers in our own lives.

A wholistic healing approach requires us to reevaluate how we lead or follow our lives. What value do we place on the kind of quality of life we are living? What values and beliefs have we adopted, and are they serving us? A reframing of how we look at life and how we might recreate ourselves becomes the context in which we can use the tools and paths for healing. The context too becomes part of the healing from trauma.

By no means do I profess that the healing modalities mentioned are the only ways. The indigenous healing practices of groups are important, for they can be the core of releasing ourselves from the stories that traumas have thrust in our paths. It would take another book to delve into and do justice to the various ways in which individuals and groups have utilized their own healing practices.

Whatever our paths, yours and mine, may we come to realize that we matter. We do have a power of life and beauty in us. We do have the strength to unfold who we are, even though for some of us our strengths are still untapped. With that unfolding, we make a difference in our own lives and in the lives of others. We all matter. We all have voices that yearn to sing our hearts' songs. We all have bodies waiting with delight to sway to the rhythm of life. We have each other to dance to the songs of life. Or, we can be mesmerized by a disharmony that disrupts our hearts and our connections with each other.

We, as individuals, as members of groups and as groups, now have the choice to be trailblazers of our own lives or to follow in the footsteps of trauma.

SECTION FOUR

Epilogue:
Walk Between Winds

The hardest path to follow
is within our own hearts.

Our greatest journey
lies not in the stories
that we are given
by society or
by our groups.

The greatest journey lies in the story
we give ourselves
when we unfold
the beauty of who we are.

—after an inspired dream

Chapter 1

WE ARE ALL RELATED

Poco a poco se camina largo. Bit by bit, one walks far. My father would say that to me when I got disillusioned about finishing a project, or when I had grown tired of trying to understand people who were *maleducados* (ill-behaved from the heart). We are trailblazers of our own lives.

On our paths we meet many different kinds of people. Some of them are like angels, helping us and encouraging us to be more of who we are—loving human beings.

Yet some of the greatest teachers I have are individuals I call "turkeys" (no disrespect to actual turkeys). These people's behaviors are disrespectful. Their actions hinder our growth. They can even literally kill us. They tempt us to be like them in the most unflattering ways of being. They tempt us to be part of their cycle of trauma, as victim and victimizers. They elicit from us feelings such as shame, embarrassment, anger, fear, revenge, and immobility at the one end, and, at the other end, they can harm us physically, sexually, psychologically, emotionally, or spiritually—and, at times, financially.

They can instill their own demons in us. Traumas can be instilled on top of generational transmissions of past group and individual sufferings, constricting life and exacerbating the feeling of merely existing from day to day.

When trauma is not the center of one's existence, life expands. We can cease to internalize the demons. We need not buy into personalizing this societal pain or family pain or individual pain as though it is of our own making.

But what *is* of our own making is unloading or jettisoning these energies from our beings, from our bodies. What *is* of our own making is understanding that healing is both an individual and group affair. What we can do and must continue to do is to heal ourselves and to help others heal, regardless of their group affiliations.

Use time as an ally to explore, give honor to yourself, expand your horizons, and become the writer of your life. Honor the pain, let go of the suffering, and become more of who you are—a beautiful, loving, and lovable person. This journey is not easy, nor is it a "quick fix." Most worthwhile transformations cannot be done overnight.

If you choose to help yourself, your community, or others in your life, consider what I am proposing. This path will help you to free yourself to be who you are, with heartfelt courage and confidence. You will find a passage into healing and to living with internal peace, no matter what the winds bring to your doorstep. You will be able to walk at your own pace. There will be no need for running. And you will find others like yourself along the way.

Healing cannot be total without neighborhoods and communities working together to let go of traumas in their midst. Otherwise, individuals who have worked so hard to be more of who they are will find themselves returning to communities of trauma, where the need to keep and use TMCS is necessary.

If their communities are in patterns that support traumas, then those folks who want to heal or are healing will move to other communities and other areas for their continued good health. Or, if they cannot move away for whatever reason, they may succumb once again to the story of trauma found in their neighborhoods, in their environment, or maybe from families that have become toxic. If they do stay, then by necessity, perhaps, they become activists in their own way, risking their health and safety.

It is therefore important that our appointed leaders, and we ourselves, develop and perpetuate non-crisis surroundings that hold the excitement of peace, rather than the lure of constant adrenaline-high activities of crises and melodrama. We must all work together to dispel the myth that peace is a void, inactive and dull.

I have met too many women who are attracted to "bad boys" because these men were exciting and a bit dangerous. In the end, those relationships did not work out. When I asked these women why they were not drawn to men who were caring, affectionate, fun, and embracing of who they (the women) were, the usual response was that such guys were boring. There was no "high." For some of these women, it was not until they had gone into recovery that they discovered the beauty they have always been, that they found peace and calm as being exciting. Now, no longer strictly within the confines of seeking safety, their imaginations and limitations are open to discoveries, to wonderment, and to healthy manifestations of excitement.

Traumas are wars that rage in our hearts, affecting how we treat ourselves and others. Traumas serve to captivate and enslave our souls. Peace is not the absence of war but an active state in which our lives can unfold and our dreams can be realized. As with addicts, detoxification from trauma's physiological effects is needed if peace is to have a chance within our hearts and with others.

To my colleagues in the health-oriented professions, I ask you to please integrate more cultural considerations, and to explore issues of societal trauma's impact on the current well-being of your clients, whether they belong to the dominant or a nondominant culture. Consider the impact of individual trauma on chronic health issues and illnesses, especially those that suddenly appear one to ten years prior to a major health issue, such as an autoimmune illness, activation of gene variants, or cancer. Also consider the long-term effects of childhood trauma or adverse childhood experiences on a client's health (including mental health).

We have the power to make a difference in our own lives and in the lives of others. Part of letting go of the "victim" belief system is reclaiming your voice and your power, as well as acknowledging the duality that trauma can set up in your life. Embrace yourself with gentleness and share that power with others. Don't impose or lecture. No '"shouldsies." Role model instead, and be open to sharing with those who wish to soar as well.

Your voice matters. Your actions always have. Choose the winds of change and warmth over the winds of trauma that may visit you in your life. How? By gently touching your Self, you will know the difference.

I have endeavored to bring together analyses, conclusions, and discoveries from different disciplines and fields. I have pointed out the need to use storytelling and dreamwork as two main ways of healing, and I have invited all of us to explore how we can integrate various healing practices, a few of which I introduced, into a way of living and healing.

There are many books, videos, and webinars you can choose from to see which ones work best for you. They explore topics such as somato techniques, energy modalities, meditation and contemplation, the value of storytelling, breath work, bodymind psychotherapy, cranial work, and EFT.

For me, it is exploring the stories that I am following in my life. What narratives honor me or not? It is about re-authoring my life. It means examining my core values: Do they serve my heart, my joy, and my love for my Self and others? Do my behaviors reflect the beauty that is in me, and do they help to create a space for others to do the same, if they so wish?

If people and situations do not honor me nor assist me in my growth, then will I gently and with compassion say goodbye to them? Please consider living in a place of *bien educado*. We can learn from each other, as well as from our own groups' ways of healing and growing.

By comprehending that we are all related, might not we reach in to reach out? Might not we experience time as an ally to give us space to see each other's soul? We can become our own trailblazers of and for life.

May the cross-section of information presented in this book stimulate you to do further exploration into your own healing and the healing of others.

Many activists and healers have argued that it is important for members of a group to use, at the core of their healing, their own traditional approach or some other approach derived from their group's heritage. I agree with this, based on my own personal healing and professional observations. This may require becoming better acquainted with the history and culture of one's group and discovering how those elements impact one's Self now.

"Group" means our family and our ancestors, but also our cultures and how traumatic events—whether human-caused or natural—can tremendously influence what we believe and how we view our world, our reality. Redefining identity is at the core of healing.

Chapter 2

JUSTICE:
BIEN EDUCADA, BIEN EDUCADO

We bring our stories into our lives. We bring our failures and losses. We bring joy and love and harmony. We bring in the range of human emotions and experiences. Some people more than others bring in the stories of traumas—of unresolved adventures and hardships. Some people bring, as their Guiding Story, traumatic events that will not let them rest, haunting them because triggers in society or in their immediate environment insist that it will happen again. And it might. Or might not.

Whatever the winds blow in, we cannot let what they bring to us dictate how we should lead our lives and how we should treat ourselves and others.

Because trauma embraces all of us in some manner, healing has to include becoming *bien educado* (or *bien educada*). We create space for our unfolding of who we always have been: love. Honoring ourselves is part of our breath. Loving is an active experience inside ourselves in such ways that celebrations inside our bodies and emotions and minds are a given. Our bodies take in delight and peace.

Being *bien educado* is being well-educated of the heart. If so, then it naturally outflows to others, to create loving space for those around you to shine or to change their behaviors if they so wish. "Well-educated of the heart" also means having healthy boundaries and creating safety for yourselves as well. We are not doormats or do-gooders that are taken advantage of by others. We know when to use fight or flight in a healthy way, when to switch from seeing time as a friend to seeing time as an enemy if there is a life threat or if the other person is being *maleducado* (not coming from the heart).

"Well-educated of the heart" means treating persons with respect and honor, with kindness, seeing them as human beings, as well as seeing our environment as part of the Beauty That Is. We are the guardians and stewards. A trust develops. We care for each other. We Are All Related.

These are terms used in many indigenous cultures. In my family, it was said in the context that we are all God's creations. Therefore, being a family, we care for one another. We take responsibility for our actions, without shame or guilt but with understanding and learning. Even when our behaviors reflect the actions considered *maleducado*, we learn and grow, asking forgiveness of ourselves and offering apologies to those we have inadvertently hurt. We learn and gravitate back to being well-educated of the heart.

The simple act of helping a neighbor, stranger, or family member contributes to creating a safe and "healing of the heart" environment. We do not say that we are altruistic when we are kind and being of help to our children, or mother or father, or brothers or sisters, or grandparents, aunts, uncles, cousins, nephew, or nieces. If we saw them as "others," perhaps that might be so. The root of the word *altruism* means "other people." If one is well-educated of the heart, there are no "others."

Examples of offerings of love can be families acting as "foster" families to other families in need. It can be choosing one person and helping that person through rough times, financially or emotionally or both. It can mean members of a spiritual or religious congregation asking other congregations to join them on a regular basis to pray fervently for a neighborhood or group of people. It can be one group helping another—for example, an LGBTQ group or individuals helping heterosexuals in areas of families and health, or African American groups or individuals helping poor white communities in areas of economic need. It can be helping groups that normally have seen you as "the other."

The point of these examples is this: Groups should not only provide tools for their own empowerment, but also reach out to other groups that traditionally might not have seen them in respectful ways. Offer. Do not impose or make it a photo-op or selfie-op. People do not have to "show off" how they are there for others. If those who are on the receiving end want those "ops," then that is a different story.

I am suggesting possibly unexpected possibilities with the purpose that all of us can reach out and expand our own environment of love and safety with bridges to other communities. We can be involved at different levels. We need not all be saints or great philanthropists to make differences in our worlds. But we can be like them with regard to their hearts and their love for humanity.

We can be like the person we know in our lives who selflessly helps others and inspires us to be more of who we are. We can become our own role models, be our own inspiration.

Addressing traumas can take on many other forms too: educating others; learning healing modalities in order to help get the trauma energies out of the bodies; or becoming great storytellers, unraveling the stories of hope and new meaning and therefore creating new myths or dreams of laughter, wonderment, and peace.

We can pass on stories of traumatic existence, or we can choose to pass on stories that promote life and love despite the traumatic themes in our lives.

Being well-educated of the heart cuts through group memberships. We Are All Related. We need to heal ourselves and all of our communities, if the latter so wish. Part of our empowerment is to help create an environment that allows us to lead healthy, peaceful, and joyful lives.

Chapter 3

WALK IN BEAUTY

Trauma can make caricatures out of us, converting us into melodramatic characters in the theater of life. Or, the story of trauma can be transformed from a melodrama into an adventure— an adventure of the soul.

Trauma can govern us, demanding that we be a supporting character in a film in which we ought to be the star. If our eyes lose sight of the prize of life, settling on simply existing or surviving— both at the individual and group levels—then traumatic effects will continue to persist. We need not play the addiction game nor be victims. We need not be players in the crisis game in order to make the vines wither that have wrapped themselves around our hearts and movements. We can utilize tools oriented toward well-being.

Trauma questions our identities and our relationship to each other. It challenges how we grieve and whether we can go on living after our existence has been threatened in some way. Trauma shakes our foundation, exposing any fault lines. It can challenge us to fall into the abyss of violence and fear of ourselves and of others—hurting all of us, and keeping us in a cycle of adrenaline highs and of victim-victimizer.

Or, we can call upon our ancestors to help us, through spiritual means and healing practices. We can acknowledge that we are the guardians of those generations yet to come. We can acknowledge and appreciate the power we have. Our reactions or responses and our worldviews will affect our descendants.

In closing, I leave you with this poem, as told to me by my mother Graciela (or "Gracielita," as she was called, or "Mami" by my friends), who came to me in a dream almost a year after her "walking on" to God. I awoke with her voice inside me, urging me to write it down. Stumbling out of bed, I went to my computer and typed what she kept repeating to me. She came to me after I had meditated and prayed to God and my angels to give me guidance before falling asleep.

Walk in beauty.
Walk, don't run.

For there is time.
Time is an ally now.

Walk, don't run.
Walk between the Winds.
For they have now given you passage.
And you have given passage to yourself.

Walk don't run.
For there is time.

Winds of life abound.

The Winds blow before you and around you,
Some beckoning and blowing and thrusting strongly beneath your feet
to the past, of what was.

Some beckoning and blowing against your back,
pushing you forward
to the future, for what will be.

Some will inspire you to fly with them upward to life
as they
touch your skin,
bring you scents of Life,
caress your hair
and murmur voices of Spirit, from Spirit.

If you run,
if you fight any of these Winds
you will never know who these Winds are.
You will not discover the Passage through.

Walk, don't run.

Walk in beauty of who you are
and say 'good day' to the Winds of change
and to those Winds which will carry you to yourself.
Walk in beauty.

Glossary and Comments

The following is a glossary of terms used regularly in this work. Definitions are based on the dictionary, research, and my own observations, as well as on feedback from colleagues and clients. I thank Harlon Dalton for allowing me to utilize his definition of *racism* and to modify it for the other "isms" in our lives.

ABUSER

One who (often) systematically, intentionally or unintentionally, perpetrates or inflicts harm on another, usually in reaction to a perceived threat to himself or herself. The threat can be seen as physical, emotional, mental, or spiritual.

In terms of societal abusers, I include those who inflict or perpetrate harm or social injustice on other groups they perceive as threats to the dominant group or to the status quo. Usually abusers justify their actions by convincing themselves that they are, in fact, the innocent victims who are simply provoked and who naturally defend themselves.

The abuser is in a personal dynamic of dominance and subordination or submission.

At the macro scale, the abusers may not see themselves as initiators of abuse because they were not historically the original abusers. This belief may exist despite their perpetuation of doing harm.

ABUSED

One who is on the receiving end of harm; one who has experienced abuse. There are many reasons as to why abused people continue to be abused. One example is the "battered spouse syndrome." Another is the feeling of "that's simply how it is" and there is no viable recourse, with the abused not realizing they are being abused — instead, only knowing that "it feels bad" and believing it is the norm to feel that way. A "learned helplessness" may have ensued.

APPROPRIATION

This term is normally used by cultural groups whose rituals, art, music, foods, and other expressions have been usurped and made over by another group without appropriately understanding the intents and bases for those expressions. In addition, the appropriating group often fails to acknowledge and appreciate the culture or the people (and their descendants) whose expressions they have usurped.

CONFLICT

An act of striking against each other; competitive or opposing action of incompatibles; antagonistic state or action (as of divergent ideas, interests, or persons); a mental struggle resulting from incompatible or opposing needs, drives, wishes, or demands from external or internal forces; a hostile encounter; a collision; a discord.

External Conflict: Conflict between two parties or two people. A person may be oblivious that he or she is in a conflict if the other person does not share his or her feelings or thoughts. External conflicts may be between more than two parties. It need only take one of the parties to experience conflict in order for conflict to exist.

Internal Conflict: Conflict within oneself, usually "triggered" by opposing or perceived conflicting feelings or thoughts within oneself. A conflict or "dissonance" may occur within the body as well (leading to a fight, flight, or freeze reaction). A trigger can activate the internal conflict, bewildering the person who is experiencing the physiological reaction.

CULTURE

The ways of knowing and having shared beliefs, customs, values, mores, and traditions—e.g., religion/spirituality, music, food, art, and treatment of individuals—shared by an ethnic/racial, religious, or social group, as well as by subcultures.

Polycultural: Because there are subcultures, a person may be polycultural. That is, a person can be a member of many groups which may have aspects of culture normally associated with ethnicity and race (e.g., gender, sexual orientation, religion, class/economic status).

Dominant culture: Originally, an anthropological term referring to the culture whose beliefs and values are used as the norm for a society. In the United States, the term *Anglo* may be used by Hispanics or Latinos when speaking about the dominant group. The term *White* is used sometimes by African Americans and Native American/First Nations people.

In recent years, the dominant group has used the term *non-White* to refer to Hispanics/Latinos. As a consequence, Hispanics/Latinos increasingly use the term *White* to refer to Anglo European Americans.

The dominant group need not be the majority in terms of population, but rather the majority in terms of wielding the power to enforce and distribute its own beliefs and values.

Nondominant culture: The culture or group which is outside the dominant (usually mainstream) culture, whose patterns and customs are not considered the norm. Since demographics are changing rapidly in the United States, all racial and ethnic groups, numerically speaking, eventually will be nondominant. However, the concepts of nondominant and "minority" can still be valid if the power is not shared equally or accessed freely by nondominant groups, such as those whose members come from lower economic levels, as well as those based on age, gender, religion, sexual orientation, disability — to name a few.

DISCRIMINATION

To make a distinction; to discern based on judgment. The ability to discriminate or make critical distinctions can be a valuable survival tool for survivors of trauma.

However, as this term is commonly used, it means to make a distinction not based on the all the facts of the situation or person and/or not based on genuine merit, but rather to discern based on unfavorable biased or bigoted perceptions.

Institutional discrimination: Discrimination (as defined above) toward a group of individuals that is sanctioned by and perpetuated by the group(s) perceived to be the dominant power in society via laws, law enforcement, media, and educational and governmental institutions. It can also be tacit in nature.

Covert and overt discrimination: Covert discriminatory practice is subtle and is felt or experienced by the targeted person or group. Someone else outside that group may not notice it. Overt discriminatory practice is obvious to those targeted as well as to others. One example is the level of law enforcement regarding safety for a group. For that group, it is obvious that there is little law enforcement for their protection. For others outside the targeted group, they may not notice the lack of law enforcement or understand why those in the targeted group are upset or in fear mode.

Individual discrimination: Discrimination which is directed toward and experienced by an individual of a group, as opposed to a whole group.

Difference between societal trauma and discrimination: Discriminatory actions may result in having a person experience societal trauma. Trauma involves unresolved fight, flight, or freeze (FFF) reactions. If the person believes that he or she was unsuccessful dealing with the discrimination, the FFF reactions will stay activated. Trauma is different from discrimination in that the receiver of discrimination need not be traumatized. That is, the person need not go into an FFF mode if she or he has learned other coping skills and mechanisms that give her or him the perception of somehow successfully dealing with the discrimination.

FAITH

Faith is not necessarily related to religion. It is a belief or trust that something, ethereal or not physical, exists that can act as a bridge between the known and the unknown. During times of transitions and crisis, this faith—for example, in God or a "Higher Power," or in one's own ability, or in the scientific method, or in a group, or in a government, or in an individual—will, in all likelihood, come through.

A crisis of faith occurs when the faith is tested and what one believed in does not appear to help. Implied in having faith is the search for another level of safety when one is not easily experiencing it during times of stress or losses.

FREEDOM

"The absence of necessity, coercion, or constraint in choice or action; liberation from slavery or restraint from the power of another or thing." Webster's Dictionary.

"The ability to have or not have what you want without it closing your heart." Stephen Levine, from *Who Dies?*

HATE CRIME

"Any act of intimidation, harassment, physical force or threat of physical force directed against any person, or family, or their property or advocate, motivated either in whole or in part by hostility to their real or perceived race, ethnic background, national origin, religious belief, sex, age, disability, or sexual orientation, with the intention of causing fear or intimidation, or to deter the free exercise or enjoyment of any rights or privileges secured by the Constitution or the laws of the United States."

The above is the definition established by the California State Attorney General's Commission on Racial, Ethnic, Religious, and Minority Violence, April 1986. Note that hate crime laws of other states may not include sexual orientation as a protected area.

The FBI uses the following definition: "A hate crime is a traditional offense like murder, arson, or vandalism with an added element of bias. For the purposes of collecting statistics, the FBI has defined a hate crime as a 'criminal offense against a person or property motivated in whole or in part by an offender's bias against a race, religion, disability, sexual orientation, ethnicity, gender, or gender identity.'"

HOMOPHOBIA

Fear of nonheterosexuals, for example, gay men, lesbians, bisexuals, and transsexuals. Originally the word pertained only to the fear of homosexuals. Fear can be internalized. For example, a male homophobe is fearful of his own elements of homosexuality.

INTIMACY

The profoundly familiar and personal connection between two people, typically developed after a long association. As C. L. Whitfield described it, "… in which two people are real with one another over time." To paraphrase him, intimate people risk being vulnerable. They share who they are, with an understanding of risk-taking and commitment. Within a healthy intimacy, people bare their souls to each other. Trust and safety are the foundation.

"ISM"

Pertaining to some form of "ism," such as racism, sexism, classism, heterosexism, and ageism. The held beliefs, ideas, attitudes, and institutional implementation (e.g., via media, law enforcement, housing, and employment) that serve to sustain the order of a particular "ism." Modified from the definition of *racism* originated by Harlon Dalton in *Racial Healing*.

In this book, "isms" such as totalitarianism, authoritarianism, communism, socialism, and capitalism are not the focus, although they certainly can create societal traumas for those not in accordance. (As an example, in a totalitarian or authoritarian state, members of certain religious faiths and nonheterosexuals, as well as certain ethnic groups, may not be welcome and even may be actively hunted down.)

Classism: Class-held beliefs, ideas, attitudes, and institutional implementation (e.g., the media, law enforcement, housing, employment) that serve to sustain a socioeconomic-based pecking order.

Heterosexism: Sexual identity-oriented held beliefs, ideas, attitudes, and institutional implementation (e.g., the media, law enforcement, housing, employment) that serve to sustain a pecking order based on sexual orientation that favors heterosexuals.

Racism: Culturally held beliefs, ideas, attitudes, and institutional implementation (e.g., the media, law enforcement, housing, employment) that serve to sustain a pecking order based on race or ethnicity.

Sexism: Gender-held beliefs, ideas, attitudes, and institutional implementation (e.g., the media, law enforcement, housing, employment) that serve to sustain a pecking order based on gender.

CULTURATION SPECTRUM

A range or spectrum having "traditional" at one end, "bicultural/polycultural" in the middle, and "assimilated" at the other end, in terms of espousing a group's beliefs and values, as well as the expressions of those beliefs and values. It is not seen as a linear process, but rather as a going back and forth.

For example, a person may be traditional in his or her beliefs in marriage roles but assimilated in other areas of life. And in yet another area of that person's life, he or she may have embraced and blended beliefs from more than one culture, thereby being bicultural or polycultural. The spectrum illustrates that we are made of many cultures, whether of race or ethnicity, religion, socioeconomic level, gender, and/or subgroups that create their own cultural expressions. Therefore, the word *group* can refer to any of the above.

Traditionalist: A person who has embraced the perpetuation of established patterns, customs, behaviors, values, and beliefs, any or all of which may be inherited or passed down, either with deliberate intent or with no understanding of them, from one generation to the next.

Biculturated or Bicultural or Polycultural: A person who has embraced and incorporated some values and beliefs, as well as the expressions of them, from another group(s), while still retaining some values and beliefs, and the expressions of them, that belong to her or his own group.

Ideally, the person chooses the best aspects of the different cultures. Usually, only two cultures are involved. However, the person, if exposed to more than two, may decide to incorporate all of them—in which case, she or he would be seen as polycultural.

Assimilated: A person who has "let go" and/or "closeted" his or her own group's ways to, instead, assume and adopt aspects of, and the ways of being of, another group, usually that of the dominant group.

PREJUDICE

A prejudgment of a person based on a particular aspect of the person's identity (e.g., race, class, gender, age, sexuality, physical appearance, religion) or situation, derived from previously learned beliefs, before getting all the facts about that particular person or situation.

Overt prejudice: Obvious words, actions, or behaviors that can be readily seen, felt, or heard by the recipient, as well as by any onlooker, as being a form of prejudice or bigotry (e.g., derogatory words, physically hitting someone).

Covert prejudice: Subtle words, actions, or behaviors that are seen, felt, or heard by the recipient of prejudice, but are not experienced by onlookers (e.g., double-meaning or "loaded" expressions, certain "meaningful" looks, subtle behaviors).

MEANING

The significance we attach to a word, phrase, and/or feeling; what one intends to communicate or convey; what is conveyed or communicated. In addition, *meaning* is what we attach to a person, place, situation, beliefs, values, etc. in terms of emotional importance to us.

If the meaning we attach is significant to a way of living, then the loss of that way of living would also be significant.

PERCEPTION

An impression or mental image experienced by an individual, based on accumulated experiences and filtered through them, typically resulting in a conceptual observation.

SAFETY

A state in which one can feel free to be oneself. To exhale with calm and peace. To enjoy life without fear.

The condition of security is threatened when there is an expectation or the actual occurrence of harm or hurt to oneself, to another person, or to a group. Traditionally, the term referred only to physical safety; it now also encompasses emotional, spiritual, and "ego" safety.

SOCIAL MOVEMENT

An organized effort to promote and attain an end; usually that end is justice and freedom. The civil rights movement is an example.

SOCIETY

Individuals who make up a group that shares patterns of relationships, institutions, and common traditions by which they live and to which they adhere.

SPIRITUALITY

The experience of one's relationship with that which is defined as "Spirit" or God, typically, but not necessarily, associated with religious practices and belief.

TRAUMA

The normal definition of *trauma* is a life-changing, disturbing, often overwhelmingly painful or stressful (physically, mentally, or emotionally) experience. Often this kind of trauma can have long-lasting effects if left unattended.

Furthermore, it can create obstacles to the growth and healing of an individual or of members of a group.

I would add that when a person perceives a failure or experiences an unsuccessful attempt(s) to deal with life-threatening situations, that person's immune system will keep fight, flight, or freeze responses active. If these responses are left active for a prolonged period of time, traumatic reactions may be created within the person's overall health.

Individual trauma: Traumatic effects (as defined above) experienced by one person. This kind of trauma, received by an individual, is not dependent on group membership.

Societal trauma: Traumatic effects (as defined above) experienced by a whole society or by a group, inflicted by an entire society through their institutions and enforcement. Societal trauma can also be carried out by members of that society toward any group targeted by the society's government and practices.

TRAUMA MECHANISMS AND COPING SKILLS (TMCS)

Trauma mechanisms are mechanisms of the body (its immune system) initiated or activated by the perception of trauma. Coping skills refer to the attitudes, behaviors, and actions initiated or activated by the perception of trauma.

These mechanisms and skills are used as tools to keep a person safe. They are created by the person, developed out of a reaction to the fight, flight, or freeze response that was initiated because of a perceived threat. Included in the TMCS are physiological reactions, which are initiated by the immune system, as well as behaviors and attitudes.

Groups as a whole may also develop TMCS as responses to societal trauma. For example, a group may develop a certain worldview full of TMCS as a way to keep safe in terms of abuser groups or of people who have threatened certain of their members and/or the group as a whole.

TRIGGERS

The stimulation of memory and associations of the past—typically painful and often traumatic experiences, resulting in a reaction to the stimulus(i).

Any person, situation, or dynamic that usually evokes a reaction along fight, flight, or freeze lines can be seen as "triggering" an individual or a group. A trigger can produce hypervigilance for, or an acute anticipation of, expressions that may precipitate trauma or danger (e.g., derogatory words or tone of voice, proximity that may portend an imminent act of harm).

When triggers occur, coping mechanisms such as hypervigilance and hypersensitivity (to movement, for example) are activated. "Normal" perception becomes skewed to highlight those triggers and minimize any other words, actions, and movements that do not portend trauma or danger. Non-crisis words may be barely heard, or movement that is not perceived as threatening may not be heard or seen by someone who is highly "triggered" by safety threats.

Tunnel-like hearing may occur even though the person evoking the trigger may be speaking normally, or words may be perceived as being shouted even though normal speech is occurring.

TRUST

A feeling of safety perceived by an individual that enables the sharing of feelings, stories, experiences, etc. with someone else. It is based on the confidence that the individual can rely on the integrity and reliability of the other person.

References and Suggested Readings

Chinua Achebe (1987), *Anthills of the Savannah*. New York: Anchor Books.

Adler, A., Ansbacher, H. L. & Ansbacher, R. R. (eds.). (1964). *The Individual Psychology of Alfred Adler*. New York: HarperTorchBooks/ Harper.

Ainslie, R. (2000, August 15). "Psychodynamics of Acculturation: A Mexican-American Experience." Charlottesville, VA: Center for the Study of Mind and Human Interactions.

Alien, P. G. (1992). *The Sacred Hoop: Recovering the Feminine in American Indian Traditions*. Boston: Beacon Press.

American Psychiatric Association. (2004). *Diagnostic and Statistical Manual TR-IV*. American Psychological Association Publication Manual of the American Psychological Association. Fourth edition. Washington, DC.

Apprey, M., Ph.D. (1998). "Reinventing the Self in the Face of Received Transgenerational Hatred in the African American Community." Paper: Center for the Study of Mind and Human Interaction, https://link.springer.com/article/10.1023/A:1023081004567

Barry, W. J. (1987). *Implementation Task Force Progress Report: Attorney General's Commission on Racial, Ethnic, Religious and Minority Violence.* California: Department of Justice.

Bar-Tal, D. (1990). "Causes and Consequences of Delegitimization: Models of Conflict and Ethnocentrism." The Society for the Psychological Study of Social Issues, 46 1), 65–81.

Bass, E. & Davis, L. (1994). *The Courage to Heal: A Guide for Women of Childhood Sexual Abuse.* New York: HarperPerennial Library.

Beinfield, H. L.Ac., & Korngold E. L.Ac. (1991). *Between Heaven and Earth: A Guide to Chinese Medicine.* New York: Ballantine Books.

Bentzen, M, Jarinaes, E., & Levine, P. (1993). "The Body Self in Psychotherapy. A Psycho-Motoric Approach to Developmental Psychology." Article. Reno, NV: Ergos Institute.

Berger, M. & Segaller, S. (1989). *The World of C. G. Jung: The Wisdom of the Dream.* New York: TV Books.

Bernhardt, P. (1992). "Individuation, Mutual Connection and the Body's Resources: An Interview with Lisbeth Marcher." Pre- and Peri-Natal Psychology Journal, 6, 28–293.

Bible (1936). *The Jerusalem Bible.* Garden City, New York: Doubleday Black, C. (1982). *It Will Never Happen to Me.* New York: Ballantine Books.

Blalock J. E. (2005, Feb.) "The Immune System as the Sixth Sense." J Intern Med. 2005 Feb;257(2):126–38. Abstract: https://www.ncbi.nlm.nih.gov/pubmed/15656872 https://onlinelibrary.wiley.com/doi/full/10.1111/j.1365-2796.2004.01441.x

Blalock, J. E. (1989, Jan.). "A Molecular Basis for Bidirectional Communication Between the Immune and Neuroendocrine Systems." Physiological Review, 69 (1), 1–32.

Boswell, J. (1994). *Same-Sex Unions in Premodern Europe.* New York: VintageBooks.

Bradshaw, J. (1988). *Bradshaw on the Family.* Deerfield, FL: Health Communications.

Bradshaw, J. (1988). *Healing the Shame That Binds You.* Deerfield, FL: Health Communications.

Brown, J. E. (1982). *The Spiritual Legacy of the American Indian.* New York: Cross Road.

Burton, J. (1990). *Conflict: Human Needs Theory.* New York: St. Martin's Press.

Carocci, M. (1997). "The Berdache as Metahistorical Reference for the Urban Gay American Indian Community." In Marie Mauze (ed.), *Present Is Past: Some Uses of Tradition in Native Societies.* New York: University Press of America, Inc., 113–129.

Chapkis, W. (1986). *Beauty Secrets: Women and the Politics of Appearance.* Boston, MA: South End Press.

Chassay, S. (1996). "Trauma as Initiation: A Shamanic Perspective on Sexual Abuse." Shamanic Application Review, 3–12.

Clark, W. R. (1995). *At War Within: The Double-Edged Sword of Immunity.* New York: Oxford University Press.

Clayman, C. (ed.) (1995). *The Human Body: An Illustrated Guide to Its Structure, Function, and Disorders.* London: Dorling Kindersley Limited.

Cloud, D. L. (1998). *Control and Consolation in American Culture and Politics: Rhetorics of Therapy.* Thousand Oaks, CA: Sage Publications.

Cose, E. (1999, June 7). "The Good News about Black America (and Why Many Blacks Aren't Celebrating)." Newsweek. New York: Newsweek, 28–40.

Craig, G. & Fowlie, A. (1997). *Emotional Freedom Techniques: The Manual.* Sea Ranch, California: Gary Craig.

Cross, Jr., W. E. (1998). "Black Psychological Functioning and the Legacy of Slavery." In Y. Danieli (ed.), *International Handbook of Multigenerational Legacies of Trauma.* New York: Plenum Press, 387–402.

Cushman, Philip. (1995). *Constructing the Self, Constructing America: A Cultural History of Psychotherapy.* New York: Addison-Wesley.

Dalton, H. L. (1995). *Racial Healing: Confronting the Fear Between Blacks and Whites.* New York: Anchor/DoubleDay Books.

Danieli, Y. (ed.) (1998). *International Handbook of Multigenerational Legacies of Trauma.* New York: Plenum Press.

Dass, R. & Gorman, P. (1985). *How Can I Help? Stories and Reflections on Service.* New York: Alfred Knopf.

Davis, L. (1951). *Allies in Healing.* New York: HarperPerennial.

Deer, P. I. (1999). "The Body as Peace: Somatic Practice for Transforming Conflict." Unpublished dissertation. Cincinnati, Ohio: Union Institute.

Dossey, L. M. D. (1993). *Healing Words: The Power of Prayer.* New York: HarperSan Francisco.

Dossey, L. M.D. (1996). *Prayer Is Good Medicine*. San Francisco: HarperSan Francisco.

Duran, E. & Duran, B. (1995). *Native American Postcolonial Psychology*. New York: State University of New York Press.

Ellis, C. (1996). *To Change Them Forever: Indian Education at the Rainy Mountain Boarding School, 1893–1920*. Norman, OK: University of Oklahoma Press.

Fischman, Y. (1990, January). "Group Treatment of Exiled Survivors of Torture." American Journal Orthopsychiatry, 60 (1), 135–140.

Fischman, Y. (1991, April). "Interacting with Trauma: Clinicians' Responses to Treating Psychological Aftereffects of Political Repression." American Journal Orthopsychiatry, 61 (2), 179–185.

Fischman, Y. (1998, January). "Metaclinical Issues in the Treatment of Psychopolitical Trauma." American Journal of Orthopsychiatry, 68(1), 27–38.

Fischman, Y., Gonsalves, C.J., Ross, J., & Torres, T.A. (1999, Spring). "The Impact of Political Repression upon Gender-Related Violence." Family Violence and Sexual Assault Bulletin, 15 (1), 21–26.

Fletcher, M. A. (2000, October 2, Monday). "Asian Americans Using Politics as a Megaphone: Growing Population Confronts Bias." Washington Post, A3.

Fowler, J. W. (1981.) *Stages of Faith: The Psychology of Human Development and the Quest for Meaning*. New York: HarperCollins.

Frankenber, R. (1993). *White Women, Race Matters: The Social Construction of Whiteness*. Minneapolis: University of Minnesota Press.

Freire, P. (1996). *Pedagogy of the Oppressed*. New York: Continuum.

Freud, S. (1989). *Sigmund Freud on Dreams*. (J. Strachey, Trans.). New York: W.W. Norton.

Gendlin, E. T. (1981). *Focusing*. Second edition. New York: Bantam Books.

Goleman, D. (1995). *Emotional Intelligence: Why It Can Matter More than IQ*. New York: Bantam Books.

Goodman, F. D. (1990) *Where the Spirits Ride the Wind*. Bloomington, IN: Indiana University Press.

Greven, P. (1977). *The Protestant Temperament: Patterns of Child-Rearing, Religious Experience, and the Self in Early America*. New York: Alfred A. Knopf.

Hadley-Garcia, G. (1990). *Hispanic Hollywood*. New York: Citadel Press.

Harrison, K. David. (2008). *When Languages Die: The Extinction of the World's Languages and the Erosion of Human Knowledge*.

Heider, J. (1986; revised, 2014). *The Tao of Leadership*. Atlanta, GA: Humanics New Age.

Herman, J. L. (1992). *Trauma and Recovery: The Aftermath of Violence: From Domestic Abuse to Political Terror*. USA: Basic Books/Harper Collins.

Herring, R. D. (1999). "Counseling with Native American Indians and Alaska Natives: Strategies for Helping Professionals."

Multicultural Aspects of Counseling Series 14. Thousand Oaks, CA: Sage Publication.

Hillman, J. & Ventura, M. (1992). *We've Had 100 Years of Psychotherapy and the World's Getting Worse.* San Francisco: Harper.

hooks, b. (1993). *Sisters of the Yam: Black Women and Self-Recovery.* Boston, MA: South End Press.

hooks, b. (1990). *Yearning: Race, Gender, and Cultural Politics.* Boston, MA: South End Press.

hooks, b. & West, C. (1991). *Breaking Bread: Insurgent Black Intellectual Life.* Boston, MA: South End Press.

Hunt, C. E. (1999, July). "Recreating the Circle: Overcoming Colonialism and Restoring Harmony in American Indian Communities." Paper presented to American Political Science Association, September 1999.

Jacoby, S. (1983). *Wild Justice and Evolution of Revenge.* New York: Harper and Row.

Jampolsky, L. (1994). *The Art of Trust: Healing Your Heart and Opening Your Mind.* Berkeley, CA: Celestial Arts.

Jung, C. (1974). *Dreams.* Hull, R.F. (trans.). New Jersey: Princeton University Press.

Kabat-Zinn, J. (1994). *Wherever You Go, There You Are: Mindfulness Meditation in Everyday Life.* New York: Hyperion.

Kalweit, H. (1992). *Shamans, Healers, and Medicine Men.* Boston: Shambala Press.

Katz, J. H. (1978). *White Awareness: Handbook for Anti-Racism Training.* Norman & London: University of Oklahoma Press.

Kingston, M. H. (1976). *Woman Warrior Memoirs of a Girlhood Among Ghosts.* New York: Vintage Press.

Kinzie, J. D. & Boehnlein, J. K. (1993). "Psychotherapy of the Victims of Massive Violence: Countertransference and Ethical Issues." American Journal of Psychotherapy, 47(1), 90–102.

Kochman, T. (1981). *Black and White Styles in Conflict.* Chicago and London: The University of Chicago Press.

Krutch, J. W. (ed.) (1965). *Thoreau: Walden and Other Writings.* New York: Bantam Books.

Krystal, J. H., Nagy, L. M., Rasmusson, A., Morgan, A., Cottrol, C., Southwick, S. M., & Charney, D. S. (1998). "Initial Clinical Evidence of Genetic Contributions to Posttraumatic Stress Disorder.' In Y. Danieli (ed.), *International Handbook of Multigenerational Legacies of Trauma.* New York and London: Plenum Press, 657–668.

Kübler-Ross, E. (1969). *On Death and Dying: What the Dying Have to Teach Doctors, Nurses, Clergy and Their Own Families.* New York: Macmillan Press.

Kübler-Ross, E. (1975). *Death: The Final Stage of Growth.* New York: A Touchstone Book. Published by Simon & Schuster, Inc.

Levine, P. A. (1996). *Nature's Lessons in Healing Trauma.* Lyons, CO: Self-published.

Levine, P. A. (1996). *Waking the Tiger: Healing Trauma Through the Body.* Berkeley, CA: North Atlantic Books.

Levine, P. A. (1998, Summer). "Memory, Trauma, and Healing." Alternative Health Practitioner, 4 (2), 115–121.

Levine, S. (1989). *Who Dies?* New York: Anchor Books/Doubleday.

Lewis, R. D. (1996). *When Cultures Collide: Managing Successfully Across Cultures.* London: Nicholas Brealey Publishing.

Lowenstein, L. F. (1997). "Impasse in Ireland: Destroying Distrust Before Disarmament." International Media, 7(3), 15–16.

Marsella, A. J., Thomas Bornemann, T., Ekblad, S., & Orley, J. (eds.) (1994). *Amidst Peril and Pain: The Mental Health and Well-Being of the World's Refugees.* Washington, DC: American Psychological Association.

Masson, J. M. (1994). *Against Therapy.* Monroe, ME: Common Courage Press.

Mauze, M. (ed.) (1997). *Present Is Past: Some Uses of Tradition in Native Societies.* New York: University Press of America, Inc.

McCall, N. (1995). *Makes Me Wanna Holler: A Young Black Man in America.* New York: Vintage Books.

McCann, I. L. Ph.D. & Pearlman, L. A. Ph.D. (1990). *Psychological Trauma and the Adult Survivor: Theory, Therapy, and Transformation.* New York: Brunner/Mazel Publishers.

Medicine Eagle, B. (1989). "Bones." From *A gift of song* [Music, CD]. Flagstaff, AZ: Mudshark Studios.Merriam-Webster's Collegiate Dictionary (Tenth edition) (1993). Springfield, MA: Merriam Webster.

Middleton-Moz, J. & Fedrid, E. (1987, July–August). "The Many Faces of Grief." Changes 8–9, 32–34.

Miller, A. (1981). *The Drama of the Gifted Child.* New York: Basic Books.

Mollica, R., Caspi-Yavin, Y., Bollini, P., Truong, T., Tor, S., & Lavelle, J. (1992). "The Harvard Trauma Questionnaire: Validating a Cross-Cultural Instrument for Measuring Torture, Trauma, and Posttraumatic Stress Disorder in Indochinese Refugees." Journal of Nervous and Mental Disease, 180(2), 111–116.

Moraga, C. & Castillo, A. (eds.). (1983). *This Bridge Called My Back: Writings by Radical Women of Color.* New York: Kitchen Table/Women of Color Press.

Moustakas, C. (1990). *Heuristic Research: Design, Methodology, and Applications.* Newbury Park: Sage Publications.

Myss, C. (1996). *Anatomy of the Spirit.* New York: Three River Press.

Myss, C. (1997). *Why People Don't Heal and How They Can.* New York: Harmony Books.

Nash, G. B. (1970). *Class and Society in Early America.* Englewood Cliffs, New Jersey: Prentice-Hall, Inc.

Nestle, J. & Preston, J. (1994). *Sister & Brother: Lesbians & Gay Men Write About Their Lives Together.* New York: HarperSanFrancisco. Harper Collins Publishers.

Nhat Hanh, T. (1994). *Zen Keys.* New York: Doubleday.

Niehoff, D. (1999). *The Biology of Violence: How Understanding the Brain, Behavior, and Environment Can Break the Vicious Cycle of Aggression.* New York: Free Press.

Northern Ireland. (April 10, 1998). Belfast Agreement. Document received from Irish representatives in May, 1998, at the Organization Development Institute Non-Violence Meeting in New Hampshire.

Parry, A. & Doan, R.E. (1994). *Story Re-Visions: Narrative Therapy in the Postmodern World.* New York: The Guilford Press.

Pelletier, K. R. (1992). *Mind as Healer, Mind as Slayer.* New York: Delta Books.

Pennebaker, J. W. (1990). *Opening Up: The Healing Power of Expressing Emotions.* New York: The Guilford Press.

Perry, B. D. (1999). "Memories of Fear: How the Brain Stores and Retrieves Physiologic States, Feelings, Behaviors, and Thoughts from Traumatic Events." https://www.semanticscholar.org/paper/Memories-of-Fear-How-the-Brain-Stores-and-Retrieves-Perry/0de5747bc47b848f9f42d97278239e815f0d8dc0

Pert, C. (1997). *Molecules of Emotions: Why You Feel the Way You Feel.* New York: Simon and Schuster.

Ridley, Louise. "The Holocaust's Forgotten Victims: The 5 Million Non-Jewish People Killed by the Nazis." HuffPost UK RELIGION section 01/27/2015 11:37 am ET Updated Dec 06, 2017 https://www.huffpost.com/entry/holocaust-non-jewish-victims_n_6555604 (retrieved August 11, 2019).

Roof, J. & Wiegran, R. (1995). *Who Can Speak: Authority and Critical Identity.* Urbana and Chicago: University of Illinois Press.

Ross, G. (2003). *Beyond the Trauma Vortex: The Media's Role in Healing Fear, Terror and Violence.* Berkeley, CA: North Atlantic Books.

Russell, K., Wilson, M., & Hall, R. (1992). *The Color Complex: The Politics of Skin Color Among African Americans.* New York: Anchor Books, Doubleday.

Sachs, S. (2000). "An Alchemy of Happiness: Poems on the Meditation of the Alchemical Process of Personal Transformation." Unpublished paper.

Sams, J. (1998). *Dancing the Dream: The Seven Sacred Paths of Human Transformation.* New York: HarperSanFrancisco.

Sandole, D. J. D. & Van der Merwe, H. (eds.) (1993). *Conflict Resolution Theory and Practice: Integration and Application.* Manchester and New York: Manchester University Press.

Satir, V. (1976). *Peoplemaking.* Palo Alto, CA: Science and Behavior Books, Inc.

Satir, V., Banmen, J., Gerger, J., & Gomori, M. (1991). *The Satir Model: Family Therapy and Beyond.* Palo Alto, CA: Science and Behavior Books, Inc.

Schaef, A. W. & Fassel, D. (1988). *The Addictive Organization.* San Francisco: Harper & Row, Publishers.

Schutzenberger, A. A. (1998). *The Ancestor Syndrome: Transgenerational Psychotherapy and the Hidden Links in the Family Tree.* (A. Trager, trans.). London and New York: Routledge.

Seligman, M. (1991). *Learned Optimism.* New York: Alfred A. Knopf.

Shapiro, F. (1995). *EMDR: Basic Principles, Protocols, and Procedures.* New York: The Guilford Press.

Shapiro, F. (1994, revised 2000, 2019). EMDR Institute website. A virtual site where practitioners and interested people can learn more about Eye Movement Desensitization and Reprocessing; included are reports of controlled studies and bibliography.

Shipler, L. K., Anand, R., & Hadi, N. (April, 1998). "Cultural Considerations in Assisting Victims of Crime." Report on needs and promising practices. National Multicultural Institute, Washington, DC. Funded by U.S. Department of Justice and Office for Victims of Crime.

Shlain, L. (1998). *The Alphabet Versus the Goddess.* New York: Penguin Arkana.

Smedes, L. B. (1984). *Forgive and Forget: Healing the Hurts we Don'tDeserve.* New York: GuidePost.

Spretnak, C. (1993). *States of Grace: The Recovery of Meaning in the Postmodern Age.* New York: HarperSanFrancisco, Harper Collins Publishers.

Stamm, B. H. (1997, Spring). "Work-Related Secondary Traumatic Stress." PTSD Research Quarterly, 8 (2). White River Junction, VT: The National Center for PTSD VA Medical and Regional.

Suomi, S. J. & Levine, S. (1998) "Psychobiology of Intergenerational Effects of Trauma." In Y. Danieli (ed.), *International Handbook of Multigenerational Legacies of Trauma.* New York and London: Plenum Press, 623–638.

Talbot, M. (1991). *The Holographic Universe.* New York: HarperPerennial.

Tan, A. (1996). *One Hundred Secret Senses.* Maine: Thorndike Press.

Tatelbeum, J. (1980). *The Courage to Grieve.* New York: Lippincott and Crowell.

Tatum, B. D. (1997). *Why Are All the Black Kids Sitting Together in the Cafeteria? And Other Conversations About Race.* New York: Basic Books.

Taylor, C. A. (1995). *Juneteenth: A Celebration of Freedom.* Madison, WI: Praxis Publications.

Tigert, L. M. (1999). *Coming Out Through Fire: Surviving the Trauma of Homophobia.* Cleveland, OH: Pilgrim Press.

Tjaden, P. & Thoennes, N. (1998). "Prevalence and Consequences of Violence Against Women. Findings from the National Violence Against Women Survey." Research in brief. Washington, DC and Atlanta, GA. National Institute of Justice, and the Centers for Disease Control and Prevention.

Traue, H. C. & Pennebaker, J. W. (eds.). (1993). *Emotion Inhibition and Health.* Toronto: Hogrefe and Huber Publishers.

United States Department of Justice. Hate Crimes Statistics. Criminal Justice Information Services (CJIS) Program. https://www.fbi.gov/investigate/civil-rights/hate-crimes

Upledger, J. E., D.O., O.M.M. (1996). *SomatoEmotional Release and Beyond.* Palm Beach Gardens: Ul Publishing, Inc.

Upledger, J. E. (1999). Website of Upledger Foundation. Graphs (of success healing rate for Vietnam war veterans and post-traumatic stress disorder) www.upledger.com and https://www.upledger.com/ptsd/

Van der Kolk, B. A., McFarlane, A. C., & Weisaeth, L. (eds.). (1996). *Traumatic Stress: The Effects of Overwhelming Experience on Mind, Body, and Society.* New York: The Guilford Press.

Van der Kolk, B. A. "The Body Keeps the Score: Memory and the Evolving Psychobiology of Posttraumatic Stress." David Baldwin's Trauma Information Pages. http://www.trauma-pages.com.

Villena-Mata, D. G. (2000, Spring). "Traumatic Conflicts: An Interdisciplinary Approach to Conflict Resolution." Nonviolent Change, XIV (3), 18–20.

Villena-Mata, D. G. (2001, January). "Revenge and Conflict Resolution." Nonviolent Change, XV (2), Winter, 17–19.

Volkan, V. D. (2000). "The Tree Model: A Comprehensive Psychopolitical Approach to Unofficial Diplomacy and the Reduction of Ethnic Tension." Mind and Human Interaction, 10 (3), 143–210.

Volkan, V. D. (ed.). (2000). Mind and Human Interaction, 11 (2). (entire issue)

Volkan, V. D. (2000, May 18). "Traumatized Societies and Psychological Care." Opening paper presented at "Crossing the Border" Dutch Adolescent Psychotherapy Organization. Amsterdam.

von Franz, M. L (1975). Carl Jung: Man and His Symbols. (Kennedy, W.H., trans.) New York: Putnam.

Walker, L. E. A. (1994). Abused Women and Survivor Therapy. Washington, DC: American Psychological Association.

Weaver, H. M. (ed.) (1999). Voices of First Nations People: Human Services Considerations. New York: The Haworth Press, Inc.

Webster's New Collegiate Dictionary. Springfield, MA: G. & C. Merriam

Wells, S. (2000, October 18). Email exchange. Re: EFT pilot study. Principal investigator, responded to my query on whether there were fight, flight, or freeze energy discharges with the EFT energy technique.

White, M. & Epston, D. (1990). *Narrative Means to Therapeutic Ends.* New York: W. W. Norton and Company.

Whitfield, C. L. (1993). *Boundaries and Relationships: Knowing, Protecting and Enjoying the Self.* Deerfield Beach, FL: Health Communications, Inc.

Wiesel, E. (1990). *From the Kingdom of Memory.* New York: Summit Books.

Williams, Jr., C. (1999). *Recovery from Everyday Racisms.* Detroit, MI: The Institute for Recovery from Everyday Racisms.

Williams, H. A. (1990, Summer). "Families in Refugee Camps." Human Organization, 49 (2), 100–109.

Williams, P. J 1991. *The Alchemy of Race and Lights: Diary of a Law Professor.* Cambridge, MA: Harvard University Press.

Winslade, J. & Monk, G. (2000). *Narrative Mediation: A New Approach to Conflict Resolution.* San Francisco: Jossey-Bass Publishers.

Woititz, J. (1986). *Struggle for Intimacy.* Pompano Beach, FL: Health Communications, Inc.

Woititz, J. (1987). *Adult Children of Alcoholics.* Pompano Beach, FL: Health Communications, Inc.

Yehuda, R., Schmeidler, J., Elkin, A., Wilson, S., Siever, L., Binder-Brynes, K., Wainberg, M., & Aferiot, D. (1998). In Y. Danieli (ed.), *International Handbook of Multigenerational Legacies of Trauma.* New York and London: Plenum Press, 639–656.